THE CLASSICAL MARXIST CRITIQUES OF RELIGION:
MARX, ENGELS, LENIN, KAUTSKY

THE CLASSICAL MARXIST CRITIQUES OF RELIGION: MARX, ENGELS, LENIN, KAUTSKY

by

DELOS B. MCKOWN

MARTINUS NIJHOFF/THE HAGUE/1975

To Anna Louise who, in wifely ways,
worked as hard as I to complete this book

PRINTED IN BELGIUM

TABLE OF CONTENTS

ACKNOWLEDGEMENTS

As is normal in carrying out a work of this kind, numerous individuals gave aid in varying ways and degrees. I should like to acknowledge the assistance of those who gave most benefically and unstintingly of their time, talents, and criticisms. The first is Dr. Donald C. Hodges of the Philosophy Department of The Florida State University who, after reading the entire manuscript, made numerous suggestions that have enhanced its worth. The second is Dr. Chester W. Hartwig of the Sociology Department of Auburn University who also read the entire manuscript and who proved to be an unfailing source of insight during several long and probing conversations. The third is Mr. Clyde I. Wolverton of the Foreign Languages Department of Auburn University who, when needed, placed his expert knowledge of German at my disposal. Should error be found in this work, no blame can be attributed to the aforementioned friends and counselors, for, in the last analysis, all responsibility is mine alone.

I am also especially indebted to Ms. Sandra Kent for her yeoman work in typing the first draft of the manuscript and to Ms. Hildegard Wolverton for her superb services in typing and in helping to correct the final draft.

Finally, I wish to express appreciation for being granted permission to quote from the following sources:

From *The Elementary Forms of the Religious Life* by Emile Durkheim, translated by J. W. Swain, copyrighted © 1915 by George Allen and Unwin Ltd., also published subsequently by Macmillan Publishing Co., Inc., New York.

From *Lenin: The Man, the Theorist, the Leader* edited by Leonard Schapiro and Peter Reddaway, copyrighted © 1967 by Leonard Schapiro and Peter Reddaway. Exerpted and reprinted by permission of Praeger Publishers, Inc., New York.

From *The Life and Death of Lenin* by Robert Payne, copyrighted © 1964 by Robert Payne and published by Simon and Schuster, Inc., New York.

From *Marxism and Ethics* by Eugene Kamenka, copyrighted © 1969 by Eugene Kamenka and published by Macmillan and Co. Ltd. With permission of Macmillan, London and Basingstoke, and St. Martin's Press, Inc., New York.

From *The Rise of Anthropological Theory: A History of Theories of Culture* by Marvin L. Harris, copyrighted © 1968 by Thomas Y. Crowell Company, Inc. With permission of the publishers.

LIST OF SYMBOLS

A-D	Engels, *Anti-Dühring*.
DN	Engels, *Dialectics of Nature*.
GI	Marx-Engels, *The German Ideology*.
LCW	Lenin, *Collected Works*.
MEB	Marx-Engels, *On Britain*.
MEC	Marx-Engels, *On Colonialism*.
MER	Marx-Engels, *On Religion*.
MESC	Marx-Engels, *Selected Correspondence*.
MESW	Marx-Engels, *Selected Works*.
MEW	Marx-Engels, *Werke*.
MG	Kautsky, *Materialistische Geschichtsauffassung*.
WYM	Marx, *Writings of the Young Marx on Philosophy and Society*.

INTRODUCTION

In view of the enormous number of works on Marxism in general and in light of the many books and articles touching on the relationship of Marxism to religion in particular, it may fairly be asked why yet another such work should be produced. My reply is that in eliciting answers to the kinds of questions posed by the methodology I have used, it was necessary to go to the primary sources almost exclusively. This is not to bemoan a sad fate but to affirm that there are notable deficiencies in the secondary sources relevant to my topic. By way of general indictment, I contend that the major difficulty with existing studies of the Marxist critique of religion is that their authors, whether expositors or critics, have failed both to specify their own presuppositions concerning religion and to approach the subject with an adequate comprehension of its many dimensions. Since, in most cases, the reader is equally unprepared, anthropologically, sociologically, psychologically, and historically, for clear and informed thought in this vast and nebulous area, the result has been widespread confusion.

As if this were not enough, numerous writers with little more than polemical interests have compounded the confusion by failing to distinguish between religion in general and their own brands of faith in particular. Others have not discriminated between the concepts of metaphysics and the supernatural items of religious belief. Some have muddled the various categories, descriptive and normative, whereby religion may be approached, understood, and assessed. Still others have mistakenly identified theology with religion and have assumed that the history and analysis of the former are identical with the history and analysis of the latter. Although it is understandable that thinkers strongly influenced by Christianity, the most theological of religions, should be predisposed to treat religion as if it were identical with the philosophy of religion, still and all, it is a serious mistake to focus so intently on the cognitive aspects of religion that its social and cultic aspects are forgotten. In that which follows, my primary concern is to give a thorough, systematic, and critical exposition of the classical Marxist critiques of religion without falling into the kinds of error just enumerated.

Since far more attention has been paid to the derivation of Marx's ideas on religion than to the comprehensive exposition and nonreligious criticism of those ideas, I have not dealt with the etiology of his views. Should the reader seek knowledge concerning the origin of Marx's ideas, he is advised to turn to the relevant works of such scholars as Hook, McClellan, Rotenstreich, Dupré, Kojève, Barnhart, and Rosen. Should he wish to learn of the non-Marxist derivation of some of Engels' and Kautsky's views on religion, he is advised to keep reading, as I know of no source other than this to which he can turn.

Having accused others of a variety of shortcomings, I hasten to describe my orientation. Since the many critical passages which follow will reveal the details of my position on specific items, it suffices here to adumbrate the perspective from which I begin. Two positive and two negative points should be noted. Positively, the first point is that my approach is entirely naturalistic. At no time in this study have I found it necessary or desirable to suppose that any given religious belief is true. Furthermore, I see no reason to suppose that the literal truth or falsity of any doctrine is important to a particular religion. On the contrary, the scientific psychology and sociology of religion require only that those who profess religious beliefs take them to be both true and sacred. Since I assume from the outset that truth and falsity are not at issue and that it is more the mode rather than the content of belief that matters to religion, no epistemological claims relative to specific religious beliefs will intrude in the pages that follow. The second positive point is that my approach is functionalistic. In other words, refusing to define religion in terms of belief in some common denominator or other, such as the supernatural, I am concerned rather to try to understand it in terms of its functions in society. Admitting that it can be dysfunctional in a variety of ways, I contend, nonetheless, as a general principle that religion and its surrogates arise and persist because they confer social benefits on a given human group and psychological benefits on the individual members of that group.

Negatively, the first point is that I shall not criticize Marxism at any time from the standpoint of an identifiable religious persuasion. Should this study constitute an advance in understanding the Marxist critique of religion, it will not be because I, unlike Luijpen and Wetter for example, have some special knowledge of God systematically withheld from Marxists.[1] The second negative point is that, despite similarities, I do not criticize religion as a Marxist unless being a naturalist and a functionalist is tantamount to being a Marxist. If it is true that every effusion of social science is partisan, then, perforce, this study is also partisan. It is, however, neither self-consciously religious nor self-consciously Marxist. Judging from the existing literature, this ought to make it refreshingly different if nothing else. Those who are gifted in the taxonomy of partisanship may classify it as they like.

It is now appropriate, having revealed my orientation, to outline the method I intend to use in giving critical exposition to the views of Marx, Engels, Lenin, and Kautsky on religion. It is a method which, as I have already said, led me to bypass secondary works very largely and to use primary sources almost exclusively. The method in question contains six points, some preliminary comment about which is now in order.

First, I have analyzed in detail what each of these thinkers believed about the etiology of religion, and I hasten to add that by etiology I do not only mean the primordial causes of religion in a temporal sense but also the subsequent springs and sources which have led to its periodic reblossoming and persistence. Those who are familiar with my topic may well be struck by the extensive treatment I have given to Marxist views on the etiology of religion, but, far from being apologetic over having made it a major theme, I take it to be one of my chief merits. To the best of my knowledge, Desroche is the only other author who has approached the etiology of religion somewhat as I have done, and in detail roughly equal to my own.[2] In dealing with what he calls the "sociographie marxiste des religions" he begins as I and proceeds for a time in much the same manner, but he does not extend his exposition beyond Marx and Engels to Lenin and Kautsky, makes no comparisons, and fails to be thoroughly critical. Terray might also have found occasion to examine Marx's and Engels' views on the etiology of religion but failed to do so.[3]

---

[1] William A. Luijpen, *Phenomenology and Atheism*, Duquesne Studies, Philosophical Series, no. 17 (Pittsburgh: Duquesne University Press, 1964), Chapter Three; pp. 140-141, 156-157 especially; Gustav A. Wetter, *Dialectical Materialism: A Historical and Systematic Survey of Philosophy in the Soviet Union*, trans. by Peter Heath (New York: Frederick A. Praeger, 1963), p. 556.

[2] Henri Desroche, *Marxisme et Religions* (Paris: Presses Universitaires de France, 1962), pp. 1-3.

[3] Emmanuel Terray, *Le Marxisme devant les sociétés "Primitives": deux études* (Paris: François Maspero, 1969), pp. 15-91.

Second, in keeping with the Marxist emphasis on the importance of historical analysis, I have tried to assemble all the significant views of Marx, Engels, Lenin, and Kautsky on the development of religion from primitive to modern times. Although this procedure is not novel, I have made critical comments on certain biblical interpretations of Engels and Kautsky which are not common to other studies.

Third, having used the etiology and history of religion as categories for assembling what might be thought of as the raw data of the classical Marxist critiques of religion, I have then sought to discover what Marx, Engels, Lenin, and Kautsky took religion to be in terms of its essence or substance.

Fourth, since it was axiomatic to them that religion *is* very largely what it *does*, I have sought to find everything contained in the raw data which is relevant to their views on the functions of religion. As might be expected, normative categories have also been revealed in the process.

Fifth, taking Marx's views on the origin, development, substance, and functions of religion as canonical, I have compared, contrasted, and assessed the opinions of Engels, Lenin, and Kautsky on the same topics.

Sixth, in addition to calling attention to the theoretical, logical, and factual errors which I take Marx, Engels, Lenin, and Kautsky to have made, I have concluded with a general assessment of the strengths and weaknesses of their critiques of religion.

I have consistently followed the method described above except for the inclusion of two sections in the chapter on Marx, the first of which deals with the unity of his thought, the second of which assess the importance to him of the criticism of religion.

When quoting or referring to Marx's and Engels' works, I have used English translations whenever possible and have referred to editions which are readily available, many in paperbacks. Whenever it has been necessary to quote from the original, I have used the *Marx-Engels Werke*.[4] In each instance, I have given the title of the subdivision cited in addition to the volume number and the page or pages at issue. In quoting or referring to Lenin's work, I have used *V. I. Lenin: Collected Works* exclusively and have referred to this *multi-volume* source as I have referred to the *Marx-Engels Werke*.[5] In referring to Kautsky's work, I have used English

---

[4] Karl Marx-Friedrich Engels, *Werke* (39 vols.; Berlin: Dietz Verlag, 1956-1970), hereinafter referred to as MEW.

[5] V. I. Lenin, *Collected Works* (45 vols.; Moscow: Progress Publishers, 1960-1970), hereinafter referred to as LCW.

translations whenever possible, but since many of his works remain in German, and are difficult to obtain, I have quoted him extensively in the original, especially at crucial points.

CHAPTER 1

MARX'S CRITIQUE OF RELIGION

RELIGION AND THE UNITY OF MARX'S THOUGHT

If one were to separate the few pages Marx devoted exclusively to religion from the thousands he wrote, it would be evident that he felt no need to deal extensively with religious phenomena. A perusal of his writings will show that normally he did not dwell intently on religion for more than two or three pages at a time, that he did not treat religion in isolation from what to him were the more significant factors of socio-economic life, and that he scattered his reflections on it widely throughout his works. Even though his references to religion often reveal intensive study and thought, they do not imply thoroughness. Moreover, they are often ill-informed. Perhaps the most accurate characterization is that his analyses were always incisive, if not always insightful, and that his criticisms were invariably trenchant insofar as they were applicable.

Marx's treatment of religion was as varied as it was scattered. On occasion he analyzed it in general with an eye to its etiology and taxonomy. On other occasions he singled out specific religions, such as Judaism or Christianity or distinct phases of religious development such as the primitive or the bourgeois, for analytic, critical, and illustrative purposes. Sometimes he drew analogies such as the ones he presumed to obtain between Catholicism and feudal agrarian society, or between Protestantism and political economy, and other times he contented himself with invidious comparisons. Marx knew the scriptures well and quoted them often for a variety of reasons, sometimes to expose exploitation and hypocrisy, sometimes to manifest irony, sometimes to convey insight, sometimes to put superstition in its place, and sometimes, one suspects, just for the fun of it.

Without presupposing anything at this point concerning the unity of Marx's thought and without any regard to the content of his various references to religion, the greater concentration of those references is to be found in works prior to 1847. If one were to list those writings of the young Marx which reveal his position on religion most clearly and completely and in which the concentration of significant references to religion is the greatest, the list would contain, as I rank them, first, "Toward the Critique of Hegel's Philosophy of Law: Introduction," written in 1843; second, two integrally related essays on the Jewish Question, also composed in 1843; third, the *Economic and Philosophic Manuscripts of 1844* (hereinafter called the *Manuscripts of 1844*); and fourth, *The German Ideology*, completed in 1846. In terms of the significance and frequency of references to religion, one work alone of the mature Marx ranks with the writings listed above. That work, rather surprisingly, is the first volume of *Capital*, published in 1867. With regard to the critique of religion it outranks by far any other work attributable to the mature Marx unless one takes *The German Ideology* to be a mature work.

A prima facie reading will reveal changes in the vocabulary of Marx's thought, in the problems which preoccupied him, and in the tenor with which he treated them. With respect to vocabulary, it is a commonplace among Marxologists that the related terms "alienation" and "self-aliena-tion" which are prominent in the early Marx disappear after 1844 as commonly used vehicles for expressing his thought. Presumably, "aliena-tion" is replaced in the later Marx by the term "exploitation." The extent to which the latter encompasses and preserves the connotations of the former is a moot question. It is also evident that the humanism which is prominent in the young Marx, particularly in the *Manuscripts of 1844*, disappears in the mature Marx. In this vein, Tucker has noted that the concept of "Man" seems to be absent in the later works having been replaced by the concept of social classes with the result that there is a kind of impersonality, uncharacteristic of the early Marx, which pervades his later works.[1]

The changing problems which preoccupied Marx at various points in his development are so clearly discernible that Löwith has not only schematized them topically but has done so in a way which must surely be acceptable to most if not all Marxologists. He says:

Marx's development can be summed up as follows: At first he criticized religion philosophically, then he criticized religion and philosophy politically, and at last he criticized religion, philosophy and politics, and all other ideologies, economically.[2]

---

[1] Robert C. Tucker, *Philosophy and Myth in Karl Marx* (Cambridge: Cambridge University Press, 1961), p. 165.

[2] Karl Löwith, "Man's Self-Alienation in the Early Writings of Marx," *Social Research*, XXI (Summer, 1954), 204.

The changes in tenor which characterize Marx's treatment of various issues are subtle and can be sensed and appreciated only by immersion in his works. In large part, these changes were probably occasioned by, and certainly associated with, alterations in his tactics which were in turn modified by his developing theory of class struggle and by his progressive identification with the proletariat.

The question is whether or not the prima facie changes which occurred in Marx's work were meant to imply the continuation and enrichment of, or the repudiation and replacement of, some or all of his earlier concepts, preoccupations, and modes of approach. Since he gave no categorical answer to this question, attempts at answering it have been circumstantial and inferential. Predictably, some Marxologists have denied that the aforementioned changes have disrupted the unity of Marx's thought while others have argued to the contrary. Equally predictably, those who have maintained that there is a significant degree of disunity have had to decide whether the young or the old Marx is the significant, the valuable Marx. In short, are the early writings to be judged, interpreted, accepted, or rejected on the basis of the late works or vice versa?[3]

A high degree of unity in Marx's thought poses no potential obstacles to the study of his critique or religion. This is true for two reasons: First, if his thought is unified and if his critique of religion is integrally related to that thought, then no special problems can be expected to arise; second, if his thought in general is unified while his critique of religion is not, then his views on religion must be taken as a special case and treated accordingly. This would be required if his critique of religion were shown to be inconsistent with itself, or inconsistent with the remainder of his unified thought, or both. But in neither case would the general unity of his thought pose problems for the study of his critique of religion.

The situation is potentially different if it can be shown that there is substantial disunity in Marx's thought. Hodges, for example, has argued that Marx outgrew the rather romantic and abstract humanism of his youth, that the emphasis on social and psychological forms of alienation, commonplace to his earlier works, is absent from his later thought, and that the terms "alienation" and "humanism" not only disappear for all practical purposes in his later vocabulary but are even used pejoratively

---

[3] Tucker, *Philosophy and Myth in Karl Marx*, pp. 168-174; Donald C. Hodges, "The Young Marx—A Reappraisal," *Philosophy and Phenomenological Research*, XXVII (September, 1966—June, 1967), 216, n. 1. Each work takes up the question of unity in Marx from different points of view; each gives a useful set of references to the works of participants involved in the controversy.

on occasion.[4] If Hodges is correct in pointing out instances of substantial disunity in Marx's thought, it is easy to see why that disunity poses a potential problem to the study of his critique of religion, for the works in which Marx first elaborated his conceptions of alienation and of humanism are writings in which he gave early expression to his views on religion. If Marx rejected certain prominent concepts of his early thought, did he also, in like manner, reject some, if not all, of his early views on religion? That is the potential problem which disunity in Marx's thought poses.

To summarize, the possibilities are four: (1) Marx's thought in general may be unified and so too may be his critique of religion; (2) his thought may be unified in general while his critique of religion may not be; (3) his thought in general may reveal disunity while his critique of religion may not; and (4) his thought in general may reveal disunity and so too may his critique of religion.

I contend that, whether or not Marx's thought is unified in general, his critique of religion is unified in particular, but before attempting to support this contention, one more problem must be dealth with. As there is no unanimity among Marxologists concerning the degree of unity in Marx's thought, so there is no agreement among them over the date which is presumed to separate the works of the young from those of the mature Marx. Hodges and Struik favor 1847 as the dividing line, whereas Tucker and Hammen prefer 1845.[5] If the latter date is more nearly correct than the former, then *The German Ideology* must be taken as a mature work. If so, it joins the first volume of *Capital* as one of two works far outstripping the other mature writings when measured by the significance and frequency of the references to religion contained therein. From the standpoint of the critique of religion, I contend that it is of no concern whether *The German Ideology* is taken as a mature work or not, nor does it matter which date is adopted as the dividing line between the young and the mature Marx.

---

[4] Donald C. Hodges, "The Unity of Marx's Thought," *Science and Society*, XXVIII (Summer, 1964), 317; "Marx's Contribution to Humanism," *Science and Society*, XXVIX (Spring, 1965), 174; "The Young Marx—A Reappraisal," pp. 217, 221-222, 225, 229.

[5] Hodges, "The Unity of Marx's Thought," p. 322; Karl Marx, *Economic and Philosophic Manuscripts of 1844*, ed. and introd. by Dirk Struik (New York: International Publishers, 1964), p. 55. All subsequent references to the *Manuscripts of 1844* will involve the edition published in Moscow: Foreign Languages Publishing House, 1961; Tucker, *Philosophy and Myth in Marx*, p. 165; Oscar J. Hammen, "The Young Marx, Reconsidered," *Journal of the History of Ideas*, XXXI (January-March, 1970), 110.

The most convincing way to demonstrate the unity of Marx's critique of religion is to begin with the works written after 1847, for in these writings every major characteristic of his position on religion, except one, appears in logical continuity with his earlier views. If interest in the continuity of these views were not at issue, one could dispense with his earlier writings and suffer no substantial loss in the assertion of his principal conclusions concerning religious phenomena. Without giving a complete catalogue of Marx's convictions involving religion and without demonstrating the aforementioned continuities at this time by citing his early writings, the following twelve points, documented exclusively with references to works written after 1847 should be sufficient to show that a high degree of unity characterized his critique of religion. First, Marx was relentless in his hostility to religious beliefs, practices, and institutions, but beyond using the spoken and written word he neither practiced nor advocated tactics designed to destroy religion forcibly.[6] Members of the working class were expected to free themselves from religious influences but in such a way that religion would die from neglect and loss of function rather than from frontal assault.[7] Second, no religious doctrine from any source was ever accepted by Marx as true. Accordingly, he never distinguished between religious belief and superstition, between true and false religion, even though he believed that some religious manifestations were more highly developed than others. He consistently referred to the objects of faith as "religious phantoms"[8] or as denizens of the "mist-enveloped" regions of religion.[9] Third, Marx always held that religion was epiphenomenal. Sometimes he made this point explicitly as he did in calling the religious world the "reflex of the real world."[10] On other occasions he made the same point implicitly, averring, for instance, that it was easy to go from the earthly core of reality to the misty regions of religion but not vice versa.[11] More often he would make the point obliquely as he did in suggesting that the feudal substructure explained Catholicism,[12] or in pointing out that bourgeois religion gave expression

---

[6] John Lewis, *The Life and Teaching of Karl Marx* (New York: International Publishers, 1965), p. 166.

[7] Karl Marx, *The Critique of the Gotha Program* (Moscow: Foreign Languages Publishing House, n.d.), p. 35.

[8] *Ibid.*

[9] Karl Marx, *Capital* (4 vols.; Moscow: Foreign Languages Publishing House, n.d.), I, 72, 372, n. 3.

[10] *Ibid.*, p. 79.

[11] *Ibid.*, p. 372, n. 3.

[12] *Ibid.*, p. 82.

to free competition.[13] Fourth, Marx held that the items of religious belief functioned as objects external to man which exercised control over him. Brain products, he noted, became independent of their producers and in turn governed them.[14] To Marx, religion was an element of ideology, and as such it both mystified and controlled its producers and developers.[15] Fifth, Marx held that the objects of religious belief not only governed man but rendered him degraded and slavish in the process. He referred sarcastically to the "sheep's nature" of the Christian,[16] criticized the "Christian slavish nature" of the English proletariat,[17] and denounced Hinduism for its degradation of man, the rightful sovereign of nature.[18] The joint implication of this point along with point four is that religious man lives in a state of alienation even though Marx used the term but rarely in his later works. Sixth, Marx always maintained that there was a close relationship between the interests of religious institutions and those of secular property whether movable or immovable. If the relationship was not one of identity, it was, at least, one of extreme similarity.[19] Seventh, Marx recognized the socially conservative functions of religion. He quoted with approval the proposition that forms of superstition which appear cruel to the individual are conservative of the Hindu community,[20] noted that when social tummult reached a certain level the barricades of religion, property, family, and order would be thrown up,[21] and pointed out that the mortgage which the French peasant held on heaven was the chief guarantor of the earthly mortgage which encumbered his small holdings.[22] "Heaven," said Marx, "was quite a pleasing accession to the narrow strip of land just won [by the French peasant during the early nineteenth

---

[13] Karl Marx and Friedrich Engels, *The Communist Manifesto*, ed. by Samuel H. Beer (New York: Appleton-Century-Crofts, 1955), p. 30 (hereinafter referred to as *Manifesto*).

[14] Marx, *Capital*, I, 72, 621.

[15] Marx-Engels, *Manifesto*, p. 29.

[16] Marx, *Capital*, I, 52.

[17] Letter, K. Marx to F. Engels, Nov. 17, 1862, Karl Marx and Friedrich Engels, *On Britain* (Moscow: Foreign Languages Publishing House, 1962), p. 538 (hereinafter referred to as MEB).

[18] Marx, "The British Rule in India," MEB, pp. 397-398.

[19] Marx, *Capital*, I, 10, 676; "Parliamentary Debates—The Clergy and the Struggle for the Ten-Hour Day-Starvation," MEB, p. 384 (hereinafter referred to as "Parliamentary Debates"); Marx-Engels, *Manifesto*, p. 35.

[20] Marx, *Capital*, II, 236-237.

[21] Karl Marx, *The Class Struggles in France: 1848 to 1850*, with an introduction by Friedrich Engels (Moscow: Foreign Languages Publishing House, n.d.), p. 203.

[22] *Ibid.*, p. 131.

century]. . . .[23] Eighth, Marx believed in the relativity of all religious ethics. He taught that religion was a part of ideology and that ideological elements change as the economic substructure changes.[24] He contended that the Teutonic-Christian family was neither absolute nor final,[25] noted that a parson may say that God wills one thing in France and another thing in England,[26] and maintained that for all practical purposes Christian ideas had succumbed in the eighteenth century.[27] Ninth, Marx asserted that there was an intimate relationship between Protestantism and political economy. Each had its cultus of abstract man, and each supported the other.[28] Protestantism was historically important in the genesis of capital, and no more fitting form of religion than it could be found for bourgeois society.[29] It was notorious for giving expression to free competition. Tenth, Marx identified the Jews with usury.[30] Eleventh, he often drew analogies between religion and economics.[31] Marx used these analogies as a means of explicating various economic mysteries. Indeed, at points one is tempted to conclude that Christianity served as a heuristic principle for his economic investigations. In passing, it is interesting to note that the two works in which he applied the greatest number of religiously inspired analogies to economics were the *Manunscripts of 1844* and the first volume of *Capital*.[32] Twelfth, Marx believed in the eventual disappearance of religion. He maintained that for several hundred years religious authority had been falling progressively into decay,[33] and he argued by implication that religion would disappear altogether when practical human relations became completely rational.[34].

Although Marx's best known and most extensive observations on

[23] Karl Marx, *The Eighteenth Brumaire of Louis Bonaparte* (Moscow: Foreign Languages Publishing House, n.d.), p. 129.

[24] Marx-Engels, *Manifesto*, p. 30.

[25] Marx, *Capital*, I, 490.

[26] Karl Marx, *Wages, Price and Profit* (Moscow: Foreign Languages Publishing House, n.d.), p. 9.

[27] Marx-Engels, *Manifesto*, p. 30.

[28] Marx, *Capital*, I, 79.

[29] *Ibid.*, pp. 79, 276, n. 2.

[30] Marx, "Parliamentary Debates," MEB, p. 378.

[31] Marx, *Capital*, I, 72, 361, 621.

[32] Marx, *Capital*, I, 361, 621, 713, 744, n. 1; *Manuscripts of 1844*, pp. 68-70, 80, 94.

[33] Karl Marx, "The Decay of Religious Authority," in *Reader in Marxist Philosophy*, ed. by Howard Selsam and Harry Martel (New York: International Publishers, 1963), p. 240 (hereinafter referred to as *Reader*).

[34] Marx, *Capital*, I, 79.

religion occur in early works, his basic position can be constructed from the later writings alone. The only prominent exception to this is the absence in the later works of any reiteration of his position on the consolatory-palliative functions of religion. Nowhere did he reaffirm his early conviction that religion is "the sigh of the oppressed creature," "the heart of a heartless world," the "*opium* of the people."[35] Marx's failure to dwell on the consolatory-palliative functions of religion does not imply that he changed his mind about the narcotic aspects of religion, but merely that he took this point to be obvious. It is tempting to speculate that the later Marx assumed the speedy demise of religion and the coming triumph of socialism to be so heartening to the proletariat that it would have been inappropriate and morbid of him to have continued mouthing the early refrain that religion was "the sigh of the oppressed creature," "the heart of a heartless world," etc. A secondary exception to the high degree of unity which exists between the views of the early and the later Marx on religion lies in the fact that his later observations on religion became increasingly scattered, terse, and sarcastic. But the slight change of focus, accompanying his later preoccupation with economics, implies neither alteration nor repudiation of his early views on religion. Therefore, since a high degree of unity exists in Marx's critique of religion, I can utilize a topical approach to the exposition of that critique with no concern over problems of internal development.

THE BEGINNING AND END OF CRITICISM

As the preceding section began with a problem, so, too, does this one. Here the problem concerns the degree of importance which should be accorded to Marx's critique of religion in relationship to his work as a whole. As might be expected, there is considerable disagreement among Marxologists as to just how important the critique of religion was to Marx. Some expositors and interpreters have accorded it great, if not paramount, importance.[36] Among these, Lewis comes to mind immediately, for in his recent biography of Marx he contends that the criticism of religion was by no means of secondary importance. One also thinks of Pascal who goes

---

[35] Karl Marx, "Toward the Critique of Hegel's Philosophy of Law: Introduction," *Writings of the Young Marx on Philosophy and Society*, ed. by Loyd D. Easton and Kurt H. Guddat (Garden City, N.Y.: Doubleday & Company, Inc., 1967), p. 250 (hereinafter referred to as "Critique of Hegel's Philosophy" and WYM respectively).

[36] Lewis, *The Life and Times of Karl Marx*, p. 58.

even further in saying that the "first and most important work" of the Young Hegelians, including Marx and Engels, "was, naturally enough, a criticism of religion."[37] To continue, Calvez concludes that to Marx the criticism of religion was indispensable for pedagogic and therapeutic reasons and that the general problem of religion pervaded his entire thought even if only implicitly.[38] To cap it off, Henri Lefebvre contends that the criticism of religion is "the prerequisite of all criticism," because "religion sanctions the separation of man from himself, the cleavage between the sacred and the profane, between the supernatural and nature."[39]

Other students of Marx, on the contrary, have contented themselves with mouthing the old refrain that religion is the opium of the people.[40] Thus, having paid their respects to the topic, they have turned their attention quickly to other topics of allegedly greater interest and have through default denied any major significance to the critique of religion. Those who would resolve the puzzle by looking to Marx for guidance are doomed to disappointment, initially at least. Though he said quite seriously, in an important early work, "die Kritik der Religion ist die Voraussetzung aller Kritik,"[41] he devoted only a few dozen pages, as I have said, to the explicit analysis and criticism of religion. The key to clarifying the problem, if not resolving it, lies in the analysis of *Voraussetzung,* a term which may mean, "beginning," "premise," "presupposition," "hypothesis," "that which is taken for granted," and the like. *Brochhaus* defines it as "das als Grundbedingung Gegebene."

Whether or not the criticism of religion is the logical presupposition of all criticism, it served as the temporal beginning for Marx's work both

---

[37] Karl Marx and Friedrich Engels, *The German Ideology,* ed. and introd. by R. Pascal (New York: International Publishers, 1947), Introduction, p. ix (hereinafter referred to as GI).

[38] Jean-Yves Calvez, *La pensée de Karl Marx* (Paris: Editions du seuil, 1956), pp. 55-57.

[39] Henri Lefebvre, *The Sociology of Marx* (New York: Random House, 1969), p. 10.

[40] R. N. Carew-Hunt. *The Theory and Practice of Communism* (London: Geoffrey Bless, 1950); George Lichtheim, *Marxism: An Historical and Critical Study* (New York: Frederich A. Praeger, 1961); John Plamenatz, *German Marxism and Russian Communism* (London: Longmans, Green and Co., 1954). These basic and well known books constitute but a small sample of works in which Marx's critique of religion is either ignored altogether or given but cursory notice.

[41] Karl Marx, "Zur Kritik der Hegelschen Rechtsphilosophie: Einleitung," MEW, I, 378.

personally and tactically. In attempting to disclose the source of Marx's personal animosity toward religion, Calvez has concluded that it did not lie in any adolescent struggle with familial religiosity but lay rather with the pervasive religious intrusions of the Prussian state.[42] Since Marx was nurtured as a liberal and a rationalist in a home characterized by freedom and tolerance, Calvez assumes that he, unlike Engels, never had to wrestle with Calvinism and Pietism.[43] This assumption is no doubt true, but it underestimates the intensity of conviction and devotion which may accompany liberal Protestantism. Payne is nearer the truth than Calvez in describing the juvenile Marx as one who, though not deeply indoctrinated, was nevertheless a serious, even a passionate Christian.[44] Whatever the exact intensity of Marx's adolescent faith may have been, he showed in early manhood many of the psychological earmarks of one who recognizes that he has been sold a bill of religious goods and that he must make expiation for his gullibility and misplaced idealism.

Furthermore, Lobkowicz misleads his readers when he says, "Contrary to most Young Hegelians, Marx never went through a period of 'religiousness'."[45] This assertion is true if it means that he was not extensively preoccupied with the ontological concerns of Hegelianized Christianity. It is also true if by "religiousness" one intends to refer either to a religious life based on mystical experience or to the pietistic experience of "being saved," but these three types of religiosity by no means exhaust the manifold varieties of religious experience. Moreover, even if Lobkowicz is correct in contending that Marx grew up among men for whom religion was no more than a matter of propriety and expediency, this in no way entails the proposition that the juvenile Marx related himself to religion in the same way.[46] In any case, it is quite clear that when he reached maturity he did not relate himself to religion as the men among whom he grew up are presumed to have done. Finally, in view of the sarcasm, irony, and innuendo to which Marx subjected religion, particularly in his mature works, it is very difficult to take Lobkowicz seriously when he says, "The utter lack of a genuine *Erlebnis* largely explains why Marx's antagonism to religion always remained completely impersonal."[47] Imper-

---

[42] Calvez, *La pensée de Karl Marx*, p. 56.

[43] *Ibid.*, p. 21.

[44] Robert Payne, *Marx* (New York: Simon and Schuster, 1968), pp. 31-32.

[45] Nicholas Lobkowicz, "Karl Marx's Attitude Toward Religion," *The Review of Politics*, XXVI (July, 1964), 329.

[46] *Ibid.*

[47] *Ibid.*, p. 331.

sonal or not, Marx's critique of religion was by no means thoroughly objective. What Lobkowicz takes to be impersonalism is often nothing but lack of interest and understanding.

In concluding this excursion, I should like to point out, first, that Marx's association with religion was indeed limited and short-lived; second, that his failure to comprehend some of the emotional dimensions of religion was probably based on his own fragmentary religious involvement; and third, that he did pass from an "extremely cerebral 'Christianity' to the atheism of the Young Hegelians" swiftly, if not so smoothly as Lobkowicz would have it.[48]

At some time during or immediately after 1837, while a student at Berlin, Marx became philosophically a naturalist, a realist, a materialist, and an atheist. One may safely assume that this process of radical inversion both accompanied and led to new perspectives on nature, society, and religion. As soon as his new position had solidified, Marx turned with his usual vehemence to the task of settling accounts with the source of his earlier disillusionment. It is in this context that his well-known tribute to Epicurus and his panegyric to Prometheus are to be understood.[49]

Turning from personal considerations to tactical concerns exclusively, it is evident that the criticism of religion was for Marx the beginning of all criticism for two reasons: First, it was the only effective means available at the time for launching a "relentless attack" on "existing conditions," and, second, it was of primary importance pedagogically and therapeutically for the benefit of the working class just then awakening to revolutionary activity.

The Young Hegelians with whom Marx aligned himself for a time perceived the regime of Friedrich Wilhelm IV, inaugurated in 1840, as both reactionary and repressive.[50] Frontal attacks on the politics of this regime were, however, perilous and practically impossible.[51] Thus attention was

---

[48] *Ibid.*, p. 330.

[49] Karl Marx, "Foreword to Thesis: The Difference Between the Natural Philosophy of Democritus and the Natural Philosophy of Epicurus," *Marx and Engels on Religion* (New York: Schocken Books, Inc., 1964), pp. 14-15 (hereinafter referred to as MER); Marx and Engels, *The German Ideology* (Moscow: Progress Publishers, 1964), pp. 147-148. This Russian edition in English contains the entire text unlike the American edition cited earlier (n. 37) which contains only Parts One and Three. Unless designated GI (Moscow), all references will be to the American edition.

[50] Engels, "Friedrich Wilhelm IV., König von Preussen," MEW, I, 446-447.

[51] Gustav Mayer, *Friedrich Engels*, trans. by Gilbert Highet and Helen Highet (New York: Alfred A. Knopf, 1936), p. 14.

diverted to religion which along with politics was one of the two greatest practical concerns in otherwise "theoretical Germany."[52] But just then good fortune in the guise of recent developments in the philosophy of religion, including the higher criticism, smiled upon the would-be opponents of the regime and suggested an avenue of attack through religion. Thus, donning the garb of parochial disputants and lapsing into abstruse theological jargon, they aimed at priestcraft in order to smite the regime, the dual objective being both to destroy traditional religion and to vanquish the existing state.[53] Seen in this perspective, Marx's early diatribes on religion assume major tactical significance. "*Religion*," said he, "is the table of contents of theoretical struggles,"[54] Moreover, "the criticism of heaven turns into the criticism of the earth, the *criticism of right*, and the *criticism of theology* into the *criticism of politics*."[55] One can, after all, turn without impediment to reject profane error when divine error has already been destroyed.

good

The didactic and therapeutic aspects of Marx's attack on religion are indistinguishable tactically. To him "religion is the self-consciousness and self-regard of man, who either has not yet found himself or has already lost himself again."[56] Born out of and sustained by alienation, religion is a mode of consciousness both false and perverted; the happiness it offers, bogus and illusory. It renders man a "degraded, enslaved, rejected, contemptible being."[57] In order to progress from these irrationalities to rationality and from perverted consciousness to truly human self-awareness, religion must be abolished, its disastrous effects transcended. Atheism, on the contrary, affirms and frees man from religious repression and heteronomy.[58] The degree to which religion is the false sun around which mankind orbits is the degree to which Marx felt obliged to weaken the gravitational pull of this illusory star in the hope of wrenching its human satellite free to determine its own course.[59]

---

[52] Friedrich Engels, *Feuerbach and the End of Classical German Philosophy*, Karl Marx and Friedrich Engels, *Selected Works* (New York: International Publishers, 1968), p. 601 (hereinafter referred to as *Feuerbach* and *MESW* respectively).

[53] Friedrich Engels, *Germany: Revolution and Counter-Revolution* (New York: International Publishers, 1969), p. 30.

[54] Letter, K. Marx to A. Ruge, Sept. 1843, WYM, p. 213.

[55] Marx, "Critique of Hegel's Philosophy," WYM, p. 251.

[56] *Ibid.*, p. 250.

[57] *Ibid.*, pp. 257-258.

[58] Marx, *Manuscripts of 1844*, p. 164.

[59] Marx, "Critique of Hegel's Philosophy," WYM, pp. 250-251.

— Nor is religion simply a form of self-deception; it is also a powerful device whereby the ruling class manipulates the working class. While the gods are at first merely the creation of alienated consciousness, once established, they compound fear and confusion, lend their sanctity to exploitive interests and become profoundly conservative forces. Keenly aware of this, Marx wanted to guide the proletariat to a correct understanding of religious repression. "Lords temporal" and "lords spiritual" were closing ranks;[60] holy men, in at least one instance, were active in an anti-industrial crusade;[61] religious penal laws abused the lower classes.[62] And the sophisticated were content to declaim hypocritically, "for us Voltaire; for the people, masses and tithes; for us pious phrases; for the people Christian practice."[63] Marx revealed all this and more on behalf of his compatriots who, in the 1840's, were still enthralled by Germanic-Christian religion and idealism. As an opening gambit in his relentless attack on existing conditions, the assault on religion cannot be overemphasized.

Granted that the criticism of religion was for Marx the personal and tactical beginning of all criticism, the question still remains as to its total significance for his thought. In short, did Marx take *Voraussetzung* to mean that the criticism of religion was the logical presupposition of all criticism? In formulating the answer to this question, it must be remembered that concern with ideology pervades his thought whether expressed early or late. If it can be maintained that the criticism of ideology was strategic for Marx, then it can also be maintained that the criticism of religion, the most visible and vociferous aspect of ideology, was also strategic. Much of the difficulty in assessing the issue lies in the blurred relationship between the tactical and the strategic in his thought. It might even be argued that nothing was strategic for Marx, since he was dealing with what he took to be self-resolving problems, and of all the problems he confronted, none seemed to be liquidating itself more rapidly than religion. The following considerations should establish this point beyond doubt.

Whenever religion was at issue, Marx's program was the reform of consciousness.[64] This would take effect progressively from the moment at

---

[60] Marx, "The Decay of Religious Authority," *The New York Daily Tribune*, October 24, 1855; *Reader*, pp. 241-242.

[61] Marx, "Parliamentary Debates," MEB, p. 382.

[62] Marx, "Anti-Church Movement—Demonstration in Hyde Park," MEB, p. 435.

[63] *Ibid.*

[64] Letter, K. Marx to A. Ruge, September, 1843, WYM, p. 214.

which man became the highest being for man. But this was precisely what Feuerbach had achieved when, in 1841, he published *The Essence of Christianity*, a work which resolved theology into anthropology. In short, Marx discerned a wave of naturalism soon to crest on a massive scale undercutting and sweeping away all the edifices of superstition, religion, and transcendentalism. Nor was this mighty wave limited to philosophy; it also appeared in science. In witness thereto, Marx wrote in 1861 that Darwin had for the first time dealt a death blow to teleology.[65]

Although theology had indeed come to grief in the fullness of time, religion having become an anachronism, Marx realized that vestiges of each would persist for a time as historical flotsam and jetsam.[66] But this did not worry him, because the religion that lingers will be dispatched in due time by the proletariat for whom theoretical ideas do not exist.[67] The modern worker can be depended on to raze all the old institutions including religion. Marx noted with satisfaction that the audience broke into applause every time Father John Bright, the English Liberal, said in a speech to the London Trade Unions that in the United States there were neither kings nor bishops.[68]

Even before theoretical German man had come to his senses through the enlightenment of Feuerbach, and well before the advanced English proletariat had spurned the Church, religious authority had been in decline. Marx wrote:

From the period of the Protestant Reformation, the upper classes in every European nation, whether it remained Catholic or adopted Protestantism, and especially the statesmen, lawyers, and diplomatists, began to unfasten themselves individually from all religious belief, and become free-thinkers so-called.[69] ~ Good

But increasing dissociation from religion did not remain the province of the upper classes, nor was it the private property of such intellectual aristocrats as Bolingbroke, Hume, and Gibbon:

This brings us down to the period of the French Revolution, when the masses, firstly of France, and afterwards of all Western Europe, along with a desire for political and social freedom, began to entertain an ever-growing aversion from religious

---

[65] Letter, K. Marx to F. Lassalle, January 16, 1861, Karl Marx and Friedrich Engels, *Selected Correspondence* (Moscow: Foreign Languages Publishing House), p. 151 (hereinafter referred to as MESC).

[66] Marx, "Critique of Hegel's Philosophy," WYM, p. 258.

[67] Marx-Engels, GI, p. 32.

[68] Letter, K. Marx to F. Engels, April 9, 1863, MESC, p. 172.

[69] Marx, "The Decay of Religious Authority," *Reader*, p. 240.

dogma. The total abolition of Christianity, as a recognized institution of State, by the French Republican Convention of 1793, and since then the gradual repeal in Western Europe, wherever the popular voice has had power, of religious tests and political and civil disabilities of the same character, together with the Italian movement of 1848, sufficiently announce the well-known direction of the popular mind in Europe. We are still witnesses of this epoch, which may be characterized as the era of democratic revolt against ecclesiastical authority.[70]

Accordingly, Marx looked confidently to the coming of the truly democratic and genuinely secular state in which religion would be unnecessary.[71] Surely, this was not too sanguine a view, since Pierre Bayle had already shown that a society composed exclusively of atheists was possible.[72] After all, it is idolatry, not atheism, which debases man. Nonetheless, Marx did not consider the promulgation of irreligious doctrine an end in itself. Desirable though the "philanthropy of atheism" was for tactical reasons, he wished to transcend all circumstances in which either the affirmation or the denial of a being beyond man was at issue.[73] According to Marx, Communism will negate the negation of theism as thoroughly as it has already negated theism.[74]

The foregoing considerations warrant three conclusions. First, the amount of time and number of pages Marx devoted to religion are not an accurate measure of its importance to him. In addition to the speed and certainty of its decline, religion was straightforward and uncomplicated to him. Accordingly, its criticism was short and simple. All that he had to do was to replace the abstract anthropology of Feuerbach with a materialistic anthropology which took real men, their economy, and the actual conditions of their social life into account. Once this was accomplished, anything that one still needed to say about religion could be said in a few pages. Having taken up the topic in his early writings with what he assumed to be sufficient penetration and thoroughness, Marx felt no need in later works to reject, revise, or reiterate what he had said initially about religion. Thus, it is not surprising that he devoted only a few dozen pages to its criticism.

Second, despite the summary treatment which Marx accorded religion, its criticism was of great tactical importance to him. If one intends to

---

[70] *Ibid.*, pp. 240-241.

[71] Marx, "Bruno Bauer, *The Jewish Question*," WYM, p. 229 (hereinafter referred to as "The Jewish Question").

[72] Karl Marx and Friedrich Engels, *The Holy Family or Critique of Critical Critique* (Moscow: Foreign Languages Publishing House, 1956), p. 171.

[73] Marx, *Manuscripts of 1844*, p. 103.

[74] *Ibid.*, p. 114; Lobkowicz, "Karl Marx's Attitude Toward Religion," p. 320.

accomplish the reformation of existing consciousness, then the abolition of false consciousness is inextricably linked with, and only slightly less important than, the creation of true and objective consciousness. The upshot is that the more completely man is subjected to the ideological control of religion, the more important the criticism of religion becomes tactically without respect to particular times and places.

Turning now to a particular time and place, it is clear that the historical, intellectual, and geopolitical conditions in which the young Marx found himself were such that religion had become not only an available target for criticism but also a vulnerable and useful one. Moreover, it was imperative at a time when the criticism of religion was rife that Marx should give his own definitive critique in order to help abolish religion by explaining it and to counteract false critiques. Thus, in the sense in which it was the obvious thing to do, the criticism of religion was the *Voraussetzung* of all criticism. But to assert with Lefebvre that this criticism was the "prerequisite" of all criticism is extreme, for if true, then the criticism of religion would have constituted for Marx the condition *sine qua non* of all criticism.[75] Despite his penchant for exaggeration, the facts do not support the notion that Marx used *Voraussetzung* to mean logical presupposition or axiom.

Third, although the criticism of religion was of paramount importance for a short time at the beginning of Marx's career and even though it may suffuse all his major works implicitly, the criticism of heaven, of religion, and of theology never attained the enduring significance which he accorded to the criticism of earth, of economics, of law, and of politics. The judgment which holds that the criticism of religion is the *Voraussetzung* of all criticism is the last half of a sentence which begins, "Für Deutschland ist die Kritik der Religion im wesentlichen beendigt. . . ."[76] In short, the criticism of ideology never quite became strategic but always remained tactical.

FROM NATURAL RELIGION TO THE RELIGION OF CIVIL SOCIETY

Introduction

There is still an immense amount to be learned about the evolution of man and the emergence of his social life from simian society. If this is the

---

[75] Lefebvre, *The Sociology of Marx*, p. 10.
[76] Marx, "Zur Kritik der Hegelschen Rechtsphilosophie: Einleitung," MEW, I, 378.

situation today, how much more must it have been so at the dawn of scientific anthropology when Marx first delivered his opinions on these matters! Furthermore, from the standpoint of modern ethology, Marx knew as little of animal behavior as he did of human evolution. Undaunted by the paucity of information his times afforded, he proceeded, nevertheless, to describe the emergence of human social life from the animal kingdom as if he knew everything relevant to an accurate description of the process.

Early in *The German Ideology*, in the context of an exposition of the interrelated phenomena of human language and consciousness, Marx developed a twofold etiology of religion which he took to explain both "natural religion" and something I have chosen for convenience to call "social religion."[77] From a literary perspective this dual etiology is curious for two reasons. First, since Marx never repeated its exposition elsewhere, except for making widely scattered references to its context, one may question whether or not it had enduring significance for his thought. Second, since Engels collaborated with Marx in writing *The German Ideology* and explicitly reaffirmed this etiology, one is curious to know which of the two initiated it. The context of their twofold etiology contains clues useful in solving this problem. In general, Marx's and Engels' views on natural religion shared much with eighteenth century atheism. Since it was commonplace in their own skeptical circles to cite fear and ignorance as the causes of natural religion, it is reasonable to suppose that on this point Marx and Engels merely reaffirmed a common heritage and that neither took precedence in influencing the other. The more significant and unusual part of their dual etiology involved the origin of social religion. Here Marx clearly took precedence over Engels and set himself apart from all others with his uniquely expressed concepts of class structure and conflict, of exploitation, and of the relationships between the socio-economic substructure of a society and its ideological superstructure.

Before giving a critical exposition of Marx's etiology of religion, I would make three points. First, since Marx neither modified nor repudiated the etiology expressed in *The German Ideology*, I contend that it played an enduring part in his thought; and as the principal author of *The German Ideology*, I attribute it to him even though Engels may have contributed to it. Second, although the understanding of Marx's etiology of religion is important to the comprehension of his critique of religion,

---

[77] Marx-Engels, GI, Section I, part (a), pp. 16-27.

it has been dealt with only perfunctorily, if at all, in the secondary sources with which I am familiar. Third, as a general theory of the origin of religion, Marx's etiology is ill-informed and illogical.

The Etiology of Natural and Social Religion

In his exposition of the interrelated phenomena of human language and consciousness, Marx noted that where there exists a relationship, it exists for a self. Thus, the relationship of an animal to other animals is not a genuine relationship since the animal cannot cognize it as such in a human way, i.e., with reference to itself. The aim of this reasoning was to establish the point that consciousness is always a social product, beginning as such and enduring as long as men shall live. Then Marx wrote:

Consciousness is at first, of course, merely consciousness concerning the immediate sensuous environment and consciousness of the limited connection with other persons and things outside the individual who is growing self-conscious. At the same time it is consciousness of nature, which first appears to men as a completely alien, all-powerful and unassailable force, with which men's reactions are purely animal and by which they are overawed like beasts; it is thus a purely animal conciousness of nature (natural religion).[78]

In addition to identifying natural religion (*Naturreligion*) with "a purely animal consciousness" of the "completely alien, all-powerful and un-assailable" forces of nature, Marx equated it with that animal behavior towards nature which is predicated on awe, if the English translation of "sich imponieren lassen" in the original can be taken to mean overawed as it is rendered in the citiation above.[79] At the very least, it means to be forcibly or strongly impressed.

An analysis of Marx's concept of natural religion reveals certain vexing difficulties of fact, of internal consistency, and of implication. With respect to fact, ethology supplies no confirmation for the notion that the animal reacts to nature as if it were a "*completely* [underlining, mine] alien, all-powerful and unassailable force." On the contrary, the animal in a natural state finds itself quite at home in the ecological niche appropriated by its species. This does not deny that the higher vertebrates sometimes exemplify caution nor that they manifest fear in fleeing danger. But if Marx were correct, one would expect animals to spend much of their time cowering before natural occurrences. On these terms it would be difficult

---

[78] *Ibid.*, p. 19.
[79] Marx-Engels, *Die deutsche Ideologie*, MEW, III, 31.

to explain the manifold phenomena of aggression and exploration which animals display.

Factual problems similar to those which confront Marx's opinions on animal behavior in response to nature also confront his views concerning very primitive human reactions to the external world. From as early as Plato's time to that of Marx, social philosophers have pondered the quality of life at the dawn of human consciousness. The difficulty with these anthropological musings is that until recently they were based only more or less, usually less, on empirical methods. The result was speculation, often insightful and provocative but speculation nonetheless, nor was Marx exempt from nonempirical speculation, as his anthropological views reveal.

Even if one agrees with Radin that man was born with fear, fear of physiological facts such as birth, disease and death, fear of the forces of nature and fear of the "collision of men with men," still there is no justification for assuming either that primitive man found nature to be completely alien or that his natural religion was tantamount to an animal response to unassailable forces.[80] In fact, there is some evidence to the contrary. Durkheim denied that the "first religious conceptions" were based on "feelings of weakness and dependence, of fear and anguish which seized men when they came into contact with the world." Apart from death rites, he was convinced that totemism, which he took to be the earliest form of religion, was based on sentiments of "happy confidence" and was associated with songs, dances and dramatic representations."[81] The point here is not to give a catalogue of opposing views on the origin of religion but to show that Marx's opinion on the essence and origin of natural religion suffers acutely from lack of information.

With respect to the consistency of his opinions on natural religion, the point is neither to deny the possibility that human religiosity is animal in origin nor that human evolution is biologically continuous with that of animals in general and of the anthropoid apes in particular; the point is that the comments Marx made about the level of animal consciousness and the characteristics of natural religion are difficult, if not impossible, to reconcile. A list of these comments, taken from *The German Ideology*, follows: (1) The "animal has no 'relations' with anything, cannot have any;" (2) "For the animal, its relation to others does not exist as a

---

[80] Paul Radin, *Primitive Religion* (New York: Dover Publications, Inc., 1957), pp. 5, 7.

[81] Emile Durkheim, *The Elementary Forms of the Religious Life* (New York: The Free Press, 1965), pp. 255-256.

relation;" (3) The most primitive human consciousness of nature is of a "completely alien, all-powerful and unassailable force;" (4) The consciousness of nature as alien, all-powerful and unassailable which men have is "purely animal consciousness."[82] Points one and two are not at issue. They are merely Marx's way of saying that animals are not self-conscious, as men are, of the actual relations in which they find themselves. The real problem occurs later when, in point four, Marx makes it appear that creatures which are less than self-conscious, and which therefore have no relations, enter, nevertheless, into a relationship with nature. It is difficult to understand how a conscious being could recognize nature as all-powerful and unassailable without recognizing its own impotence, but this would imply self-knowledge. It is equally difficult to understand how an animal could recognize nature as an alien force without viewing itself as a stranger in the ambience of nature. Moreover, to conclude that nature is completely alien, the animal would either have to possess innate knowledge to this effect or else be able to arrive at conclusions based on induction. As if this were not enough, Marx identified natural religion with "a purely animal consciousness" of alien nature and also with animal behavior in response to alien nature, but without distinguishing between animal consciousness and animal behavior.[83] Since there may well be a difference, one would like to know what it is along with examples of religiosity in animal behavior.

Marx's conception of natural religion contains implications of extreme interest to anyone analyzing his critique of religion. Assuming, for a time, that the etiology of religion is as he conceived it and further that the concept of natural religion is beset neither by factual nor by logical difficulties, the most pertinent question for Marxism is whether or not natural religion still exists as a constituent of contemporary religion. In attempting to answer this question, a dilemma emerges. If natural religion, or something akin to it, still exists among modern people, then Marx failed to develop an adequate sociology of religion, and, if so, his critique can hardly be sound in all respects. If, on the other hand, natural religion no longer exists, it may prove to have been discontinuous with contemporary religion: the latter requiring a different etiology, the former becoming irrelevant. Since the analysis of this hitherto unrecognized dilemma is as intriguing as it is illuminating, I hasten to scrutinize each of its horns.

[82] Marx-Engels, GI, p. 19.
[83] Ibid.

If three modifications are made, Marx's concept of natural religion will attract considerable support among anthropologists. First, the precise relationship between animal consciousness and human self-consciousness must be ignored. Second, instead of assuming that the earliest primitives confronted the external world as if it were completely alien, all-powerful, and unassailable, it suffices to recognize that they faced an environment that was often hostile, destructive, and difficult to assail. Third, the possible occasions for primitive awe, wonder, and fear must not be limited to natural pyrotechnics nor to economic dangers but should be extended, as Radin has shown, to include the physiological facts of birth, sex, disease, death, and to various types of human aggression.[84]

When these modifications are made, one is left with a conception which holds that responses based on awe, wonder, and fear are sometimes, and perhaps frequently, associated in one way or another with religious beliefs and practices. This modified concept, which I shall continue to call "natural religion" for the sake of convenience, is unobjectionable provided that etiological considerations are not allowed to dominate; that religion is broadly defined so as to include elements of totemism, fetishism, euhemerism, and magic; and that responses based on the feelings of joy, exuberance, and celebration are allowed now and again to play a role in religion as well as responses based on the feelings of awe, wonder, and fear. Even if one minifies the importance of joy, exuberance, and celebration in religion and emphasizes awe, wonder, and fear in order to remain more nearly in the spirit of Marx, natural religion appears to be an enduring element in human society.[85]

Having introduced the concept of natural religion, Marx promptly dropped it. If, instead, he had pursued the phenomena associated with it, he would have been led, even on the basis of the limited data available to him, to the fundamental distinction between the sacred and the secular, to magic as a pretechnical attempt at coercing elements in the environment, to the religious behavior associated with the so-called "rites of passage," to the religious aspects of disease and healing, and, above all, to the rites of the dead. Marx had nothing to say about these phenomena, nor did he take the slightest account of them in his sociology of religion. If he had investigated them, he would have been forced to recognize that religion

---

[84] Radin, *Primitive Religion*, pp. 5-7.

[85] J. Milton Yinger, *The Scientific Study of Religion* (London: The Macmillan Company, 1970), p. 7; James W. Gladden, "The Condition of Religion in Communist Europe—Twenty Years After Tobias," *Lexington Theological Quarterly*, VI (October, 1971), 102.

is more broadly based than he was otherwise willing to admit. Malinowski illustrated this point in part when he wrote:

In a maritime community depending on the products of the sea there is never magic connected with the collecting of sellfish or with fishing by poison, weirs, and fish traps, so long as these are completely reliable. On the other hand, any dangerous, hazardous, and uncertain type of fishing is surrounded by ritual. In hunting, the simple and reliable ways of trapping or killing are controlled by knowledge and skill alone; but let there be any danger or uncertainty connected with an important supply of game and magic immediately appears. Coastal sailing as long as it is perfectly safe and easy commands no magic. Overseas expeditions are invariably bound up with ceremonies and ritual.[86]

Clearly, these religious responses have nothing to do with the forces of production including property relationships, with social relations in contradiction to the forces of production, or with consolatory projections based on false consciousness predicated in turn on the contradictions in productive forces, in social relationships or both.

When Marx dropped the concept of natural religion in *The German Ideology* and reverted quickly to his more characteristic approach to religion, his hidden but untenable premise must have been that when man gained technological competence in dealing with his environment, natural religion would be no more, i.e., man would cease to respond to nature as if it were alien, all-powerful, and unassailable; as if he were but an awestruck beast.[87] One may grant that the history of man is the narrative of progressive technical competence and corresponding secularization without assuming that the process is ever to be completed or that natural religion is ever to be abolished. Despite immense technological achievements, the forces of nature still wreak havoc on the inhabitants of earth; despite impressive advances in medicine, disease still flourishes; and in the end, death takes all. Moreover, to say this is to say nothing of the instances of human aggression which lead to the crises to which most men respond religiously in part at least. To write further of the sacred and the profane or to comment on the totemistic elements associated with hearth and home is to carry owls to Athens.

The second horn of Marx's dilemma is as illuminating as the first. Immediately after identifying natural religion with awestruck animal responses to nature, he affirmed that this behavior was "determined by

---

[86] Bronislaw Malinowski, "Culture," *Encyclopaedia of the Social Sciences* (New York: The Macmillan Company, 1931), p. 630.

[87] Marx, "Review of G. Fr. Daumier's *The Religion of the New Age*," MER, p. 95.

the form of society and *vice versa*," though he did not give details of this allegedly reciprocal conditioning.[88] Then he wrote:

Here, as everywhere, the identity of nature and man appears in such a way that the restricted relation of men to nature determines their restricted relation to one another, and their restricted relation to one another determines men's restricted relation to nature, just because nature is as yet hardly modified historically; and, on the other hand, man's consciousness of the necesity of associating with the individuals around him is the beginning of the consciousness that he is living in society at all. This beginning is as animal as social life itself at this stage. It is mere herd-consciousness, and at this point man is only distinguished from sheep by the fact that with him consciousness takes the place of instinct or that his instinct is a conscious one.[89]

Equating herd consciousness with tribal consciousness, he announced that the latter received its development and extension through increased productivity, increased needs, and through what is fundamental to both, "the increase of population."[90] With these developments, a division of labor occurred, first in the sex act, then spontaneously in ways predisposed by differences in strength, dispositions, needs, etc., and finally in the division of mental from physical labor.[91] Then he concluded:

From this moment onwards consciousness *can* really flatter itself that it is something other than consciousness of existing practice, that it is *really* conceiving something without conceiving something *real*; from now on consciousness is in a position to emancipate itself from the world and to proceed to the formation of 'pure' theory, theology, philosophy, ethics, etc.[92]

But what, one may wonder, is the religious content of the theology which is based on pure theory? Is it a theology of natural religion either as Marx defined the concept or as I have modified it? Is it a theology of animal consciousness of alien nature, of the physiological fears associated with rites of passage, of economic want without respect to modes of production, or of human hostility and aggression? Is it a theology of hearth and home, of group solidarity, in short, of totemism? Is it fetishistic, magical, or euhemeristic? The answer to all these questions in *The German Ideology* is a resounding, "No." Marx wrote:

But even if this theory, theology, philosophy, ethics, etc. comes into contradiction with the existing relations, this can only occur as a result of the fact that existing

[88] Marx-Engels, GI, p. 19.

[89] *Ibid.*, pp. 19-20.

[90] *Ibid.*, p. 20.

[91] *Ibid.*

[92] *Ibid.*

social relations have come into contradiction with existing forces of production. . . ."[93]

And, he concluded:

It is self-evident, moreover, that 'spectres,' 'bonds,' 'the higher being,' 'concept,' 'scrupple,' are *merely* [underlining, mine] the idealistic, spiritual expression, the conception apparently of the isolated individual, the image of very empirical fetters and limitations, within which the mode of production of life, and the form of intercourse coupled with it, move.[94]

Even if Marx's progression from natural religion to social religion and pure theology is logically consistent and suffers neither omissions nor mistakes of fact, the basis of natural religion and the foundation of pure theology are different. The one is an animal response to natural forces, the other is a reflection in consciousness of contradictions in socio-economic life. Natural religion and social religion are, therefore, discontinuous but not contradictory. It may be pointed out that *The German Ideology* is an early work and is not, accordingly, to be taken too seriously; but a work which is admittedly self-clarificatory is not to be rejected merely because its principal author did not publish it.[95] In any case, Marx's concept of natural religion constitutes a spot of infection, to use a phrase he enjoyed, which makes his critique pathological. If he had made the concept anthropologically respectable, he would have had to revise and supplement his explanation which held that religion was fundamentally a consolatory phenomenon based on false consciousness produced in turn by contradictions between the forces of production and the relations of production corresponding to them. He would also have had to recognize that religion will not necessarily wither and die just because a classless society abolishes these contradictions.

Although the concept of natural religion is uniquely expressed in *The German Ideology*, some of its contextual elements appear elsewhere in Marx's works. In *Pre-Capitalistic Economic Formations*, he referred to primitive man as "*a generic being, a tribal being, a herd animal*—though by no means a 'political animal' in the political sense."[96] Presumably, the members of the human herd became individualized through the "process of history." "Exchange itself," he said, "is a major agent in this individuali-

[93] *Ibid.*

[94] *Ibid.*, p. 21.

[95] Marx, "Preface to a Contribution to the Critique of Political Economy," MESW, p. 184.

[96] Karl Marx, *Pre-Capitalist Economic Formations*, ed. and introd. by E. V. Hobsbawm (New York: International Publishers, 1964), p. 96.

zation. It makes the herd animal superfluous and dissolves it." [97] In the first volume of *Capital*, Marx wrote:

Those ancient social organisms of production are, as compared with bourgeois society, extremely simple and transparent. But they are founded either on the immature development of man individually, who has not yet severed the umbilical cord that unites him with his fellowmen in a primitive tribal community, or upon direct relations of subjection. They can arise and exist only when the development of the productive power of labour has not risen beyond a low stage, and when, therefore, the social relations within the sphere of material life, between man and man, and between man and Nature, are correspondingly narrow. This narrowness is reflected in the ancient worships of Nature, and in other elements of the popular religions.[98]

Thus, three elements from the context of natural religion, found in *The German Ideology*, reappear. They are: (1) belief in the herd or tribal nature of primitive man; (2) the belief that economic factors are instrumental in human development from its animal origins; and (3) the belief that narrowness in relationships between man and man and between man and Nature characterize primitive life. Regrettably, Marx neither showed how nor why this narrowness reflected itself in Nature worship. Without bothering to develop the concept, he also mentioned in passing something called "popular religions." It is hazardous to draw inferences concerning the beliefs enumerated above beyond the obvious fact that he entertained them from as early as 1845 until as late as 1867. Whether or not the natural religion of *The German Ideology* is identical with the Nature worship mentioned in *Capital* is anybody's guess.

Before turning from the origins of religion to its more developed manifestations, a word about fetishism is in order. In the heat of parochial debate, Marx once characterized this primitive form of faith as "the *religion of sensuous appetites*."[99] Accordingly, the fetish is anything taken to have inherent powers which in fact it does not have. If one ignores nonsensuous appetites, whatever they might be, and takes no account of the theology which is based on pure theory, then fetishism refers to any religious act of a coercive or magical sort. As such, the concept is vacuous for the scientific study of religion. Little wonder then that *The Encyclopedia of Religion and Ethics* lacks Marx's definition of fetishism

---

[97] *Ibid.*

[98] Marx, *Capital*, I, 79.

[99] Marx, "The Leading Article in No. 179 of the *Kölnische Zeitung*: Religion, Free Press, and Philosophy," WYM, p. 115 (hereinafter referred to as "Article No. 179").

while containing those of Comte, Spencer, and Tylor![100] Making a contribution to the taxonomy of religious phenomena was, of course, not what Marx had in mind. His intention was to appropriate this term from the context of religion in order to apply it pejoratively to commodity production:

There is a definite social relation between men, that assumes, in their eyes, the fantastic form of a relation between things. In order therefore, to find an analogy, we must have recourse to the mist-enveloped regions of the religious world. In that world the productions of the human brain appear as independent beings endowed with life, and entering into relation both with one another and the human race. So it is in the world of commodities with the products of men's hands. This I call the Fetishism which attaches itself to the products of labour, so soon as they are produced as commodities, and which is therefore inseparable from the production of commodities.[101]

Thus, the concept of the fetish plays no significant role in Marx's views on religion.

Asiatic and Ancient Religions

Having dealt with Marx's etiology of religion, the task at hand is to survey his views on the development of religion from primitive times to his own century. "In broad outlines," he wrote, "we can designate the Asiatic, the ancient, the feudal and the modern bourgeois methods of production as so many epochs in the progress of the economic formation of society."[102] In this section and in the three which follow it, the object is to examine his opinions on the types of religion which he thought appropriate to the stages of this economic schema.

Although Marx referred both to the Asiatic and ancient modes of production, he did not differentiate them sharply, distinguish them clearly from the Germanic and Slavonic modes which he also mentioned, nor describe in detail how any of the four emerged from their common primitive matrix.[103] A similar inattention to detail characterized his views on the Asiatic and ancient religions. By Asiatic religions, Marx meant those east of Asia Minor; by ancient religion, the Greco-Roman primarily.[104] Nature worship was the only characteristic he explicitly

---

[100] W. G. Aston, "Fetishism," *Encyclopedia of Religion and Ethics* (New York: Charles Scribner's Sons, 1925), V, 894-898.

[101] Marx, *Capital*, I, 72.

[102] Marx, "Preface to Critique of Political Economy," MESW, p. 183.

[103] Marx, *Pre-Capitalist Economic Formations*, pp. 19-25.

[104] Letter, K. Marx to F. Engels, June 2, 1853, MESC, p. 97.

attributed to both,[105] but in saying that "the 'true religion' of the ancients was the cult of 'their nationality'," he could have had orientals in mind as well as occidentals.[106] If so, that would constitute a second common characteristic.

Marx assumed that the history of the East appeared as a history of religion because of "*the absence of private property* in land." That was the "real key," he thought, "even to the oriental heaven."[107] But what of the occidental heaven, of the Elysian Fields of the Greeks, of their Islands of the Blest? In failing to predicate the existence of these beliefs on the absence of private property in land, did Marx intend to distinguish between Greco-Roman and Asiatic religions? If so, this constitutes the only distinction he drew between the two. Although no definite conclusion can be reached, I take the distinction to be apparent, not real, and think it the product of an oversight.

When he spoke of Asiatic religions, Marx had those of the Near East in mind more often than those of the Far East. The only prominent exception to this was Hinduism. Even though he knew more of its modern manifestations than of its ancient expression, Marx took Hinduism as a whole to be the religious nadir of human degradation. Two references alone, neither of which requires comment, show that he held it in contempt:

Yet, in a social point of view, Hindustan is not the Italy, but the Ireland, of the East. And this strange combination of Italy and of Ireland, of a world of voluptuousness and of a world of woes, is anticipated in the ancient traditions of the religion of Hindustan. That religion is at once a religion of sensualist exuberance, and a religion of self-torturing asceticism; a religion of the Lingam and of Juggernaut, the religion of the Monk, and of the Bayabere.[108]

Elsewhere he added:

We must not forget that this undignified, stagnatory, and vegetative life, that this passive sort of existence evoked on the other part, in contradistinction, wild, aimless, unbounded forces of destruction, and rendered murder itself a religious rite in Hindustan. We must not forget that these little communities were contaminated by distinctions of caste and slavery, that they subjugated man to external circumstances instead of elevating man to be the sovereign of circumstances, that they transformed a self-developing social state into never changing natural destiny, and thus brought

---

[105] Marx, *Capital*, I, 79; Karl Marx and Friedrich Engels, *On Colonialism* (Moscow: Foreign Languages Publishing House, n.d.), p. 37 (hereinafter referred to as MEC).

[106] Marx, "Article No. 179," WYM, pp. 115-116.

[107] Letter, K. Marx to F. Engels, June 2, 1853, MESC, p. 99.

[108] Marx, "The British Rule in India," MEC, pp. 31-32.

about a brutalizing worship of nature, exhibiting its degradation in the fact that man, the sovereign of nature, fell down on his knees in adoration of Hanuman, the monkey, and Sabbala, the cow.[109]

Returning from the Far East to the ancient Near East, a comment concerning Marx's attitude toward biblical Judaism is in order. In view of the great importance traditionally accorded to the Hebrews for their role in the development of Western Civilization, particularly in the provinces of religion, morality, and law, Marx's failure to comment on biblical Judaism may seem a glaring omission. But, omission or not, it was perfectly consistent with his critique of religion. Since Marx was convinced that the objects of religious belief were merely conceivable and in no way actual or even possible, it would have been absurd for him to have graced one set of conceivables with his approbation while denying it to others. Thus, he did not find Hebrew monotheism praiseworthy, belief in one god being to him as ridiculous as belief in many. By the same token, he did not regard as worthy of comment the social morality of the eighth and sixth century prophets, a morality usually held in high esteem, particularly in view of its ethical alternatives and background. Moreover, he found nothing noteworthy in the sectarian and theological developments of post-exilic Judaism. Theocratic legalism and apocalypticism left him equally uninterested.

Marx ignored primitive Christianity as completely as biblical Judaism and showed no interest in attempting to establish the original Christian kerygma, canon, and creed. He saw no significance in discovering precisely how primitive Christianity differentiated itself from the various Jewish sects contemporaneous with it, nor did he find worthwhile to posit an original Christianity by which subsequent developments in doctrine, ritual, and morality could be judged with respect to consistency with or divergency from that original. After all, why bother to distinguish one body of nonsense from another or why establish a canon of nonsense with which to measure developments in the same nonsense? As a result of this attitude, Marx took genuine Christianity to be whatever in fact it was at any given time without reference to its primitive content. Thus, the Catholicism of the Middle Ages was a Christian to him as primitive Christianity, however different the two might have been, and bourgeois Protestantism was as Christian as either despite even further differences. This attitude plus Marx's conviction that religion was never what it

---

[109] *Ibid.*, pp. 36-37.

seemed to be or said of itself enabled him to establish a religious typology with which any religion became precisely what he wanted it to be.

Roman Catholicism

Turning now from the Asiatic and ancient modes of production with their archaic ideologies, we come to a new mode of production and to a religious ideology admirably suited to it. The mode of production in question is the feudal, as it developed in Europe during the Middle Ages, and its accompanying ideology is, of course, Roman Catholicism. Though Marx had very little to say of the Roman Church, probably because it did not merit serious criticism, four points can be pieced together from his scattered comments on the subject. First, the Roman Church "reigned supreme" during the Middle Ages due entirely to the social and economic relations of feudalism which required and determined it.[110] In no sense did it develop independently of those requirements as a result of any inherent virtues. Priests, it must be remembered, grow and flourish on a peasant economy.[111] Second, there can be no doubt that Marx regarded Catholicism as idolatrous and fetishistic.[112] Moreover, according to him, it had created in the Middle Ages a period of "realisierten Unvernunft," of perfected irrationality.[113] Third, the authoritarian structure, moral heteronomy, distant deity, and external religiosity of Catholicism had revealed and promoted religious estrangement.[114] This could be seen clearly in the emergence of its legions of priests, those "inevitable middlemen" between the Good Shepherd and the sheep.[115] Fourth, since Luther and the Reformation had already moved to negate priests and to destroy outward religiosity, and since feudalism had lost its struggle to survive in the eighteenth century, it was to be expected that Roman paganism and priestcraft would wither away.

Protestantism

Long before the actual demise of feudalism, its executioners and gravediggers had been called forth and, since the sixteenth century in

---

[110] Marx, *Capital*, I, 82, note.

[111] Marx, "Review of G. Fr. Daumier's *The Religion of the New Age*," MER, p. 95.

[112] Marx, *Manuscripts of 1844*, p. 93.

[113] Marx, "Vorrede," *Differenz der demokritischen und epikureischen Natur-philosophie nebst einem Anhange*, MEW, Supplement, I, 261.

[114] Marx, *Manuscripts of 1844*, p. 79; *Capital*, I, 744, n. 1.

[115] Marx, *Capital*, I, 744, n. 1.

particular, had gone about their business with relish and industry. These harbingers and executives of doom were the rising bourgeoisie, and their mode of production was capitalistic. And what, one may ask rhetorically, was their religion? Marx answered:

The religious world is but the reflex of the real world. And for a society based upon the production of commodities, in which the producers in general enter into social relations with one another by treating their products as commodities and values, whereby they reduce their individual private labour to the standard of homogeneous human labour—for such a society, Christianity with its *cultus* of abstract man, more especially in its bourgeois developments, Protestantism, Deism, &., is the most fitting form of religion.[116]

To Marx, Protestantism was more than the most fitting form of religion for bourgeois society. It was also important in the development, of what society insofar as it had played an integral part in the process of primitive accumulation and in the degradation of legions of people to the ranks of the proletariat.

Despite the intellectual vacuity of Protestantism and its manifold ties with the quintessence of exploitive economies, it was to Marx progressive when measured by earlier religions. With grace and perception, he wrote:

Luther, to be sure, overcame bondage based on *devotion* by replacing it with bondage based on *conviction*. He shattered faith in authority by restoring the authority of faith. He turned priests into laymen by turning laymen into priests. He freed man from outward religiosity by making religiosity the inwardness of man. He emancipated the body from its chains by putting chains on the heart.

But if Protestantism was not the true solution, it was the true formulation of the problem. The question was no longer the struggle of the layman against the *priest external to him* but of his struggle against *his own inner priest*, his *priestly* nature.[117]

In short, the progressive element in Protestantism lay in the autonomy it claimed and promoted. The theological trifles and doctrinal quibbles whereby the reformers distinguished themselves from the papists were to Marx less than insignificant. What Luther and his compatriots had done of real significance was to abolish the heteronomy of the spirit required by Catholicism.[118] With the abolition of the priestly middleman, the Protestant took a gigantic stride away from religious estrangement toward the emancipation of the spirit. Once that was fully achieved, the task then would be simply to strip the "religious" from "religious autonomy," leaving human autonomy which, when added to human rationality shorn

---

[116] *Ibid.*, p. 79.
[117] Marx, "Critique of Hegel's Philosophy," WYM, p. 258.
[118] Marx, *Manuscripts of 1844*, p. 94.

of all ideology and fetishism, would enable man to determine his own purely human future.

In his salad days Marx had referred to Christianity, in various contexts, as the "apex of religious development,"[119] as the *"essence of religion,*[120] as "religion itself."[121] Though he did not continue to write in this vein in later years, and never made the point explicitly, the impression is strong that he had the Lutheran tradition in mind including its role in civil society and its theological development to the time of Hegel. Clearly, Protestantism was religion perfected when compared with nature worship, Hinduism, Catholic idolatry, or even with Anabaptist sectarianism. Marx, it must be remembered, scorned sectarianism for its lack of universality.[122]

It is noteworthy and ironic that Marx referred to Luther more than to any and to all other reformers. He ignored Calvin completely and deigned to speak of the Anglican reformation only in the context of its role in the primitive accumulation of capital through expropriation of Catholic properties, enclosure acts, and the like.[123] In light of historical, cultural, and psychological factors it is not surprising that Marx felt a greater affinity for Luther than for the other Protestant reformers, but what is surprising is the use to which he put some of Luther's views. On several occasions in each of volumes one and three of *Capital* he quoted Luther with approbation. The topic was usury, the sum and substance of Luther's views on which were (1) that all who take more or better than they give are usurers whether in lending, buying, or other kinds of business;[124] (2) that those who, albeit in the guise of service, rob and deprive others of nourishment as surely kill their victims as murderers do;[125] (3) that Christians, unlike the Heathens who recognized usurers for what they were, have transmuted their vices into virtues and have come practically to worship them;[126] and (4) that since society hangs the small thief and since, next to the Devil, there is no greater enemy of mankind than the

---

[119] Marx "Notes to the Doctoral Dissertation: Platonism and Christianity," WYM, p. 58.

[120] Marx, "Root Errors of Political Speculation: On Hegels' 261-69," WYM, p. 174.

[121] Marx, "Reflections of a Youth on Choosing an Occupation," WYM, p. 39.

[122] Letter, K. Marx to J. B. Schweitzer, October 13, 1868, MESC, pp. 257-258.

[123] If those who prepared the *Personenverzeichnis* contained in each volume of MEW made no mistake, Marx never mentioned Calvin in print.

[124] Marx, *Capital*, I, 192, n. 1; *Capital*, III, 340, n. 56.

[125] Marx, *Capital*, I, 592, n. 1; *Capital*, III, 386, 597.

[126] Marx, *Capital*, I, 592, n. 1.

big thieves who are usurers, they ought to be hunted down and beheaded.[127]

The irony becomes apparent when Luther's views on usury, quoted and applauded by Marx, are juxtaposed with his own view that Protestantism is the most fitting form of religion for bourgeois society, for a society based on "naked self-interest," "callous 'cash payment'," and "direct, brutal exploitation," in short, for a usurious society.[128] If the greatest Protestant reformer vehemently attacks the very practices which his religion is allegedly best suited to uphold, what one may wonder, constitutes the congruity between Protestantism and bourgeois economy?

Since Marx presumed that religious thought was the epiphenomenal reflection of the real world, he cited what seemed to be a body of evidence sufficient to confirm his supposition. Moreover, he apparently assumed that all relevant evidence would confirm his opinion. Thus, he was neither open to criticism nor assiduous in searching for disconfirmatory evidence. Nowadays, it is commonplace to regard a proposition for which all evidence is confirmatory and none disconfirmatory as vacuous. But he was not troubled by such methodological niceties as this and spent no time in specifying which conditions would have to obtain if there were to be incongruities between a mode of production and its religious superstructure. Yet there are incongruities of this type, and they are not merely the historical leftovers of antecedent modes of production. In view of Christian dualism and rejection of the world, to say nothing of eschatology, John Herman Randall, Jr. has observed that it is a marvel which "passes all human comprehension" that Western man devoted . . . to "pleasure, prosperity and power" should even have given "lip service to Christian ethics."[129] In short, one must entertain the possibility that Western man has been Christian in spite of his economic and social structures rather than, as Marx would have it, because of them.

Non-Biblical Judaism and Judaized Christianity

Most fitting though his religion is to the bourgeois mode of production, the Protestant is not the only denizen of civil society; there is also the Jew, a religious type which, according to Marx, civil society produces

---

[127] *Ibid.*, p. 593, note.

[128] Marx-Engels, *Manifesto*, p. 12.

[129] John Herman Randall, Jr., *The Role of Knowledge in Western Religion* (Boston: Starr King Press, 1958), p. 45.

from its own "entrails."[130] Lest it seem anachronistic that modern capitalism should produce a type of creature presumably in circulation since the time of Father Abraham, a word of clarification is in order. By "civil society" Marx meant those social relationships which he thought were required and developed by the bourgeois mode of production, particularty insofar as that mode of production had gained freedom from political control. In short, civil society was to him the sphere of economic egoism, of Hobbes' *bellum omnium contra omnes*, in which communal ties were dissolved leaving only atomistic and hostile individuals using each other for private ends and falling thereby into the grip of alien powers.[131] This, then, is the type of society which excretes the Jew, even as the spider brings forth the substance of its web, but what precisely, is the Jew?

Just as Marx ignored the biblical Jew, so he ignored the medieval Jew whether orthodox, rationalistic, or Kabbalistic, and so, too, he ignored the modern Jew whether messianic, Chasidic, or Reformed. Nothing distinctly theological, ethico-legal, or cultic associated with Judaism interested him. In a well-known polemic on the Jewish Question, he made it clear that he was not concerned, as Bruno Bauer mistakenly was, with the Sabbath Jew but rather with the everyday Jew whose secret lay not in the sacred but in the profane.[132] To Marx the real foundation of Judaism was egoism of the very sort epitomized in civil society. Subjectively, the basis of the worldly Jew was practical need;[133] bargaining was his cult; and money, "the alienated essence" of human life and labor, was his jealous god.[134] Developed by commercial and industrial practice, the Jew had no nationality, because the merchant's greed knew no limits, patriotic or otherwise.[135]

The ubiquity of the merchant-Jew had been enhanced, as Marx saw it, by Christianity which had completed "the alienation of man from himself and from nature" and which, in its claim to transcendence over all lesser ties, had made "national, moral, and theoretical relationships external to man."[136] To summarize, the full development of Protestant Christianity

---

[130] Marx, "Bruno Bauer, *The Capacity of Present-Day Jews and Christians to Become Free*," WYM, p. 245 (hereinafter referred to as "Jews and Christians").

[131] Marx, "The Jewish Question," WYM, p. 227.

[132] Marx, "Jews and Christians," WYM, p. 243.

[133] *Ibid.*, p. 245.

[134] *Ibid.*, pp. 243, 246.

[135] Marx, "Jews and Christians," WYM, p. 246; Marx-Engels, *The Holy Family*, p. 147.

[136] Marx, "Jews and Christians," WYM, p. 247.

had enabled the economic sector of society to escape the toils of political and communal control. In this way, civil society came into being and in perfecting itself permitted Judaism to reach its highest development.

Thus, Judaism had grown so powerful and pervasive, to Marx, that it had already become the spirit of the economically advanced Christian nations and had in fact come to dominate Christianity in North America where even the Christian ministry had become an article of commerce.[137] Whenever and wherever the Christian had forsaken his other-worldly theorizing and had turned to satisfy his egoism through practical activity, he had become a Jew, and his religion, arising in Judaism, had returned again home.[138] In this manner, though he did not use the term, Marx created the "Judaized Christian." Since the egotism, atomized individualism, and alienation of the bourgeois, of the Jew, and of the practical Christian were identical, all were one, and their religions were one.

Marx's religious type consisting of the Jew and the Judaized Christian prompt three critical observations. First, when he declared that money was the jealous god of Israel he was indulging neither in metaphor nor in homiletic hyperbole. With equal seriousness, he also averred that the basis of Judaism was practical need or egoism. But this is a banality. If one denies that religion is a gift of God and affirms rather that it is the offspring of socio-economic factors, then it is trite to select Judaism, as one religion among many, and announce that it is based on practical need or egoism. By way of contrast, which religion, one might ask, is based on impractical need or is composed of devotees devoid of self-referential concerns. William James made the point memorably when he said, "Religion, in short, is a monumental chapter in the history of human egotism."[139] Although there can be little, if any, doubt that the majority of Jews believe Judaism to be compatible with worldly success, the same could be said of all so-called practical peoples. Despite the evidence of mystic and monastic minorities, it is unthinkable that ordinary people concerned with daily practicalities should possess a religion largely, if not totally, antithetical to their everyday problems and interests. Such a religion might survive in the monastery, where the practicalities are those of the next world, but not in the home, the field, the market place, the military establishment, or even in the public temple. In these precincts, a

---

[137] *Ibid.*, p. 244.

[138] *Ibid.*, p. 247.

[139] William James, *The Varieties of Religious Experience* (New York: Random House), p. 480.

given religion must supply adequate reinforcement for the life style in favor; if not it will either be reformed to the point at which it sacralizes the dominant social values or it will be neglected by the majority and become the private preserve of sectarians, cranks, and the like. Marx made no contribution to the scientific study of religion when he identified Judaism with egotism.

Second, if Marx did not use the term "Jew" merely as an epithet but meant to designate a religious type, and if neither ethnic nor theological considerations were at issue for him, then a problem of limits arises. Who or what, for example, is the person who thinks himself to be a Jew, who is thought to be one by others, but who does not fit the role of the Judaized Christian of bourgeois society? What, for instance, of the Essenes or the Therapeutae? Perhaps they were really Mahayana Buddhists. More importantly, what of the Chasidic movement which developed in Poland and spread to the Ukraine? Since the overwhelming majority of these naive and lyrical mystics were either peasants or poor farmers, untouched alike by the bourgeois world or by the intellectual Jews of the Enlightenment, perhaps they were really Catholics. To go further afield, what is one to think of the prosperous Chinese businessmen of Southeast Asia or of the economically successful Jains and Parsees of India? Jews, it would seem, all Jews! The foregoing comments are not intended to disparage every effort at developing a religious typology. The point is that if there are to be typologies, scientifically useful to the study of religion, then criteria must be established which take into account the complexities of religion and which set limits to the categories used in describing, explaining, and interpreting religious phenomena.

Third, the type which Marx intended when speaking of the Jew and of the Judaized Christian was fallaciously based. Even if one agrees that all theological systems are false, the fallacy remains. Marx noticed that Judaism functioned in such a way as to reinforce and to sacralize the ways of free enterprise, and he descried the same functions in Protestantism; therefore Jews were Protestants or Protestants were Jews, whichever way one wanted it. Construed as an Aristotelian syllogism, figure two, the argument contains an undistributed middle class.

Some might argue that since the great majority of Marx's opinions on Judaism appeared in early works, they are neither to be taken too seriously nor assumed to be his last word on the subject. But the evidence, both explicit and implicit, indicates no significant change of mind, if any. In mature works on economics he continued on occasion to associate the Jew with the merchant and the monopolist,[140] and once, at least, he called the monetary interests of Gentile capitalists "inwardly circumcised Jews."[141] In terms of bulk, the implicit evidence is far greater than the sum of all explicit references, but it is no less decisive. In summary, Marx's views on Judaism, whether early or late, were consistent with his general opinions concerning the etiology, nature, functions, and future of religion. Among these opinions, the last merits further comment.

An exposition of the process through which Marx believed Judaism would be abolished is important not only because it reveals consistency in his thought concerning the future of religion in general but also because it clarifies what he took to be the relationships between church and bourgeois state. The occasion for these views was a parochial dispute with Bruno Bauer who had mistakenly concluded that Jews would have to reject Judaism before they could enjoy full citizenship.[142] Aware that the Jewish Question differed from country to country,[143] Marx contended that wherever the state, as in North America, had developed fully and had become secular and democratic, religion could survive as a private matter.[144] Thus, in fully developed states, Jews would obviously not have to renounce their religion to enjoy political emancipation. Having triumphed over Bauer, Marx strove to establish the thesis that even though Judaism could survive political emancipation, neither it nor any other religion could exist in conditions of human emancipation.

To distinguish political from human emancipation as Marx did, seven points must be presupposed. First, to him, political emancipation was synonymous with the conditions of the secular democratic state. Second, such a state was "the final form" of the existing order and an immense improvement over the religio-political tyrannies of the past including the so-called Christian state.[145] Third, although the democratic state permitted the continuation of religion when relegated to the sphere of "private right," the actual persistence of religion implied a defect in the state which tolerated it.[146] Fourth, the democratic state could coexist with civil society, i.e., political emancipation was compatible with capitalism. Fifth, the conditions of human emancipation, like those of political emancipation,

---

[140] Marx, *Pre-Capitalist Economic Formations*, p. 84; *Capital*, I, 79.
[141] Marx, *Capital*, I, 154.
[142] Marx, "The Jewish Question," WYM, pp. 217-220, 232.
[143] *Ibid.*, p. 221.
[144] *Ibid.*, p. 222.
[145] *Ibid.*, p. 227.
[146] *Ibid.*, p. 222.

are secular and democratic. Sixth, human emancipation, unlike political emancipation, is antithetical to civil society, cannot coexist with it, and will destroy it. Seventh, human emancipation will not only abolish political and economic servitude but will also abolish religion.

For Marx, the normative goal and the temporal end of prerevolutionary, or of "prehistoric," social development were one and the same. Both goal and end were characterized by the concept of human emancipation described in the early articles on the Jewish Question. The characteristics of human emancipation are the same as those Marx envisioned when, in the first volume of *Capital*, he spoke of a time when the "practical relations of every-day life," of men in relation to each other and to nature, would all be perfectly intelligible and reasonable.[147] The conditions of human emancipation and the characteristics of Marx's vision in *Capital* are also identical with the attributes of the classless society. To achieve the classless society, the characteristics of civil society must be destroyed, i.e., money, bargaining, alienation, exploitation, and egotism must and will be abolished by being transcended. In the process of abolition and transcendence, men will renounce the life of atomized hostile individualism and will achieve, or re-achieve, the kind of collective social existence which is their true species-life.[148] To the democratic life politically will be added the democratic life economically..

If the economic life of civil society is to be abolished, it is clear in Marx that the religion of civil society must also be annihilated. Hence, the Jew and the Judaized Christian as such must go. They will remain as individuals, but as individuals denied their monetary deity and shorn alike of bargaining consciousness and marketing mentality. Those who live to participate in the conditions of human emancipation will be secular and democratic in all things social and economic. The truly human life will meet all the general needs and supply all the benefits which men in former times vainly sought in the comforting illusions of religion. Unafraid of their surroundings, undaunted by their future, and released from the irrationalities and restraints of class society, emancipated men will neither make religion nor miss it.

THE SUBSTANCE AND FUNCTIONS OF RELIGION

Introduction

It is notoriously difficult to know precisely *what* is being dealt with

---

[147] Marx, *Capital*, I, 79.
[148] Marx, "The Jewish Question," WYM, p. 231.

when religion is at issue. There are at least three reasons for this. First, the etymology of the word "religion" is uncertain. It may come from the Latin *religare* meaning to bind together or from *relegere* meaning to study seriously. The result is that while the Latin may be suggestive of possibilities, it is deficient in explicatory power. Second, those who rely on ordinary usage to determine meanings cannot hope for reliable assistance in this case, because in ordinary usage people infuse the word "religion" with normative dimensions and take their own religion to be the paradigm of all religion, whether it is or not. The result is that ordinary usage will in most, if not all, cases reveal a conception of religion which is valuative, idiosyncratic, and unfit for philosophical or scientific purposes. Third, it is debatable whether or not there is any single belief, type of belief, or set of beliefs essential to all religions. William James, for instance thought there was a set of fundamental convictions common to all religion,[149] but John Dewey thought otherwise and refused to employ "religion" as a meaningful concept, preferring rather to speak adjectivally of "the religious."[150] On occasion, Dewey referred to specific religions but only in the sense of identifiable social entities evolving in history. The point of this dispute is that if there is no fundamental belief essential to all religions, then religion cannot be defined in terms of intellectual content, natural or supernatural. If so, those who seek essential characteristics for religion must look elsewhere. Some have concluded on the basis of psychological investigations that, quite apart from specific beliefs, the unitary core of religion stems from the affective aspects of human nature and that religion is intimately associated with such feelings as dependence, awe, veneration, devotion, exaltation, unity and the like.[151] Others, especially in the twentieth century, have taken a sociological approach and have concluded that religion is to be understood in terms of its functions, i.e., in terms of the way it confers meanings, sacralizes types of behavior, discourages other types of behavior, and celebrates values.[152] But those who utilize affective or functional approaches to religion, or both, are still confronted with problems of definition. It is not at all clear, for example, just where the line is to be drawn between the sacred and the secular when feelings of dependence, awe, veneration, devotion, exaltation, unity and the like

---

[149] James, *The Varieties of Religious Experience*, pp. 475-476.

[150] John Dewey, *A Common Faith* (New Haven: Yale University Press, 1934), pp. 3-14.

[151] James H. Leuba, *A Psychological Study of Religion: Its Origin, Function, and Future* (New York: AMS Press, Inc., 1969), Appendix, pp. 346-351.

[152] Yinger, *Scientific Study of Religion*, Chapters One and Three especially.

are at issue. Furthermore, those who utilize a psychological method in studying religion run the constant risk of confusing its etiology with its essence or, what is worse, of unwittingly converting the former into the latter. The functionalist is also confronted with definitional problems, for he must determine whether or not and, if so, where lines are to be drawn between religious beliefs and opinions which are admittedly metaphysical but not religious, between religious practices and magic, between religion and morality, religion and patriotism, religion and aesthetics. Moreover, since the functionalist approaches religion from a social perspective, he risks defining it so abstractly that it becomes vapid and unrecognizable not only to ordinary people but more especially to individuals of exceptional religious experience; the saint, the prophet, and the mystic.

Although attempts at defining religion may be a source of delight to dialecticians, they can be unnerving to those who prefer clear and distinct categories. If at the end of a massive volume on religion, the authors conclude that religion cannot be defined, the reader may justly wonder *what* the book was about, why the authors thought the mountains of data they had assembled were relevant to the putative topic or nontopic, and whether or not they were victimizing him with an elaborate intellectual trick.[153] One gets the same feeling of uncertainty when at the beginning of a classic work on the sociology of religion he is told that an examination of definitions of religion is beyond the scope of the book.[154]

But investigators who attempt to define religion may create as much confusion as those who expatiate on the subject without determining what the subject is. If, on the one hand, the investigator defines religion so narrowly that he has a clear and distinct conception of what it is, then he is liable to have chosen one perspective on the subject in ignorance of the claims made for other perspectives, to have permitted the insinuation of normative elements into his definitions, and to have ignored relevant data. Too narrow a definition of religion results in the creation of such more or less dubious categories as "true" and "false religion," "quasi-religion," and even "pseudo-religion" to take account of the siblings, look-alikes, and other relations of religion arbitrarily excluded by unwarranted narrowness.

On the other hand, there is currently a tendency among sophisticates in the field to define religion in a manner so inclusive that anything taken

---

[153] William Graham Sumner and Albert G. Keller, *The Science of Society* (4 vols.; New Haven: Yale University Press, 1927), II, 1428.

[154] Joachim Wach, *Sociology of Religion* (Chicago: University of Chicago Press, 1944), p. 13.

most seriously and given top priority qualifies as being religious. This tendency is understandable when one takes into full account such considerations as (a) all serious attempts at definition known to exist, beginning with the *incomplete* list of forty-eight specimens collected and arranged under three major headings by Leuba;[155] (b) the ten pitfalls to be avoided when defining religion enumerated by Ferm;[156] (c) all types of relevant data; and (d) all the valid claims of the several methods of approaching the subject. These considerations are so formidible that those who would still attempt to define religion must perforce do so with great caution. The result has been a number of definitions so broadly conceived that for most, if not all, purposes, they appear to be tantamount to no definition at all. I have in mind such recent attempts as those of Hutchison who defines religion as a *"system of holy forms"* and Tillich who defined it as "ultimate concern."[157] If the definition is so broad that one cannot use it in discerning the limits of religion, then the circle is closed and one is again in the position of the author who gives no definition but expatiates nevertheless on he knows not precisely what.

With the preceding paragraphs I have intended neither to boggle the reader's mind nor to enervate his will. Nor have I meant to imply that the task of understanding religion is hopeless, for when definition is impossible, characterization may yet be possible; when absolutes are inappropriate, probabilities may be in order; and when sharp lines of demarcation cannot be drawn, areas of limited overlap may be tolerable. What I have tried to do, on the contrary, is to make the reader aware of the enormous complexity of religion.

Marx never defined religion comprehensively, but he did recognize some of its functions. More surprisingly, he also characterized the substance or content of religious belief, though in a limited and peculiar way. This assertion will seem patently false, at first, in light of his belief that religion had neither essence nor history and that its teachings were false. But when one views religious belief in the context of Marx's opinions on the etiology of religion, it becomes clear that religious belief does have content of a type which endures for a time. I will return to this topic later. What

[155] Leuba, *Psychological Study of Religion*, Appendix, pp. 339-361.

[156] Virgilius Ferm, "Religion, the Problem of Definition," *An Encyclopedia of Religion*, ed. by V. Ferm (Paterson, New Jersey: Littlefield, Adams & Co., 1959), pp. 646-647.

[157] John A. Hutchison, *Paths of Faith* (New York: McGraw-Hill Book Company, 1969), p. 5; Paul Tillich, *Systematic Theology* (3 vols.; Chicago: University of Chicago Press, 1951-63), I, 12-14.

I wish to pursue next is the point that Marx's views on the etiology of religion involve normative considerations which cast doubt on the scientific basis and merit of his critique.

Marx did not differentiate cognitively between religion and superstition, nor did he regard some religious beliefs as more nearly true than others. Moreover, he always referred to mysticism pejoratively. Finally, he never defined religion in terms of what he thought it ought to be or do. But in what can only be called normative terms, Marx took one manifestation of religion to be preferable, in one respect at least, to all others. I refer to the autonomy required and promoted by Protestantism. But this characteristic was by no means adequate to make religion permanently valuable, for, far from thinking of religion in terms of what it ought to be, Marx thought that it ought not to be at all and proceeded to adumbrate a future society in which it would not and could not exist.

The future society to which I refer is, of course, the classless society in which man is to live his genuine *species-life*, is to enjoy human emancipation, and is to relate himself rationally and intelligibly to others and to nature. Without getting involved in the question of strict determinism, of whether or not Marx was making a necessity out of virtue, there can be no doubt that he believed that forces were afoot which were to destroy capitalism and to eventuate in a new society.[158] There can also be no doubt that he took the new society to be more desirable, more truly human, than existing class societies and that he worked for its realization. When Marx's vision of the classless society is added to his philosophical anthropology, it is clear that his views on man and society, despite their scientific pretensions, are shot through with normative assumptions. Over and again, he judged existing men by what he thought man should and would be and measured existing societies by the classless society of the future.

At no point do normative considerations play a greater role in Marx's thought than in his views on the etiology of religion. In this context he made the extraordinary observation that religion is the "self-consciousness and self-regard of man who has either not yet found or has already lost himself."[159] The one who has not yet found himself is the primitive human being who possesses natural religion; the one who has already lost himself is the practitioner of what I have called social religion. In that which follows, I shall be concerned with the latter.

---

[158] Marx, *Capital,* I, 763.
[159] Marx, "Critique of Hegel's Philosophy," WYM, p. 250.

The Substance of Religion

To Marx, practical human activity involved in material production and reproduction was the condition *sine qua non* of religion. Within the social process whereby men produce their means of subsistence, divisions of labor occur which lead, on economic grounds, to the development of various forms of society. In each form of society involving the division of labor, contradictions occur between the mode of production of that society and the social relations erected thereon. The result is that contradictions engendered by the division of labor lead to conditions of alienation in which men are separated from the full appropriation of the items they produce, are set against their fellows through competition, and are manipulated by the productive activities in which they must engage.[160] To summarize, practical material activity involving divisions of labor which lead to socio-economic contradictions and to forms of alienation, when taken together, provide the conditions out of which religion is born and by which it is sustained. These conditions, however, are merely sufficient and not necessary. I shall return to this point shortly.

Insofar as it is possible to separate the means whereby religion is created from the conditions of its creation, one is justified in concluding that at a certain time in the development of human society, the contents of religious belief are projected by the spontaneous acitivity of alienated human self-consciousness and imagination.[161] In addition to being alienated, this mode of consciousness is false, inverted, and perverse.

That which has been projected on the basis of the conditions described above can be characterized as (a) "sublimates of material life processes";[162] (b) an element of ideology along with metaphysics, ethics, and law;[163] (c) a derivative source of alienation limited to the realm of consciousness;[164] (d) a reflex, or series of reflexes, determined by forms of society;[165] (e) irrationality;[166] and (f) an inessentiality based on stages of material production.[167]

In characterizing religion, Marx emphasized over and again his conviction that it was an inessentiality. Expressed negatively, this meant to him

---

[160] Marx-Engels, GI, pp. 16-27.
[161] Marx, *Manuscripts of 1844*, p. 73.
[162] Marx-Engels, GI, p. 14.
[163] *Ibid.*
[164] Marx-Engels, GI (Moscow), p. 168.
[165] Marx, *Capital*, I, 79.
[166] Marx, "Critique of Hegel's Philosophy," WYM, p. 250.
[167] Marx-Engels, GI (Moscow), p. 168.

(1) that religion was not its own *causa sui*;[168] (2) that it was not the handiwork of God; (3) that it was not the product of human self-consciousless *per se*; and (4) that it was in no way caused by what some might assume mistakenly to be the permanent essence of man.[169] Expressed differently, the human being, to Marx, possessed neither a religious faculty nor a unique mode of religious apperception. Furthermore, religion had no biological basis and was not required by any permanent features in social life nor by any forms of interaction between biological and cultural elements. Expressed positively, religion was an inessentiality for Marx first, because the contents of religious belief were in no sense empirical but were merely conceivable; second, because religious projections were both reflective of and determined by distinct forms of socio-economic life, thus having no history; and third, because religion was abolishable, having neither occasion nor function in the classless society. To complete the case for the inessentiality of religion, it is important to show not only that it is abolishable but also that it never had to develop in the first place, for if there are forces of any sort which necessitate human religiosity, religion gains a measure of essentiality. To complete the denial of essentiality to religion, Marx did not treat material activity as the cause of religion but merely as the condition in which it could occur. Furthermore, practical activity, the division of labor, socio-economic contradictions, and alienation did not necessitate religion, as Marx understood it, but merely served as sufficient conditions in which religion could develop its spectral nature.

In Marx's conceptual scheme, the inessential, however, is neither the vapid nor the void at all times. Throughout the several millenia during which divisions in labor, exploitation, and class society have developed, conditions have arisen in which religious conceptions have been projected by human beings enthralled by alienated self-consciousness and imagination. Through the alchemy of belief these projected conceptions have also been objectified in such a manner that they have become powers external to man which threaten him, deny him autonomy, and render him servile. Powers such as these constitute, for Marx, the peculiar substance or content of religious belief. Limited to the realm of inessentiality though they may be, they are coeval with exploitive class society and exercise dominion over men as long as any form of that society endures.

Those powers, projected in alienation, limited to conception, and

---

[168] *Ibid.,* pp. 161-162.
[169] *Ibid.,* p. 168.

hypostasized by belief, which degrade and enslave man are the gods. For a variety of reasons Marx referred to them now and again throughout his writings and even called some by name, such as Jehovah, Moloch, Vishnu, and Plutus. In most respects he conveived of the gods in much the same way any nonbeliever would, but at two points his convictions were exceptional. First, he attributed a peculiar characteristic to the deities which no one to my knowledge had ever seriously done before, and second, he conceived of the gods in such a manner as to render them unfit to carry out many of the functions that religion manifestly carries out. I will take up the first of these contentions immediately but will defer the second one until my exposition of Marx's views on the functions of religion.

To Marx, the metaphysical nature of the gods and of money had a common denominator. At least four reasons can be given for this exceptional position. First, both the gods and money have a purely conceptual basis. Marx wrote:

Real dollars have the same existence imagined gods have. Has a real dollar any mode of existence other than in conception, though in man's general or rather communal conception? Take paper money into a country where this use of paper is not known, and everyone will laugh at your subjective concept. Come with your gods into a country where other gods prevail, and people will prove to you that you are a victim of fictions and abstraction.[170]

Lest it be thought that this passage is atypical of Marx, it should be noted that as late as the closing pages of the third volume of *Capital* he wrote of the "mystic nature" of capital as he had written earlier in the first volume of the "mysterious nature" of commodities.[171] In each case, the mystic and the mysterious were to be understood, along with the merely conceptual, as counterfeits of the empirical. Accordingly, those who put their confidence in the "illusions of the monetary system" were as surely deluded as were the suppliants of the gods.[172] In either situation, they were victimized by the same metaphysical inessentiality.

Second, in addition to their purely conceptual being, both money and the gods share some of the same predicates and carry out some of the same functions. In 1843, while dealing with the Jewish Question, Marx wrote:

Money is the jealous god of Israel before whom no other god may exist. Money degrades all the gods of mankind—converts them into commodities. Money is the

---

[170] Marx, "Notes to the Doctoral Dissertation: Reason and the Proof of God," WYM, p. 65.

[171] Marx, *Capital*, III, 806, 809; *Capital*, I, 72.

[172] Marx, *Capital*, I, 82.

general self-sufficient *value* of everything. Hence it has robbed the whole world, the human world as well as nature, of its proper worth. Money is the alienated essence of man's labor and life, and this alien essence dominates him as he worhips it.

The god of the Jews has been secularized and has become the god of the world. The bill of exchange is the Jew's actual god. His god is only an illusory bill of exchange.[173]

A year later, in a different context, he added:

The very *relationship* of things and the human dealings with them become an operation beyond and above man. Through this *alien mediation* man regards his will, his activity, and his relationships to others as a power independent of himself and of them—instead of man himself being the mediator for man. His slavery thus reaches a climax. It is clear that this *mediator* becomes an *actual god*, for the mediator is the *actual power* over that which he mediates to me. His worship becomes an end in itself.[174]

Third, on one occasion at least, Marx explicitly included religion and wealth in the same category. While criticizing Hegel for assuming religion and wealth to be "*spiritual* entities," mistakenly based on "abstractly sensuous consciousness," Marx pointed out that even on the correct basis of "*humanly* sensuous consciousness" religion and wealth were "but the estranged world of human objectification."[175] One might add that just as man has less the more he projects into God, so he has less the more he projects into capital. In each case, the end result is greater alienation than before.

Fourth, Marx conceived of gold as a fetish and referred explicitly to the "fetish worshippers of metal money."[176] The fetish and fetishism are, of course, religious categories which he often used in characterizing economic phenomena.[177] Said Marx, "Modern society, which . . . pulled Plutus by the hair of his head from the bowels of the earth, greets gold as its Holy Grail. . . ."[178]

I do not mean to imply that Marx never used metaphors, similes, and analogies in a lighthearted and merely suggestive way. He did, but, on some occasions when he used what appear at first blush to be mere figures of speech, he meant to be descriptive and to be taken literally.

---

[173] Marx, "Jews and Christians," WYM, p. 246.

[174] Marx, "Excerpt Notes of 1844", WYM, p. 266.

[175] Marx, *Manuscripts of 1844*, p. 150.

[176] Marx, *Capital*, I, 133; *Manuscripts of 1844*, p. 123.

[177] Friedrich Delekat, "Vom Wesen das Geldes," *Marxismusstudien* 3, with a Foreword by Erwin Metzke (Tübingen: J. C. B. Mohr [Paul Siebeck, 1954]), p. 65.

[178] Marx, *Capital*, I, 132-133.

Nowhere is this more apparent than in his comparisons of money with the gods. In the context of the European colonial system, he once wrote of western industrial-commercial supremacy that it was the strange God who perched himself on the altar cheek by jowl with the old Gods of Europe and one fine day with a shove and a kick chucked them all of a heap. "It proclaimed surplus-value making as the sole end and aim of humanity."[179]

The Functions of Religion

If one rejects Marx's peculiar conception of the supernatural and reverts instead to the more traditional content of western religious belief, it is evident that he understood religion more in terms of function than of content. His writings support this contention, both explicitly and implicitly, even though he did not devote so much as a single page exclusively to the analysis of the functions of religion *per se*. Explicitly, he once noted in passing that religion constituted one of the activities of the human group,[180] and elsewhere he wrote insightfully of religious functions apart from the idiosyncratic content of any specific beliefs.[181] Implicitly, it is clear that he conceived of the gods as thought-entities which exerted power over estranged individuals and carried out certain functions in alienated human society. Regrettably, Marx scattered his views on the functions of religion widely throughout his works, never developed their implications fully, and gave neither a general statement of his functional approach to religious phenomena nor a methodological justification of it. The result is a set of views which, though true in certain particulars, leaves much to be desired.

Marx's scattered and fragmentary views on the functions of religion can, doubtless, be classified in a variety of useful ways. Upon surveying their range and scope, I have categorized them under the headings of (1) spontaneous functions; (2) manipulative functions; (3) reflective functions; and (4) miscellaneous functions. In so doing, I recognize that there are areas of possible overlap between each of these categories and that one can approach them from different perspectives; from the psychological perspective of the individual or from the social vantage point of the group, from the standpoint of the exploiter or from that of the exploited, and from the internal viewpoint of the devotee or from the external viewpoint of the scientific observor. Though Marx had little to say on

---

[179] *Ibid.*, p. 754.
[180] Marx, *Pre-Capitalistic Economic Formations*, p. 80.
[181] Letter, K. Marx to J. B. Schweitzer, October 13, 1868, MESC, pp. 257-258.

these matters explicitly, and seldom repeated himself, he suggested much by implication.

Despite the indelible association between Marx and the assertion that religion is the opium of the people, the expression neither originated with him nor was he the first in his circle of acquaintances to use it.[182] Nevertheless, it is the best known of all his characterizations of religion. Significantly, it makes no reference to the prima facie content of any specific belief associated with any particular religion but refers rather to a function carried out, presumably, by all religions. What Marx said is, "Religion is the sigh of the oppressed creature, the heart of a heartless world, as it is the spirit of spiritless conditions. It is the *opium* of the people."[183] This functional description of religion as a pain killer, written early in his career, constitutes the most gentle treatment Marx ever accorded religion. Though he never repeated these, for him, almost maudlin sentiments, his writings reveal the continued recognition that religion carries out palliative and consolatory functions. I have called these functions spontaneous, because they are not foisted on the masses by exploitive interests. Moreover, the deceptions associated with them are self-deceptions and not the result of collusion and contrivance.

No sooner has the point that religion functions as an opiate been made, however, than two serious questions arise. They are: (1) How great is the range of the ills which religion attempts to palliate; and (2) how suitable are the gods, as Marx conceived them, for consoling human beings in distress? The first question requires an empirical answer which can be supplied only by a scientific study of all relevant data or types of data. In seeing how Marx answered this question, one positive and one negative point must be considered. Positively, Marx always associated religion (excluding natural religion) with the existence of classes. For him, man was the real enemy of man, not nature and not the gods. Negatively, except in part when dealing with primitive man, Marx never associated religion with those aleatory elements in man's natural environment which are usually referred to as the vicissitudes of life. He took no notice of the healing deities, such as Asclepius, ignored the fertility gods such as Astarte, brushed aside the fetishes of the Earth Mother designed to aid women in childbirth, spurned the gods and demigods which assure safe passage from place to place as well as from the beginning of life to its

---

[182] Zvi Rosen, "The Influence of Bruno Bauer on Marx's Concept of Alienation," *Social Theory and Practice*, I (Fall, 1970), 60.

[183] Marx, "Critique of Hegel's Philosophy," WYM, p. 250.

end, and paid heed neither to the gods of the underworld nor to the gentle saviors, such as the Amida Buddha, who welcome the blessed dead to unity with God and reunion with their loved ones in the celestial kingdom. Yet each of these archetypal deities has had, or still has, its cult, its funcionaries, and its devotees.

Since it is impossible to assume that so learned a man as Marx could have been ignorant of these gods and of their several functions, one is left with the conviction that he deliberately ignored them perhaps because they had but the most tenuous relationship, if any at all, with modes of production and social evils. Whatever the case, Marx fixed his penetrating but radically limited gaze only on those palliative and consolatory functions of religion which respond exclusively to the socio-economic conditions with which men afflict each other and themselves. In what appears to be the willful disregard of enormous amounts of data, he failed to consider the palliative and consolatory functions of religion which respond to those natural, physical, nonsocial conditions which constitute a significant proportion of the crises and contingencies of human life. In so doing, Marx unwittingly classified himself with Strauss and Stirner whom he once criticized for having begun with real religion and theology and having determined as they went along what these were to mean.[184] In summary, the range of ills to which religion may respond as an opiate is for all practical purposes unlimited and immensely broader than Marx was willing to admit. Hence, although what he had to say about this aspect of religion may be true, it is not the whole truth.

The second of the questions posed above concerns the suitability of the gods, as Marx understood them, for carrying out the palliative and consolatory functions of religion. It will be remembered that the gods are presumed to be thought-entities which are projected with such intensity of alienated belief that they become independent of man, appear as alien

---

[184] Marx-Engels, GI, p. 5. Here Marx refers to David Friedrich Strauss (1808-1874) author of the influential book, *Das Leben Jesu,* and to Max Stirner (1806-1856) author of *Der Einzige und sein Eigentum.* Although Marx specifically mentions Strauss and Stirner, often calling the latter "Saint Max," the text explicitly refers to the "entire body of German philosophical criticism from Strauss to Stirner" which would include such luminaries as Bruno Bauer, Ludwig Feuerbach, and Moses Hess along with a number of lesser lights among the Young Hegelians of the Left. Marx's contention was that, as a group, they had begun with real religion (*wirklichen Religion*) and actual theology (*eigentlichen Theologie*) as these were found in traditional form in European society, had then reinterpreted each in Hegelian categories for a time, and had finally altered each in keeping with their progressive rejection of Hegelianism.

beings, and exercise power over him. If the gods really are as Marx thought them to be, one is perplexed as to how they could serve as an opiate for those who call upon them for this purpose.

There are approximately five circumstances in which the religious man may be threatened by what he believes. First, he may, as Job, be threatened by the sheer overwhelming power of the Lord. Second, he may be subject to a trickster deity or to one who uses his power capriciously. Third, he may fear in this life the righteous anger of the god whose standards he has not met. Fourth, he may dread the final confrontation with the deity after death. Fifth, he may fear the demonic more or less continuously. In view of these common beliefs, it cannot be denied that religion presents the believer with certain unique frights, but if these were greater, worse, or more enduring than the evils of the world, religion would be unintelligible, and one would expect men to flee it in search of solace in the world. But this is not the case.

The god of infinite power is also a god of love and hence need not be feared by the pious. If there are tricksters about, well, there are also guardian angels. The good god cannot really be capricious, for his goodness will not permit. The deity who demands righteous conduct is good enough to reveal objective standards so that men will know precisely what to do. In cases of human failure he is, happily, quick to forgive. The god of the dead is a threat but only to the wicked. As for Satan, he will get his just deserts in due time, and the good God will at last have no rival. Should the great high God become too remote and alien, a Mediator will come. Should the Mediator become assimilated to the Godhead, there is always the Blessed Virgin. Consider too the treasure troves of merit which the saints have accumulated for us men and our salvation. If all else fails, there are always penances to be performed, rituals to be undertaken, good works to be done, and heartfelt prayers to be said. The gods which Marx assumed that people believe in are more nearly their devils than their gods. Few, if any, go to devils for consolation.

In turning from religion as "the general ground of consolation," Marx discerned another of its functions, namely its sanctioning function. He asserted explicitly that religion served as the "moral sanction of the world."[185] He also observed implicitly that various kinds of action and passion might be "sanctified by religious fanaticism."[186] Furthermore, in speaking of the barricades of religion, property, family, and order, he

---

[185] Marx, "Critique of Hegel's Philosophy," WYM, p. 250.
[186] Marx, "The Indian Revolt," in MEC, p. 131.

testified to his belief that religion functioned conservatively in class society, justifying the differing moralities of various stages of social development and sanctioning their values.[187]

To contend that Marx was aware of the sanctioning function of religion is to suggest neither that he was thorough in his analysis of this phenomenon nor entirely correct in assessing it. At the outset, there is a problem of classification. Although Marx was content to categorize the palliative and consolatory functions of religion as spontaneous, he was strongly disposed to regard its sanctioning function as exclusively manipulative. For example, once when criticizing various types of reactionary socialism in the *Manifesto*, he noted that the French and English aristocracies began suddenly and uncharacteristically to favor socialism during the period epitomized by the revolutionary year of 1830. Having much to fear from the emerging bourgeoisie and the revolutionary proletariat they were evoking, he contended that the aristocracy in order to arouse sympathy "was obliged to lose sight, apparently, of its own interests, and to formulate its indictment against the bourgeoisie in the [pretended] interest of the exploited working class alone."[188] But he continued:

Nothing is easier than to give Christian asceticism a socialist tinge. Has not Christianity declaimed against private property, against marriage, against the state? Has it not preached in the place of these, charity and poverty, celibacy, and mortification of the flesh, monastic life and Mother Church? Christian socialism is but the holy water with which the priest consecrates the heartburnings of the aristocrat.[189]

Marx had an exceptionally keen eye for hypocrisy and a sharp nose for ulterior motives. The quotations above indicate that what he discerned in religious sanctioning was the fraudulent manipulation of religion in such a way as to support those moral structures suitable to the interests of the dominant class. Marx did not seriously consider the possibility that religion might sometimes function spontaneously and innocently in such a manner as to sanction the morality, or some elements of the morality, of an entire society without respect to the class divisions within it. In classifying the sanctioning function of religion as basically manipulative, he made a serious error.

At one point in *The German Ideology*, Marx touched upon the relationship between instinct in the animal and consciousness, or intelligence, in

---

[187] Marx, *Eighteenth Brumaire*, pp. 25-26; *Class Struggles in France*, p. 203.
[188] Marx-Engels, *Manifesto*, p. 33.
[189] *Ibid.*, p. 35.

man.[190] In so doing, he occupied briefly the position from which Bergson was later to launch his analysis of the relationship between what he called "static religion" and the "closed society."[191] Whereas Marx quickly dropped his consideration of instinct in animals and consciousness in man and turned at once to deal with the division of labor and class interest, Bergson, on the contrary, analyzed the relationship between animal instinct and human intelligence extensively. The results of Bergson's work not only have wide-ranging significance for the understanding of religion but also constitute a serious challenge to Marx's critique of religion.

Briefly stated, Bergson argued that gregariousness is essential to the survival of certain animal species and that gregariousness is made possible in animals by virtue of instinctive patterns which determine and limit the behavior of the organisms in question. With man, however, a novel event occurred in organic evolution, for in this species intelligence has largely supplanted instinct. This poses an enduring problem for the species, because while it continues to require the values of gregariousness, the instinctive basis for it has been lost. Bergson concluded that to fill the void morality developed as the social surrogate for instinct. At its most fundamental or "static" level morality is neither the product of individual consciousness nor of reflection but is simply the totality of the mores and folkways traditionally sanctioned by a given human community. Passed from one generation to the next through habituation, imitation, and education, it functions to establish roles, to set acceptable limits to behavior, and to provide the stability requisite to the survival of the human group. Conceived in this way, morality functions among men as instinct functions among other gregarious animals. Despite the necessity of morality in general, however, specific moralities are more or less fragile. Since traditional moralities are not rational in the sense of being based consciously on empirical knowledge and logical demonstration, often being based instead on the most fortuitous of elements, they are susceptible to the corrosive attacks of human intelligence. Necessary to the human groups yet ever threatened by human intelligence, morality requires supernatural support to strengthen and maintain its sanctioning activities against free inquiry and criticism. In this way, Bergson believed that religion developed in primitive or "closed" societies. Thus the gods were called forth to set limits on the potential divisiveness of intelligence. Since

---

[190] Marx-Engels, GI, p. 20.

[191] Henri Bergson, *The Two Sources of Morality and Religion* (Garden City, N. Y.: Doubleday and Company, Inc., 1954) Chapters One and Two especially.

their wills were decisive, even if irrational, their judgment final, and their power over man very great, they could bolster any given way of life and could, moreover, be depended on to favor the way of life traditionally sanctioned, individual human criticisms notwithstanding.

Bergson may have associated the origin of "static" religion in the "closed" society too closely with the sanctioning function of morality to have given an adequate etiology of religion especially in view of its other functions, and he may have overemphasized the role of intelligence in social dissolution. Nevertheless, he had a considerable body of anthropological data, not available to Marx, with which to work. On the whole, I take his analysis of the relationship between the morality of a human group and the sanctioning function of religion to be sound.

One of the most important implications of this position is that religion can have value for a total society insofar as social stability is requisite for the survival and reproduction of the group, insofar as morality is indispensable in achieving that stability, and insofar as religion is instrumental in maintaining the moral system in question. Religion may sacralize felt values which are shared generally by the whole group, may come to the defense of ancestral claims to a given territory, for example, and may support the self-esteem of a people vis-à-vis the barbarian, the gentile, the pagan and the like. The upshot of this is that in analyzing the sanctioning function of religion, one is not justified in focusing exclusively, as Marx did, on the manipulative use of religion by the ruling class, for there are occasions when religion carries out sanctioning functions taken to be beneficial to an entire society by its members without respect to class interests.

In addition to the mistake he made by underestimating, if not ignoring altogether, the spontaneous and society-wide aspects of the sanctioning function of religion, Marx misunderstood the nature of religious relativism. In response to the suggestion that the Communists could soon be silenced if only the authorities would develop the social principles of Christianity, he said:

The social principles of Christianity have now had eighteen hundred years to develop and need no further development by Prussian consistorial councillors.
The social principles of Christianity justified the slavery of Antiquity, glorified the serfdom of the Middle Ages and equally know, when necessary, how to defend the oppression of the proletariat, although they make a pitiful face over it.[192]

It should be noted in passing that neither the sanctioning function nor the

---

[192] Marx, "The Communism of the Paper *Rheinischer Beobachter*," MER, p. 83.

moral relativism which Marx discovered in Christianity are unique to that religion. With minor alterations, they also characterize the relationships between other historic religions and the cultures in which they are lodged. Accordingly, what Marx said of Christianity in this context can be generalized, and what I shall say of what he said is applicable to other religions as well.

Broadly speaking, the quotation above contains an accurate description provided that one ignores sectarian movements within Christianity, whether socially atavistic or progressive, and focuses instead on the general drift of its organized orthodox forms. Marx was also justified in attacking as false and prententious both the assertion that Christianity was the bearer of divine truths and the claim that it was the custodian of eternal moral principles. The legions of inconsistent theologies which have appeared indicate that Christians have yet to decide what precisely the truths were which God allegedly revealed in Christ. Furthermore, no theoretical foundation for Christian ethics acceptable to all informed parties has yet been developed and probably never will be. So much, then, for divine truths and eternal moral principles. Here Marx was on solid ground. Where he lost his footing was in associating the chameleon-like nature of Christian ethics too closely with conscious manipulative activities reflecting class interests and in assuming that religion would carry out its sanctioning role only on behalf of the morality of class society.

It cannot be denied that institutionalized religion has vested interests surprisingly like those of the ruling elite; that it insinuates itself into secular institutions; that the members of its hierarchy arrogate authority and power unto themselves; that religious functionaries proclaim the unsupported contents of faith as if they were established facts; that they do not always believe what they proclaim, practice what they preach, nor exemplify what they say of their religion; that the pious do their share of posturing and posing; that in differing ways and in varying degrees organized religion participates in the full range of evils which characterize secular life. When taken together, this amounts to the cant, deceit, and exploitation which Marx perceived in religion and for which he loathed it. Still and all, even if none of this were true and hypocrisy were never at issue, religion would have to change in changing societies, even while denying change, would pronounce its benediction over different socio-economic structures at different times and places in witless innocence of what it was doing, would celebrate relative values as absolute, and would baptize freshly assimilated goals as if they were perfectly consistent with its ancient values.

Even if one could assume with certainty that the palliative-consolatory aspects of religion will disappear in the classless society, having no functions to perform, this does not imply that the sanctioning functions of religion will vanish. Whereas the Scriptures hold that with God all things are possible, I contend that with man all gods are possible. The point is that although Marx would have rejected the proposition vehemently, he could just as well have had the blessings of the Most High as not. Any religion sufficiently plastic to have sanctioned slavery, feudalism, and capitalism can surely reconcile itself to socialism. This is all the more true if the religion in question has been successful in leaving its Jewish homeland to abide cheek by jowl first with Neo-Platonists, then Aristotelians, and finally with modern science, to say nothing of its wondrous adaptability to such differing governmental forms as monarchy, oligarchy, and democracy.

In addition to the palliative-consolatory and sanctioning functions of religion, Marx also detected what I have chosen to call a reflective function. This function is neither spontaneous in the sense of meeting the needs of exploited people nor manipulative in the sense of supporting ruling class interests. It is a revelatory function which discloses the way in which the substructure of a society reflects itself in ideology. Although bourgeois investigators would not likely recognize this function, it was evident to Marx that the interests of the ruling class would be transmogrified into appropriate conceptual phantoms and that economic conflicts would reappear as ideological struggles.[193]

Under the heading of miscellaneous functions, I should like now to consider briefly the alienating function of religion, its expressive functions, and its intellectual function. Along with its soothing activities, religion also alienates human beings, according to Marx. He observed that it is the expression of real suffering and also the "protest against real suffering."[194] Since he never returned to give these opinions adequate expression, one is at a loss to know precisely what he had in mind. It is tempting to speculate that he was acknowledging the prophetic tradition in the Judeo-Christian religion. It is equally enticing to hypothesize that by dropping the point he left well enough alone, for it would have been incongruous, if not impossible, for him to have permitted a critical or prophetic thread to run through religion as he understood it. On one occasion, he also made the point that religion was the "generalized theory of this world, its

---

[193] Marx, "Preface to the Critique of Political Economy," MESW, p. 183.
[194] Marx, "Critique of Hegel's Philosophy," WYM, p. 250.

CHAPTER 2

ENGELS' CRITIQUE OF RELIGION

ENGELS' ROLE IN THE CRITICISM OF RELIGION

At first glance it appears as if the scholarly pursuits of Marx and Engels were related inversely. Whereas Marx began with a critique of religion, then moved on to deal with philosophy and socio-political issues, and finally turned with increasing preoccupation to economic investigations, Engels, beginning with economic matters, ended with works which had much to do with religion but little with economics. To illustrate further, while Marx was producing the introduction to his proposed critique of Hegel's philosophy of law and was writing two essays on the Jewish Question, Engels was working on a book entitled, *The Condition of the Working Class in England*, and was producing "Outlines of a Critique of Political Economy." One could also point out that while Marx was pottering about with the materials which were eventually to comprise the second and third volumes of *Capital*, Engels was writing *The Dialectics of Nature and Anti-Dühring*. But this inverse relationship is trivial insofar as their critiques of religion are at issue. It becomes important only if it misleads the reader into thinking that Marx, in turning to economic studies, repudiated his earlier views on religion or that Engels had never criticized religion atheistically before he produced the economic writings which led to collaboration with Marx.

Unlike the problematical role of religion in the Marx household, religion in the Engels' household was straightforward and transparent. Friedrich Engels not only came from a home notorious for the most perfervid fundamentalism but also from that part of Germany in which Pietism and evangelical preaching were most highly regarded.[1] During the first seventeen years of his life, Engels was steeped, if somewhat rebelliously, in authoritarian faith and intolerance, in orthodoxy and in trust in the literal

---

[1] Gustav Mayer, *Friedrich Engels*, p. 4.

inspiration of the Scriptures.[2] Those who have escaped the toils of this kind of religion will not be surprised to learn that he could break with it only by passing through a season of travail, brief in his case but agonizing nonetheless.[3]

While living in Bremen in 1839, Engels began to settle accounts with his erstwhile faith by producing a set of writings called, "Letters from the Wuppertal." In these so-called letters, written under a pseudonym, Engels cast a critical and descriptive eye toward the "sanctimonious valley" from which he had come. In view of his preoccupation with the mindless mysticism of pietistic religion, with its strongly Calvinistic flavor in the valley of the Wupper, with its bigoted preaching, and its intolerance of all things papist, one can only conclude that these writings never transcended the parochial insofar as a general critique of religion is concerned.[4] Their principal significance lies, first, in the fact that Engels had grown bold enough at nineteen to write them and, second, in the fact that he had already noticed the irrelevance of Pietism for the laboring masses.

From the standpoint of his development as a critic of religion, the most important event in Engels' Bremen days was his reading of Strauss' book, *The Life of Jesus*.[5] This pioneering work in biblical scholarship not only prompted him to cry, "Adios Glauben!" but also converted him into an enthusiastic Straussian.[6] Becoming a disciple of Strauss was not, however, an end in itself for Engels. On the contrary, his new position led him quickly to interest in speculative theology and thence to the absolute idealism of Hegel. These budding interests were stimulated and facilitated by Engels' removal from Bremen to Berlin in 1841 where he fulfilled military obligations. Once in Berlin, Engels learned from and collaborated with the Young Hegelians who were just then girding to do intellectual battle with various reactionary tendencies in Prussia associated with the accession of Friedrich Wilhelm IV to the throne in 1840. Amongst the most radical of Young Hegelians, Engels wrote an article in 1842 in which he bemoaned the fact that though Friedrich Wilhelm IV had been raised a free spirit, he had sought to transmogrify the existing state into a highly

---

[2] Edmund Wilson, *To the Finland Station* (Garden City, N. Y.: Doubleday and Company, Inc., 1953), p. 130; Yelana Stepanova, *Friedrich Engels* (Moscow: Foreign Languages Publishing House, 1958), pp. 6-7; Mayer, *Friedrich Engels*, p. 5.

[3] Ernest Czóbel, "Die Hauptetappen der politischen Tätigheit von Engels," in *Friedrich Engels, Der Denker* (Basel: Mundus-Verlag, 1945), p. 20.

[4] Engels, "Briefe aus dem Wuppertal," MEW, I, 419-420.

[5] See above, Chapter I, note 184.

[6] Letter, F. Engels to W. Graeber, October 8, 1839, MEW, II, Supplement, 419.

theologized form of Christian state. The result was grotesque, because theology at that time was, according to Engels, "die Vermittlung und Vertuschung absoluter Gegensatze."[7]

A set of three articles attacking Schelling's philosophical theology constitutes Engels' most important literary achievement during his Berlin days. As he perceived it, Schelling had been called to the University of Berlin to defend the reactionary trends which then characterized Prussian life. As an apologist for the regime, Schelling attacked all that was progressive in Hegelianism. Accordingly, it seemed appropriate to Engels to defend Hegel insofar as possible and to undercut Schelling simultaneously. In an article entitled, "Schelling and Revelation," the most important member of the set philosophically, Engels accused Schelling of rejecting the valid achievements of Hegel in order to reintroduce mysticism and scholasticism into philosophy.[8] Although the article is by no means essential to an understanding of the content of Engels' critique of religion, it is important in that it was the first work of a Young Hegelian to proclaim atheism, a tribute to Engels' grasp of Feuerbach's book, *The Essence of Christianity*.[9]

When Engels departed Berlin for Manchester, England in 1842, it might have been expected that he would do little toward consolidating his position on religion, but not so. In his "Review of Thomas Carlyle's *Past and Present*," published less than two years after his arrival in England, he showed continued progress as a critic of religion. Noteworthy among the convictions he expressed were, first, his belief that religion was an emptying of human content which was then transferred so as to constitute God, the divine phantom; second, his assertion of the essential falsehood and hypocrisy of religion; third, his contention that after Christianity had reached abstract, or philosophical, expression there could be no further religious development but only extinction; fourth, his call to non-violent war on religion; fifth, his belief that religion would be abolished when man returned to correct self-consciousness; sixth, his trust in the atheism of the age as a means conducive to complete human emancipation; and seventh, his affirmation that it was the members of his own persuasion who took history seriously and not members of opposing groups, despite loud cries to the contrary.[10]

[7] Engels, Friedrich Wilhelm IV, König von Prussen, MEW, I, 447.

[8] Engels, "Schelling und die Offenbarung," MEW, II, Supplement, 191.

[9] Ernest Czóbel, "Die Hauptetappen der politischen Tätigheit von Engels," p. 22.

[10] Engels, "Review of Thomas Carlyle's *Past and Present*," *Reader*, pp. 234-237, 239.

In view of the preceding paragraphs, it is clear that Marx's and Engels' views on religion had, for all practical purposes, converged into a single position before the inauguration of their renowned collaboration in 1844. Moreover, he provided confirmation for Marx's view that religion was about to be abolished. When Engels first went to England, he was surprised upon being told by Chartists that religion was the most important thing for Englishmen, even for the working class.[11] He agreed that this had been true in the latter years of the eighteenth century, but by 1845 when he published *The Condition of the Working-Class* in England the situation had changed dramatically. By that time the workers were no longer religious and the clergy were in a bad odor.[12] Independent thought among the "great unwashed" had put agnosticism in England almost on a par with the Established Church.[13] "Atheism," said Engels, "was nearly self-evident to the workers."[14] Christianity was already in its last stage.[15]

After the completion of *The German Ideology* in 1846, Marx never again found time to deal with the loose ends which had been left therein, nor did he return to the topic of religion except to summarize his views in passing or to encapsulate them in short bursts of trenchant criticism. Engels, on the contrary, did return to those loose ends in *Feuerbach* (1886) and did turn again to consider religion rather extensively, although twenty-five years intervened between *The Peasant War* (1850), in which he had much to say of religion, and the research which eventuated in a short piece entitled, *Socialism: Utopian and Scientific* (1877), and in the more extensive work, from which the former had been taken, entitled, *Anti-Dühring* (1878). In the three preceding works taken together with *The Dialectics of Nature*, on which Engels labored from 1873 to 1886, and with *The Origin of the Family, Private Property and the State* (1884), he dealt with religion as a summarizer and systematizer of, and as an apologist for, the critique of religion Marx and he had forged in the years leading up to 1846.

In his declining years, Engels, unlike Marx, took sufficient interest in the results of biblical scholarship to use them as grist for the Marxist

---

[11] Leopold Schwarzschild, *The Red Prussian* (London: Hamish Hamilton, 1948), p. 125.

[12] Engels, *The Condition of the Working-Class in England*, MEB, p. 159 (hereinafter referred to as *Condition of Working-Class*).

[13] Friedrich Engels, *Socialism: Utopian and Scientific* (Moscow: Foreign Languages Publishing House, n.d.), pp. 19-20 (hereinafter referred to as *Socialism*).

[14] Engels, "Emigrant Literature," MER, p. 142.

[15] Engels, *Feuerbach*, MESW, p. 630.

mill. Although Engels' articles entitled, "Bruno Bauer and Early Christianity," "The Book of Revelation," and "On the History of Early Christianity," published in 1882, 1883, and 1894-95, respectively, seem at first blush to be too parochial to be of much use in developing or supporting a general critique of religion, they are significant insofar as Engels sought therewith to verify Marx's historical materialism.

When one considers Engels' "Letters from the Wuppertal," written in 1839, and then turns to consider his article on the history of early Christianity, the last installment of which was published in the year of his death, it is no exaggeration to say that the criticism of religion was for him the beginning and the end of all criticism.

FROM THE INCEPTION OF RELIGION TO ITS TRANSCENDENCE

The Etiology of Religion

Twice in *Anti-Dühring* Engels dealt with the origin of religion much as Marx and he had treated the subject in *The German Ideology*. Although Engels did not re-employ the term *Naturreligion* as it appears in the latter work, it is clear that he still had the same concept in mind when he wrote *Anti-Dühring*. He noted at one point in the book that when men "made their entry into history" they were "still half animal, brutal, still helpless in the face of the forces of nature, still ignorant of their own strength."[16] And to this he added elsewhere in the same work, "All religion . . . is nothing but the fantastic reflection in men's minds of those external forces which control their daily life, a reflection in which the terrestrial forces assume the form of supernatural forces."[17] Having satisfied himself that man's initial religious response was one of fear before the ravages of almighty nature, Engels proceeded to note that threatening social forces also play a role in religion:

It is not long before, side by side with the forces of nature, social forces begin to be active—forces which confront man as equally inexplicable, dominating him with the same apparent natural necessity as the forces of nature themselves.[18]

In this manner, Engels made explicit a point which I believe Marx and he intended to make in *The German Ideology*, but a point to which they failed to give definitive expression.

The point in question is that religion, in temporal terms, is at first a

[16] Friedrich Engels, *Anti-Dühring*, 3rd ed. (Moscow: Foreign Languages Publishing House, 1962), p. 247 (hereinafter referred to as A-D).

[17] *Ibid.,* p. 433.

[18] *Ibid.*

response to nature and later a response to social conditions. Marx attempted to unite natural religion and social religion by saying of natural religion that it "was determined by the form of society and *vice versa.*"[19] Since I have already shown that he failed to achieve a unified etiology for natural religion and for the pure, abstract, theological religion allegedly characteristic of the social relationships of class society, it remains to be seen whether or not Engels escaped the resulting dilemma into which Marx fell.

It was an egregious error to presume, as both Marx and Engels did, that primitive man became religious when he first recognized his helplessness in the presence of rampant nature. It was equally mistaken to think that primitive man next became religious when he recognized his vulnerability to threatening social forces. It is not primitive man who experiences these confrontations on the first and second days of creation, as it were; it is the human infant, neither primitive nor civilized. In order for an infant to survive and develop to the point of becoming religious, there must be a social matrix as well as a natural environment. As far as the infant is concerned, the one does not precede the other, nor are the two carefully distinguished during the first few years of the child's life. Since the individual who confronts nature as nature is already a socialized being, it is nonsensical to provide a temporal schema for the appearance of those environmental conditions to which men in fear respond religiously.

This error is all the more puzzling in view of Engels' essay entitled, "The Part Played by Labour in the Transition from Ape to Man," published in 1876, two years before *Anti-Dühring.* He wrote, "It has already been noted that our simian ancestors were gregarious; it is obviously impossible to seek the derivation of man, the most social of all animals, from nongregarious ancestors."[20] He made the same point in abbreviated form in *The Dialectics of Nature,* a work begun five years before the completion of *Anti-Dühring* (1878). [21] Since primitive man did not cease being gregarious when he departed the animal world and entered history, Engels ought to have realized that he could no longer postulate fully grown, but nonsocialized, primitives who at the dawn of creation became religious out of their fear of awesome natural forces and then, later on, out of their fear of threatening social forces.

[19] Marx-Engels, GI, p. 19.

[20] Engels, "The Part Played by Labour in the Transition from Ape to Man," MESW, p. 360.

[21] Friedrich Engels, *Dialectics of Nature* (New York: International Publishers, 1940), p. 282 (hereinafter referred to as DN).

If human society is taken to have emerged from simian gregariousness and if religion is presumed to have developed from two sources of fear temporally ordered, then the sequence established by Marx and reiterated by Engels must be reversed. But to do this is to lodge the origin of religion in simian gregariousness. Had they been induced to convert the order, Marx and Engels would have had difficulty localizing the origin of religion, because they knew next to nothing of primate society and were always at pains to claim uniqueness for the kind of work, requisite to human subsistence, which led to the threatening social forces to which they thought men responded religiously. Thus, one is left to wonder what types of social forces, threatening or not, they might have found in primate society conducive to religion.

The attempt at lodging the origin of religion in primate society is not an idle one. Morris, in *The Naked Ape* (a book of sufficient significance to merit a rejoinder by John Lewis),[22] has recently attempted to do just that by hypothesizing that God is the idealized surrogate for the dominant male typical of primate social groups and that "in the behavioural sense, religious activities consist of the coming together of large groups of people to perform repeated and prolonged submissive displays to appease a dominant individual."[23]

In addition to the logical problems raised above, it now appears that Marx and Engels overemphasized the role of fear in general in the creation of religion. Montagu writes:

It is a mistaken view, widely prevalent, that nonliterate peoples live in a constant state of terror, in abject fear of the supernaturals who are ever ready to pounce upon and punish them for their transgressions. The truth is that the magico-religious systems of nonliterate peoples, on the whole, permit people to live their lives quite as happily and as free from fear as do the most advanced religious systems of the literate peoples of the world. The morality of nonliterate peoples is a functional and fundamentally integrative, as well as regulative, factor of society and gives support to social codes or moralisms.[24]

Animism

In *Feuerbach,* Engels gave vent for the first time to an animistic etiology of such basic ideas as God, the soul, and immortality. In one respect, it is

[22] John Lewis and Bernard Towers, *Naked Ape or Homo Sapiens?* (London: Garnstone Press, 1969).

[23] Desmond Morris, *The Naked Ape* (New York: McGraw-Hill Book Company, 1967), pp. 178-181.

[24] Ashley Montagu, *Immortality, Religion, and Morals* (New York: Hawthorn Books, 1971), p. 116.

not at all unusual that he should have done so, but in another respect it is most surprising that he did so. In 1871, E. B. Tylor published *Primitive Culture*, a work which was to become a landmark in the investigation of primitive mentality. In a letter dated August 9, 1871, Engels sent a list of books, along with their prices to one Pjotr Lawrowitsch Lawrow. The list contained *Primitive Culture* along with books by Lecky, Lubbock, and Maine.[25] Nearly a month later, Engels sent a slightly expanded list, including these titles minus the prices, to the same individual.[26] Then he fell silent on the subject of Tylor until 1884 when he wrote to Bernstein, "All that humbug by Tylor, Lubbock and Co. about endogamy, exogamy and whatever else that rubbish is called has now been definitely squashed."[27] Since the humbug to which Engels referred was not included in *Primitive Culture*, but in a later work, one may conclude that he followed Tylor's progress to some extent. Both Marx and Engels knew Tylor's earlier book entitled, *Early History of Mankind* (1865). Marx cited it;[28] and Engels mentioned it.[29]

Despite the lack of conclusive evidence, it is probably safe to assume that both Marx and Engels knew the contents of *Primitive Culture*, but Marx did not deign to speak of it and gave no indication of having been influenced by it relative to the etiology of religion. Engels, however, not only mentioned *Primitive Culture* but also expressed some of its most famous conclusions as if they were his own, without bothering to acknowledge their source. It is unimportant whether or not Engels acquired these conclusions through primary sources or simply absorbed them from the era's intellectual atmosphere. The point is that he knew something of Tylor's work as might have been expected. The surprising element is that Engels adopted Tylor's views on the origin of religion as if they were not only compatible with his own opinions but also with those of Marx. Although Tylor's etiology of religion does not contradict Marx's position in all respects, the two viewpoints tend to be mutually exclusive.

Lest there be confusion as to precisely which of Tylor's ideas Engels adopted, I shall quote from *Feuerbach*, the one and only work in which

---

[25] Letter, F. Engels to P. L. Lawrow, August 9, 1871, MEW, XXXIII, 261.

[26] Letter, F. Engels to P. L. Lawrow, September 1, 1871, MEW, XXXIII, 275.

[27] Letter, F. Engels to E. Bernstein, January 1, 1884, MESC, p. 442.

[28] Marx, *Capital*, II, 438-439.

[29] Friedrich Engels, *The Origin of the Family, Private Property, and the State* (Moscow: Foreign Languages Publishing House, n.d.), p. 11 (hereinafter referred to as *Family, Property, and State*).

he gave a typically animistic explanation of such religious conceptions as the soul, the gods or God, and immortality:

From the very early times when men, still completely ignorant of the structure of their own bodies, under the stimulus of dream apparitions came to believe that their thinking and sensation were not activities of their bodies, but of a distinct soul which inhabits the body and leaves it at death—from this time men have been driven to reflect about the relation between this soul and the outside world. If upon death it took leave of the body and lived on, there was no occasion to invent yet another distinct death for it. Thus arose the idea of its immortality, which at that stage of development appeared not at all as a consolation but as a fate against which it was no use fighting, and often enough, as among the Greeks, as a positive misfortune. Not religious desire for consolation, but the quandry arising from the common universal ignorance of what to do with this soul, once its existence had been accepted, after the death of the body, led in a general way to the tedious notion of personal immortality. In an exactly similar manner the first gods arose through the personification of natural forces. And these gods in the further development of religions assumed more and more an extramundane form, until finally by a process of abstraction, I might almost say of distillation, occurring naturally in the course of man's intellectual development, out of the many more or less limited and mutually limiting gods there arose in the minds of men the idea of the one exclusive God of the monotheistic religions.[30]

The preceding paragraph is a reasonably accurate distillation of Tylor's views expressed in Chapters Eleven through Seventeen of *Primitive Culture*.

There are three reasons why Engels' adoption of the foregoing views is most surprising. In the first place, if the animistic approach is correct, then certain conceptions of major significance to most, if not all, religions may or may not be associated with reactions to nature based on fear. It will be remembered that Marx had always been at pains to emphasize the role of fear in the etiology of religion as Engels, too, had been up to this point. In the second place, by Engels' own admission, the idea of immortality did not arise initially in the context of consolation but in the context of explanation.[31] In view of the profound importance Marx attached to the palliative and consolatory functions of religion, it is odd that Engels should have made this admission. He did assert that a consolatory aspect eventually attached itself to the idea of immortality, but he neither specified when this alteration occurred nor did he give a reason as to why it would have occurred at a particular time. In the third place, from the perspective

---

[30] Engels, *Feuerbach,* MESW, pp. 603-604.
[31] *Ibid.,* p. 604.

of animism, the belief in gods, spirits, and the immortality of souls (which defines religion for Tylor) involves explanatory concepts of biomorphic and psychomorphic origin which have little, or nothing, to do with modes of production and exchange of commodities. The question, then, is whether or not Marx's etiology of religion with its strongly sociomorphic orientation, involving class structure, socio-economic contradictions, and ideology, can include cogmogonic and etiological myths and religious conceptions based on biomorphic and psychomorphic models. I judge that Marxism cannot be reconciled with Tylor's animism without losing its most distinctive characteristics.

It is most unlikely that Engels intended to develop Marx's critique of religion beyond its original dimensions and equally unlikely that he was conscious of introducing any elements in *Feuerbach* which would modify the position on religion which he and Marx had long since forged. What, then, happened to Engels? Did Tylor's animistic explanation of religion seem so overwhelmingly evident that Engels had perforce to syncretize it with Marx's critique, whether the two were compatible or not?

It may well be that Engels found Tylor's animistic approach congenial, because it reinforced and supplemented a tendency in his own thought for which there was little or no support in Marx. I refer to the tendency of recognizing that various religious concepts are taken by those who believe in them to refer to beings, powers, or principles which have explanatory significance, often of cosmic dimensions. It would be absurd to suggest that Marx did not know this item of information, since he had ridiculed Proudhon at length for finding all manner of economic categories "slumbering in the heart of God the Father" and for using Providence as a locomotive for moving all sorts of economic and historical baggage.[32] But to Marx the concept of God was so vacuous and inessential, so utterly reflective, and so patently counterfeit that he could not seriously entertain the idea that anybody might believe in the idea for explanatory reasons in addition to those he had characterized as ideological.

Even though he ridiculed Dühring much as Marx had ridiculed Proudhon, Engels could and did understand how the concept of God might be used, albeit mistakenly, as an explanatory principle.[33] In the *Dialectics of Nature* he noted that when those of prescientific mentality failed to explain an occurrence with reference to the natural they simply

---

[32]   Letter, K. Marx to P. V. Annenkov, December 28, 1846, MESC, p. 45; *The Poverty of Philosophy* (Moscow: Foreign Languages Publishing House), p. 114.

[33]   Engels, A-D, pp. 86, 102.

ascribed it to the supernatural,[34] and in *Anti-Dühring* he pointed out that, for some, God was merely another word for "initial impulse."[35] Thus, although Engels disbelieved in God, noting with satisfaction that the evolutionary scheme of things left no room for deity and that the old teleology had gone to the Devil, still he was sufficiently rationalistic, along with Tylor, to recognize that some people, ranging from ignorant savages to various misguided sophisticates, might believe in the supernatural as a force ultimately explanatory of natural occurrences.[36] When Engels pointed out that the first gods arose "through the personification of natural forces" and then proceeded to evolve in such a manner as to eventuate in the one god of theism, congruently with the development of man's intellectual powers, he was closer to Tylor than to Marx.[37]

By way of summary and conclusion, three points can be made. First, I think it most probable that Engels intended to maintain intact the etiology of religion first presented in *The German Ideology* and that he proposed no wayward developments. But in giving later expression to it in *Anti-Dühring*, he made its initial error more obvious than it had originally been, the error being that of portraying the fully grown primitive as one who in the first place quaked in religious fear before the awesome presence of nature and as one who in the second place, after a suitable period of development, responded with religious fear to the alien powers of society.

Second, whether by design or not, Engels allowed natural religion to persist and interact with social religion. Marx, it will be remembered, had tried to bridge the gap between man's first and second religious responses by contending that natural religion was "determined by the form of society and *vice versa*." But at this crucial juncture, Marx, regrettably, gave neither a description of the kinds of interaction he had in mind nor any evidence of their existence. Moreover, he dropped all further consideration of natural religion at this point and focused exclusively on social religion. Engels, however, did not annihilate natural religion as an ongoing element in human faith, nor did he divert all attention from it:

As to the realms of ideology which soar still higher in the air—religion, philosophy, etc.—these have a prehistoric stock, found already in existence by and taken over in the historical period, of what we should today call bunk. These various false conceptions of nature, of man's own being, of spirits, magic forces, etc., have for

[34] Engels, DN, pp. 231-232.
[35] Engels, A-D, p. 77.
[36] Engels, DN, p. 187.
[37] Engels, *Feuerbach*, MESW, p. 604; A-D, p. 474.

the most part only a negative economic element as their basis; the low economic development of the prehistoric period is supplemented and also partially conditioned and even caused by the false conceptions of nature. And even though economic necessity was the main driving force of the progressive knowledge of nature and has become ever more so, it would surely be pedantic to try and find economic causes for all this primitive nonsense.[38]

Entirely in keeping with this, Engels had written earlier:

The fantastic figures, which at first only reflected the mysterious forces of nature, at this point acquire social attributes, become representatives of the forces of history. At a still further stage of evolution, all the natural and social attributes of the numerous gods are transferred to one almighty god, who is but a reflection of the abstract man.[39]

When Engels announced that various false conceptions having a negative economic basis "supplemented," "partially conditioned" and "even caused" the low economic development of prehistoric man, he went beyond Marx's obscure assertion that natural religion and the form of society were reciprocally determined. But in making explicit the point that the initial basis of *Naturreligion* continues along with the historical development of religion, Engels posed a problem which Marx never confronted.[40]

Third, in adopting animistic interpretations, Engels, wittingly or unwittingly, developed a broader basis for understanding religion than did Marx and in effect minimized the importance of economic factors. Despite the fact that the animistic approach now seems somewhat dated, moot, and overly rationalistic, particularly in its portrayal of logical though grossly ignorant savages inventing rational explanations for certain psychic phenomena, still it provides a more adequate basis for understanding religion than the one Marx developed with its unique but overextended sociomorphic model predicated on modes of production, division of labor, and socio-economic contradictions.

Earlier I suggested that it remained to be seen whether or not Engels fell into Marx's dilemma of postulating discontinuous etiologies of natural and social religion. The record indicates that Engels did fall into this dilemma initially but that he progressively extricated himself from it, perhaps without fully recognizing either the problem or his partial escape from it.

Spontaneous and Artificial Religion

The course of religion from its inception to the demise of its ancient forms in the West, coincident with the full expansion of the Roman Empire

[38] Letter, F. Engels to C. Schmidt, October 27, 1890, MESC, p. 505.
[39] Engels, A-D, pp. 433-434.
[40] *Ibid.*, p. 434.

and the emergence of Christianity, provided Engels with the opportunity for introducing his concept of "spontaneous" religion. This type is to be understood as the opposite of what he called "artificial" religion, a mode typified by Christianity and Islam. Having called attention to Engels' use of these categories, it remains to clarify what he meant by them. From within the context of man's primordial religious behavior, composed of fear reactions, fantastic mental reflections, and the personification of natural forces, the individual religions of antiquity emerged. These religions, uninterested in proselytes, were common to unified tribal groups and were limited in efficacy to the geographic region claimed by the group.[41] The gods of these antique religions were ethnic or national deities which flourished with a tribe's expansion and became moribund with its eclipse.[42] According to Engels the principal characteristic of all archaic religions, exemplified alike by the religion of the primitive Aryans and Negro fetish worshippers, was spontaneity.[43] By this he meant that they arose initially without conscious deception, contrivance, or manipulation. But sooner or later in the course of their development, all spontaneous religions suffered the inevitable intrusions of priestly mendacity.

The only difference between spontaneous and artificial religions which Engels noted explicitly is that the latter employ deception including "falsification of history" from their inception.[44] Among prime examples of artificial religion, as he saw it, were Christianity, the eschatological sects of Judaism, and Islam, that "fake religion."[45] Engels was annoyed by the apocalyptic genre of sacred writing including Daniel from the Old Testament, Enoch from the Intertestamental Period, and Revelation from the New Testament. The authors of these works, fully cognizant of their deceptions, wrote of the past as if it were yet to happen, but in a manner agreeable to themselves.[46] Engels could have found equally flagrant examples of the misuse of history in the Synoptic Gospels and in the Book of Acts. I am thinking of such passages, for instance, as Matt. 2:15 in which Hosea's reference to the nation of Israel is interpreted as applying to

[41] Engels, *Feuerbach*, MESW, p. 628.

[42] *Ibid.*, p. 613.

[43] Engels, "Bruno Bauer and Early Christianity," MER, p. 194 (hereinafter referred to as "Bauer").

[44] *Ibid.*

[45] *Ibid.*, p. 195; Letter, F. Engels to K. Marx, approx. May 24, 1853; MESC, p. 96.

[46] Engels, "On the History of Early Christianity," MER, p. 327 (hereinafter referred to as "Early Christianity").

Jesus; Matt. 2:23 in which a nonexistent prophecy is utilized in justification of calling Jesus, "the Nazarene;" and Acts 2:25-28 in which King David is blithely assumed to have spoken of Jesus as his Lord. Needless to say, there is no historical justification at all for having construed passages from the Old Testament in this manner. But, still and all, what did Engels gain toward the understanding of religion by dividing it into spontaneous and artificial types? Very little, it would seem, particularly in view of the fact that he could not decide to what extent Christianity was artificial and to what extent spontaneous. He had the same difficulty with Islam and would have had the same trouble with Judaism had he investigated it thoroughly.

Primitive Christianity

"A religion like the Christian," said Engels, "cannot be destroyed through ridicule and invective *alone*, it has to be *overpowered scientifically*, i.e., *historically explained*, and that cannot be managed even by the natural sciences."[47] Accordingly, in order to expedite the abolition of religion, Engels set out to smite Christianity. His first blow consisted in categorizing it as an artificial religion.[48] In so doing he sought to burden it with the cross of duplicity in addition to all the other evils, endemic to religion in general, which it bore. To castigate a religion for construing history perfidiously is not, however, to explain it, but merely to characterize an aspect of it. As Engels said:

A religion that brought the Roman world empire into subjection and dominated by far the larger part of civilized humanity for 1,800 years cannot be disposed of merely by declaring it to be nonsense gleaned together by frauds.[49]

His task, then was to explain the origin and development of Christianity in such a way as to make intelligible the reasons why the Roman Empire preferred this slave-taught faith to its many rivals.[50]

Engels undertook his first extensive examination of the origin and development of Christianity in a short work entitled, "Bruno Bauer and Early Christianity," published in 1882 (hereinafter referred to as "Bauer"). He not only paid tribute to Bauer as a pioneer in New Testament scholarship but also adopted uncritically many of the latter's convictions

---

[47] Engels, "From the Second Manuscript of 'Notes on Germany'," *The Peasant War in Germany* (Moscow: Foreign Languages Publishing House, 1956), p. 232 (hereinafter referred to as "Notes on Germany" and *Peasant War* respectively).

[48] Engels, "Bauer," MER, pp. 194-195.

[49] *Ibid.*, p. 195.

[50] *Ibid.*

concerning the early church and its literature. In his highly selective reiteration of some of Bauer's conclusions, Engels sought to explain Christianity in strictly human and material terms, rejecting both the "mystical" understanding of the faithful, who thought that their religion had been heaven-sent in the fullness of time, and the idealistic interpretation of Bauer who regarded Christianity as the expression of a necessary phase in the development of human consciousness. Christianity, on the contrary, came into being in a much more mundane manner according to Engels.

The imposition of Roman social, political, legal, and economic conditions on conquered peoples destroyed the efficacy of the ethnic and national gods of antiquity, but the destruction of archaic religion did not annihilate human need for religion at the time but left a void into which a legion of religions poured, each offering its interpretations and consolations in exchange for public acceptance.[51] Christianity triumphed over its rivals because it was more fitted to meet the religious needs of the time than they were. Among its assets were (1) the possession of both eastern (Philonic and Judaic) and western (Stoic) ideological elements;[52] (2) the proclamation of one god at a time when vulgar philosophy (Platonism) and religion had made monotheism acceptable;[53] (3) the lack of idiosyncratic rituals associated with ethnic and national cults;[54] (4) the possession of a universal concept of sin explanatory of current decadence and depravity;[55] (5) the possession of an attractive set of doctrines, the most important being that of the Incarnation and Atonement of the Logos, which gave hope and consolation to the wretched of the earth;[56] and (6) the capacity of absorbing the ancient gods and their functions.[57] Taken together, these points reveal the universality of Christianity in contradistinction to the particularity of the dying religions of antiquity. Since Christianity was more suited to the conditions of the times and met more of the religious needs of people than any other available faith, it is only natural that the Roman world should have adopted this brand of fraudulent nonsense and not some other.

Philosophical naturalists will applaud Engels for having rejected super-

---

[51] Engels, "Bauer," MER, pp. 198-202; *Feuerbach*, MESW, p. 629.

[52] Engels, "Bauer," MER, pp. 196-197; "The Book of Revelation," MER, p. 207 (hereinafter referred to as "Revelation").

[53] Engels, "Bauer," MER, p. 197.

[54] *Ibid.*, p. 203.

[55] *Ibid.*, pp. 203-204.

[56] *Ibid.*, p. 196.

[57] Engels, "Early Christianity," MER, p. 329.

natural explanations of Christianity. They will also commend him for integrating economic considerations with other explanatory factors in giving a thoroughly naturalistic account of Christian origins. Moreover, anyone familiar with the period will agree that Engels dealt with historical facts long since recognized as pertinent. But the question is, "Wherein does his account of the origin and development of Christianity contain anything uniquely Marxist?" The record indicates that, Marxist or not, Engels undertook to do more than he could accomplish in trying to explain Christian origins, that he fell into an obvious inconsistency in the attempt, and that he paid little more than lip service to historical materialism in the process.

Engels failed to give a satisfactory account of early Christianity because he was not an expert in the field and because the requisite knowledge was not available in the nineteenth century. Furthermore, he was misled by Bauer and by Ferdinand Benary whose opinions concerning the Book of Revelation he adopted uncritically. Three examples will suffice to show what I mean. First, in dating Revelation in A.D. 68 and in assuming it to have been the earliest New Testament work, Engels either forgot or ignored the fact that all the writings of Paul antedated the year in question. Since Paul's theology, probably completed by A.D. 65, was far more highly developed than that of Revelation, Engels had no basis for concluding that the Christianity of A.D. 68 was exemplified in Revelation. It apparently did not occur to him that he might be dealing with sectarianism in this book rather than with temporal priority and doctrinal purity. Second, though Engels, unlike Marx, is to be praised for trying to establish a kerygmatic canon with which to measure Christian development, he chose a dubious standard in picking Revelation rather than Acts 2:22-36, 3:13-26, 4:10-12, and 10:34-43 plus related passages in the Gospels and I Cor. 15:3-8 which many now take to contain the earliest Christian proclamation or kerygma, material which not only antedates Revelation but also the theological developments of Paul. Third, Engels, following Bauer, attempted to show that Christianity was a Philonic-Stoic amalgam, that Philo was "the real Father" of this religion and that Seneca was its "uncle." In light of recent knowledge, this hypothesis has been rejected in favor of viewing Christianity as a blend of Jewish apocalyptic and Gnostic redemption mythology.[58] The details of the

---

[58] Rudolf Bultmann, *Kerygma and Myth*, ed. by Hans W. Bartsch, trans. by Reginald H. Fuller (Society for the Publication of Christian Knowledge, 1954), pp. 15-16.

preceding examples need not concern us further. They merely show in aggregate that Engels was unfit to make definitive statements about the origin of Christianity.

Far more serious than these mistaken details, however, was his almost total ignorance of apocalyptic thought and eschatological sectarianism in Intertestamental Judaism. Of nearly equal importance was his lack of information concerning the influence of Greek mystery religions on Paul's Epistles, influences which antedated Gnostic and Philonic influences on John's Gospel. It would have been illuminating, in one way or another, if Engels had attempted to explain the Jewish sects including the Sadducees, Pharisees, Essenes, Zealots, and Christians on the basis of class struggles, exploitation, and contradictions between modes of production and the social relations based thereon, but he did not. To have attempted to do so would only have complicated a skein of history already too complex for him to unravel.

The inconsistency in Engels' treatment of early Christianity is evident. Having begun by branding it an artificial religion in 1882, he proceeded to call it spontaneous the following year:

Christianity, like every great revolutionary movement, was made by the masses. It arose in Palestine, in a manner utterly unknown to us, at a time when new sects, new religions, new prophets arose by the hundred. It is, in fact, a mere average, formed spontaneously out of the mutual friction of the more progressive of such sects, and afterwards formed into a doctrine by the addition of theorems of the Alexandrian Jew, Philo, and later on of strong stoic infiltrations.[59]

This is a most damaging statement, because it makes Christianity the revolutionary work of the masses, rather than that of conniving priests bent on distorting history. Three years later, he struck a balance, whether intentionally or not, by saying that Christianity was a more or less artificial religion.[60] But to say this is also to say that it was a more or less spontaneous religion which is to say nothing distinctive about any religion. It merely affirms that along with the institutionalization of a given religion, an elite group develops which has vested interests in that religion, whether in conjunction with pious aims or not.

In "Bauer," Engels invoked the familiar Marxist concept of classes while attempting to give a naturalistic explanation of Christianity. The classes he discerned in the Roman world were "rich people" including

[59] Engels, "Revelation," MER, p. 207.
[60] Engels, *Feuerbach*, MESW, p. 613.

land owners and usurers; "propertyless free people"; and "the great mass, the slaves."[61] Of these groups Engels said:

But in all classes there was necessarily a number of people who, despairing of material salvation, sought in its stead a spiritual salvation, a consolation in their consciousness to save them from utter despair. This consolation could not be provided by the stoics any more than by the Epicurean school, for the very reason that these philosophies were not intended for common consciousness and, secondly, because the conduct of the disciples of the schools cast discredit on their doctrines. The consolation was to be a substitute, not for the lost philosophy, but the lost religion; it had to take on a religious form, the same as anything which had to grip the masses both then and as late as the seventeenth century.[62]

In Roman times, it should be added, the majority of those "pining for such consolation" were slaves. To summarize, a number of people from all three classes of the Roman world were attracted to Christianity, but more came from the lowest class than from the other classes. What is noteworthy, one may wonder, about the fact that more converts came to Christianity from the most numerous class? If people from all classes were "necessarily" attracted to it, why go to the trouble of involving the concept of classes at all? Did Engels in educing this concept, provide a useful conceptual tool, or was he simply reciting an oft repeated bit of Marxist litany?

Instead of merely mentioning classes, he could have performed a service if he had (a) shown in detail the role of class struggle in the development of Christianity; (b) pursued thoroughly such instances of class hostility as those contained in Luke 6:20-26 and I Cor. 1:26-28; (c) correlated Christian sect appeal with economic class membership; (d) revealed how and why economic contradictions in the Roman Empire in the first century A.D. made the rich despair of material salvation; and (e) discussed how upper class converts perceived Christianity at the point of their recruitment. Did they, for example, see it as a reflection of class struggle, perceive it as a way of justifying the status quo, or view it as a means of diverting the revolutionary impulses of the masses into harmless ideological channels? Beyond affirming the proposition that economic and social factors play some part or other in religious developments, Engels did little more than mention the right words when he invoked classes and class struggle to explain the origin and development of Christianity.

The same point can be made with reference to other passages in Engels. In *Feuerbach*, for instance, he observed that the Roman world adopted

---

[61] Engels, "Bauer," MER, p. 199.
[62] *Ibid.*, p. 202.

Christianity because that religion best fitted the "economic, political and ideological conditions" of the time, but Engels neither showed why the economic conditions of the time were fundamental to the political and ideological conditions nor how the latter were related to the former.[63] In a similar vein in "Bauer" he wrote, "Religions are founded by people who feel a need for religion themselves and have a feeling for the religious needs of the masses."[64] Although one would expect economic and social conditions to have some relationship to religious needs, Engels never undertook the empirical task of developing a catalogue of such needs to prove his point. Having failed to do this, it is not clear that *all* religious needs are related to socio-economic conditions, nor is it clear precisely how those needs are so related.

Engels was probably better informed on religion than Marx, certainly more sensitive to its complexities, and somewhat less doctrinaire. Accordingly, he found it impossible to do justice to religion on the limited basis composed of the premises supplied by Marx. The result was that, while trying to remain true to his mentor, he introduced new premises, made damaging concessions, fell into inconsistencies, and, more often than not, merely paid lip service to historical materialism.

When dealing with the origin and development of the early church in particular, Engels revealed the same ambivalence which characterized his famous letter to Bloch. By way of introduction, he had written as late as 1887 that Marx had provided "the proof that all man's juristic, political, philosophical, religious and other ideas are derived in the last resort from his economic conditions of life, from his mode of production and of exchanging the product."[65] To clarify this apodictic statement, Engels wrote saying that (1) he and Marx, to make their point, had overemphasized the economic element in history at the expense of the interaction of other social factors with the economic; (2) that they had never said that the economic element was "the *only* determining one"; (3) that "various elements in the superstructure . . . also exercise their influence upon the course of the historical struggles and in many cases preponderate in determining their *form*"; and (4) that among the various "conditions" under which human beings produce and reproduce life the economic ones are "ultimately decisive."[66]

Close attention will reveal that Engels began by construing the economic

[63] Engels, *Feuerbach*, MESW, p. 613.
[64] Engels, "Bauer," MER, p. 197.
[65] Engels, "Juristic Socialism," MER, p. 272.
[66] Letter, F. Engels to J. Block, September 21-22, 1890, MESC, p. 498.

aspect as the ultimately determining element ("das *in letzer Instanz* bestimmende Moment") but that he apparently ended by construing it as a necessary condition ("bestimmten Voraussetzungen und Bedingungen").[67] Having granted that economic elements (causes, factors, or influences) were not the only ones operative in history but that there were other efficacious influences which interact with them, even predominating in certain ways, Engels was in danger of giving parity to all the causal elements in question. In order to retain priority for economic influences, he announced that they were "ultimately decisive" and that they constituted the basis of all else. But in so doing, he seems to have translated them from the realm of determining causes into that of necessary conditions. Nothing is gained in this manner, however, for the economic factor cannot be made decisive among sufficient causes by being construed as a necessary condition. Moreover, once construed in this manner it is neither unique nor first among equals but is simply one of an indefinite number of conditions necessary for the production and reproduction of life. Although it is true, for instance, that man must eat before he makes religion, it is also true that he must breathe before he eats; yet Engels would have been most reluctant, I presume, to explain religion with respect to breathing. Accordingly, despite appearances to the contrary, I doubt that he meant to construe economic factors as necessary conditions having no causal efficacy in the production and reproduction of life. What he wished to do was to make economic factors regnant over all sufficient causes of religion. But his adoption of Tylor's animism ran counter to this intention and led him to say that beliefs in such nonsense as spirits, magic forces, and the like (having only negative economic bases) acted detrimentally on primitive man's impoverished economy.

Despite the inadequacies catalogued above, Engels was basically correct about the early church in at least four particulars. First, he recognized that Nicene Christianity was astonishingly different theologically and ritually from the faith proclaimed at Pentecost.[68] Closer inspection would have shown him that equally radical changes had also occurred in church government and organization, in the appeals of Christianity, and in its functions in society. Second, it was clear to him that syncretistic forces of remarkably diverse origins had acted profoundly in the transmogrification of a Jewish sect into a world religion.[69] Third, he admitted that there was a

---

[67] Letter, F. Engels to J. Block, September 21-22, 1890, MEW, XXXVII, 463.
[68] Engels, "Early Christianity," MER, p. 328; *Feuerbach*, MESW, p. 629.
[69] Engels, *Feuerbach*, MESW, p. 629; "Bauer," MER, p. 197.

spontaneous and unknown, if not mysterious, element in the surging development of Christianity which could only be explained in terms of its manifold capacities to meet the religious needs of the time.[70] Fourth, in view of the compatibility of Christianity with the socio-economic conditions of the Roman world, Engels concluded that it was neither imported into that world nor superimposed upon it but that it was the home grown product of that world.[71] Although it is an oversimplification to suggest that an entity called the "Roman world" produced its own religion, he was basically correct in recognizing that Christianity came not as an alien but somehow as a member of the family. Had Engels developed an adequate functional approach to religion and come thereby to an understanding of religious adaptability, he would neither have been so elated to discover the kinship of Holy Mother Church with the profane world nor could he have continued to think that economics explains this congruity in the last analysis.

Roman Catholicism

Unlike the attention he lavished on ante-Nicene Christianity, Engels maintained but little interest in detailing the development of orthodox Catholicism beyond the fourth century. In general terms, the church, as might be expected, became not only the religious counterpart of feudalism but also its international center, its clergy the principal representatives of medievalism, their theology merely its ideological reflection.[72] So vacuous was this reflection to Engels that he denied that the Christian Middle Ages bequeathed anything of intellectual value to subsequent generations.[73] Moreover, the high prelates of the church, despite their spiritual virtuosity, ruled with all the naked force and guile of secular lords and often for identical ends. When brutality failed to suffice in exploiting their subalterns and dependents, they resorted to all the "subterfuges of religion" including excommunication, the employment of forged documents, and the fabrication of signs and wonders with which to bamboozle the ignorant and superstitious masses.[74] Engels noted with satisfaction that by the eighteenth century Catholicism was already *"beneath all criticism."*[75] The only kind of Christianity worthy of critical attention was German

[70] Engels, "Revelation," MER, p. 207.
[71] Engels, "Early Christianity," MER, p. 324.
[72] Engels, *Feuerbach*, MESW, p. 629; *Socialism*, p. 27; *Peasant War*, p. 44.
[73] Engels, DN, p. 4.
[74] Engels, *Peasant War*, p. 44.
[75] Engels, "Notes on Germany," *Peasant War*, p. 232.

Protestantism which merited attention because it alone had a theology into which one could set one's philosophical teeth.[76] Regrettably, Engels failed to clarify just why he, a Marxist and a despiser of ideology, should have favored German theology above all other brands of Christian nonsense.

Protestantism

Engels, the apostate, not only preferred German theology to other varieties of ghostly science but also preferred Protestantism as a whole to Catholicism in general. To refine matters even further, he valued certain types of heretics and sectarians, such as Anabaptists, above Lutherans, Calvinists, and Anglicans. The value of Protestantism lay with the progressive movement whose "ideological costume" it was. The movement in question was the bourgeois movement which together with the rise of science during and after the renaissance broke papal dictatorship and progressively dissolved feudal ties and medieval thought. The corollary of this attack on religio-political absolutism and heteronomy was the emergence of a sense of individual responsibility and autonomy hitherto undreamed of in the Christian Middle Ages. Protestant progressivism in these particulars, however, was contradicted by conservatism in other particulars. For example, Luther, the celestial radical who was to Rome what Copernicus was to superstition, was nevertheless a mundane conservative who sided with the rising burghers against the peasants in the infamous war of 1525.[77] To continue, the democratic and republican elements of Calvinism which emboldened the middle class to assault Popes and Kings also gave them the basis for lording it over the working class.[78] Finally, though the rising bourgeoisie had benefited greatly from science, Protestants frequently outdid Catholics in persecuting those who, like Servetus, undertook the free investigation of nature.[79] Whatever its benefits, Protestantism, like the rest of Christianity, was already in its last phase and about to vanish.[80]

To Engels there were at least five reasons why the imminent abolition of religion was guaranteed. First, the bourgeois destruction of feudalism necessitated the withering away of Catholicism which was merely the ideological manifestation of feudal relations. Second, in like manner, the approaching collapse of capitalism would doom Calvinism, the para-

---

[76] *Ibid.*

[77] *Ibid.*, p. 62 ff.

[78] Engels, *Socialism*, p. 34.

[79] Engels, DN, p. 8.

[80] Engels, *Feuerbach*, MESW, p. 630; A-D, p. 435.

digmatic reflection of bourgeois conditions. Third, modern science no longer found God useful as an explanatory principle nor did it have further need of teleology. Fourth, materialism had put both Christian theology and philosophical idealism to rout. Fifth, the workers of England, the bellwethers of their kind, had shown by putting agnosticism on a par with Anglicanism that the masses were no longer turning to religion for succor and consolation. Despite his belief in the abolition of religion, Engels did not think that Christianity would vanish without trace.

Kline has noted that Engels was more positive than Marx in his conviction that science would supersede religion.[81] This may be true provided that one assumes that Christianity is nothing but its theology and ecclesiastical structure and provided that one emphasizes Engels' views in *The Dialectics of Nature,* a work which has no parallel in Marx. But if one looks in particular at Engels' book on the Peasant War (1850), at his articles entitled, "The Book of Revelation" (1883), "On the History of Early Christianity" (1894-95), and at his introduction to Marx's *The Class Struggle in France* (1895), it is clear that for over forty years Christianity was more to Engels than its theology and hierarchy. These writings indicate that it was to be transcended, not merely abolished, and that in the process certain valuable characteristics were to be preserved to reappear in socialism.

Proletarian Christianity

Engels went to astonishing lengths in associating early Christianity with socialism and in drawing parallels between the two movements. It must be remembered that to him Christianity, like modern socialism, was a mass movement of oppressed peoples recruited from the working classes by sectarians opposed to the established order.[82] Indeed, socialism became dominant in the early church, insofar as conditions permitted,[83] and gave vent, albeit in religious tones, to the demand for the abolition of all classes.[84] Even as Christians once preached with assurance and conviction that salvation was at hand, so socialists in the modern world proclaim a forthcoming salvation with equal vigor and certainty.[85]

---

[81] George L. Kline, "Hegel and the Marxist-Leninist Critique of Religion," *Hegel and the Philosophy of Religion,* ed. and introd. by Darrel E. Christensen (The Hague: Martinus Nijhoff, 1970), p. 195.

[82] Engels, "Revelation," MER, p. 206; "Early Christianity," MER, p. 316.

[83] Engels, "Early Christianity," MER, p. 317.

[84] Engels, A-D, p. 147.

[85] Engels, "Early Christianity," MER, p. 316.

It is now, almost to the year, sixteen centuries since a dangerous party of overthrow was likewise active in the Roman empire. It undermined religion and all the foundations of the state; it flatly denied that Ceasar's will was the supreme law; it was without a fatherland, was international; it spread over all countries of the empire, from Gaul to Asia, and beyond the frontiers of the empire. It had long carried on seditious activities in secret, underground; for a considerable time, however, it had felt itself strong enough to come out into the open. This party of overthrow, which was known by the name of Christians, was also strongly represented in the army; whole legions were Christian. When they were ordered to attend the sacrificial ceremonies of the pagan established church, in order to do the honours there, the subversive soldiers had the audacity to stick peculiar emblems—crosses—on their helmets in protest. Even the wonted barrack bullying of their superior officers was fruitless. The Emperor Diocletian could no longer look on while order, obedience and discipline were undermined. He interfered energetically, while there was still time. He promulgated an anti-Socialist—beg pardon, I meant to say anti-Christian—law.[86]

It was clear to Engels that the revolutionary elements of early Christianity including its proletarian demands, socialistic practices, and chiliastic expectations were short-lived. They were in fact moribund by the time of Constantine when Christianity became the official religion of the Roman Empire, expressed itself systematically in creedal affirmations, and established its hierarchy. But they were revitalized from time to time, even in the Middle Ages, official dogma and hieratic repression notwithstanding. The revolutionary elements of Christianity reappeared among such heretics as the Waldenses who called for the abolition of private property and for the return to New Testament Christianity which was tantamount to the wholesale rejection of the established church.[87] In greater or lesser degree the Cathari, the Lollards, and the Flagellants also demanded radical changes in Christendom and thus, along with the Waldenses and numerous lesser ascetic and mystical sects, kept revolutionary religion alive.[88]

The restoration of exuberant vitality did not occur, of course, until the Protestant Reformation. At that time two great revolutions took place. The first was associated with what Engels called the "burgher heresy." This was the heresy of Luther and Calvin, a heresy which in holy tones proclaimed the class interests of the rising bourgeoisie and sounded the death knell of declining feudalism and Catholicism. The second revolution was associated with what Engels called the "plebian heresy." This was the heresy of Thomas Münzer and the Anabaptists, a heresy which was not

[86] Marx, *Class Struggles in France*, Introduction, pp. 40-41.
[87] Engels, *Peasant War*, p. 55
[88] *Ibid.,* pp. 58-59.

only antifeudal and anticlerical but was antibourgeois as well. It demanded civic, religious, and economic equality for all classes; indicted the institutions of class society whether Protestant or Catholic; and opposed the ruling classes whether bourgeois or aristocratic.[89] Despite the mysticism and chiliastic fantasies associated with the Anabaptist movement, its aims were as terrestrial as celestial.[90] In short, its program, though couched in theological jardon, had revolutionary implications for social life.

The immediate result of the plebeian heresy was the Peasant War, a class conflict between the burghers and the masses which constituted the most "critical episode" of the Reformation.[91] Since Münzer did not fully understand the relationship between economic and social realities and since the times were not yet ripe for a successful proletarian revolution, the plebeian heretics were defeated, the revolutionary elements of Christianity, which they represented, suppressed. These elements did not die, however, but in Engels' view were being restored to vigorous well-being. The difference lay in the fact that revolutionary Christianity was no longer being nursed back to health by the sacred hands of religionists but by the secular hands of socialists.

The point I have been attempting to make is neither that Engels made no mistakes in assessing the revolutionary intentions of primitive Christianity nor that he was entirely correct in explaining the Reformation. The point, rather, is that he found enduring characteristics in Christianity which were not to vanish with the evaporation of its theology and the dessication of its hieratic structure. Christianity's appeal to the wretched of the earth, its universalism, and its revolutionary antipathy to the ruling classes and their established order were such valuable traits to Engels that they were to transcend the dissolution of the religious vehicle which had borne them hitherto and were henceforth to lodge in the all-conquering heart of scientific socialism.

When Engels enumerated the similarities between revolutionary Christianity and socialism, including their mutual sectarianism,[92] when he cited Ernst Renan to the effect that one could get a better idea of primitive Christian communities by looking at local sections of the International Working Men's Association than at contemporary parish churches,[93] and

[89] *Ibid.*, pp. 54, 59, 141.

[90] *Ibid.*, p. 71.

[91] Engels, *Peasant War*, p. 54; "Notes on Germany," *Peasant War*, p. 222.

[92] Engels, "Early Christianity," MER, p. 316.

[93] Engels, "Revelation," MER, pp. 205-206; "Early Christianity," MER, pp. 317-318.

when he observed that contributions were not coming in to the International any faster than St. Paul received a love offering from the Corinthians, he removed himself as much from the spirit of Marx as his adoption of animism had set him apart logically from the latter's etiology of religion.[94] In total effect, these two divergencies are breathtaking.

THE MASKS AND DISGUISES OF RELIGION

I have already classified Marx's views on the functions of religion under four headings. These same headings, the spontaneous, the manipulative, the reflective, and the miscellaneous, can also be used in giving exposition to Engels' opinions on the same topic. Somewhat arbitrary, admittedly, these categories will serve the ends of systematic exposition well enough, even though some of the topics to be dealt with might have been classified differently.

Although Engels did not undertake a systematic functional analysis of religion, he recognized that it carries out certain operations. Moreover, he regarded some of these as spontaneous inasmuch as pious fraud and manipulation by ruling classes played no initial part in them. This is the only sound interpretation of his assertion that religions are founded by people who need them and who understand the religious needs of the masses.[95] The kind of needs Engels had in mind primarily were those which prompt men to seek palliation and consolation. The rise of Christianity illustrated this to him admirably, for at a time of universal decadence and wickedness it appeared with the proclamation of atonement and the promise of universal salvation.[96]

On two additional occasions Engels verged on other spontaneous functions of religion but failed to pursue the opportunities afforded him. In the first place, when he adopted the animistic etiology of religion and said in *Feuerbach* that it was not the desire for consolation but the need to solve a quandary arising from various psychic phenomena that led to the idea of immortality, he bore witness to the intellectual function of religion. From time immemorial, it has operated so as to give people conceptual frameworks with which to relate themselves to the mystery and power of the universe and with which to find meaning and purpose for

---

[94] Engels, "Early Christianity," MER, p. 318.
[95] Engels, "Bauer," MER, p. 197.
[96] Engels, "Bauer," MER, pp. 196, 202; "Early Christianity," MER, pp. 328-329.

their lives individually and collectively.[97] The fact that no religious system can be shown to be literally true detracts in no way from its conceptual function, for that function is not an end in itself, such as pure science, but is rather a means whereby biosocial and psychological needs may be met.[98] Thus, it is irrelevant to those who enjoy the benefits of religion that Engels regarded their beliefs as bunk.

He also bore witness to the spontaneous operation of religion when, in the second place, he correlated the rise and fall of antique religions with the rise and fall of the ancient peoples who possessed them.[99] If he had pursued these phenomena in depth he might well have recognized that religion in general operates so as to facilitate the process whereby the individual identifies himself with the sacred history, values, and goals of the group to which he belongs. In other words, it assists him in coming to know who and what he is and where he stands in the scheme of things.[100]

Engels knew that one of the major functions of religion was to sanction traditional ways of life. In so doing it became a profoundly conservative force, preserving the past, freezing the present, and thwarting the future.[101] The question is whether the sanctioning function of religion is to be classified as spontaneous or not. I have categorized it as manipulative rather than spontaneous, because even though religion may be innocent to Engels at its inception, it is quickly institutionalized. Once this process is under way, vested interests are served and a tool is provided whereby the ulterior aims of the ruling class may be realized. Engels observed with scorn that the English bourgeoisie, secularists at heart, were clinging ever more tightly to religion in the latter days of the nineteenth century in the hope that it might sustain the very morality which had been designed to keep the revolutionary masses down.[102]

Marx had contended that economic conflicts, whether recognized as such or not, would reappear as ideological struggles. Engels, in complete agreement, added nothing of substance to this point but illustrated the reflective function more frequently and more arrestingly than Marx had done. He opined that among the popular uprisings of the Christian West

[97] Montagu, *Immortality, Religion, and Morals*, p. 72.

[98] *Ibid.*, pp. 85-86.

[99] Engels, "Bauer," MER, p. 201.

[100] Erich Fromm, *The Sane Society* (Greenwich, Conn.: Fawcett Publications, Inc., 1965), pp. 64-66.

[101] Engels, *Feuerbach*, MESW, p. 631; A-D, p. 434; DN, pp. 79-80; *Socialism*, p. 49.

[102] Engels, *Socialism*, pp. 38-39, 48-49.

the "religious disguise" was only "a flag and a mask" for attacks on the antiquated economic order.[103] As a rule it could be said, according to Engels, that up to his time class struggles had always been "clothed in religious shibboleths" and that class interests were normally concealed behind a "religious screen."[104] Turning from the general rule to specific instances, he observed that the first uprisings of peasants and plebeians in the Middle Ages had been hidden behind "religious masks."[105] The struggle against the church at that time was in reality a disguised struggle against feudalism.[106] That same disguise was worn even more effectively several centuries later by the bourgeois-plebeian movement we call the Reformation. Calvinism, for example, was but the "ideological costume" of the advanced bourgeois revolution, whereas the chiliastic sectarianism of Münzer was merely a cloak for proletarian interests.[107]

In using such terms as "religious disguises," "religious masks," and "religious screens," Engels gave a colorful account of Marx's views on the relationship between socio-economic and ideological struggles and provided a possible vantage point from which to view these interrelated phenomena. It is not the only vantage point, however, nor is the view it affords altogether satisfactory. If Engels had been less concerned with apologetics and more interested in giving a dispassionate portrayal of the functions of religion, he would have noticed that class interests are not the only interests which are reflected in religion and that economic struggles are not the only conflicts disguised by theology. That class interests and economic struggles are the most fundamental of interests and struggles, now reflected and now disguised by theology, has yet to be demonstrated.

The religion of a cohesive group functions in such a way as to sacralize most, if not all, of the felt values of that group and to abominate whatever it commonly loathes or despises. Religion as a functioning entity in society would be impossible if that which a group esteemed were not valued by its own benign deities and also impossible if the same spirits were systematically to applaud everything regarded by the group as wicked. The Heavenly Father most assuredly supports the approved interests of Catholics and simultaneously loathes all heresy and schism. With equal certainty the same God applauds the sacred aims of Protestants and

---

[103] Engels, "Early Christianity," MER, p. 317, n. 1.
[104] Engels, *Peasant War*, p. 54.
[105] Engels, "Early Christianity," MER, p. 317.
[106] Engels, *Socialism*, p. 28.
[107] Engels, *Feuerbach*, MESW, p. 630; *Peasant War*, p. 70.

despises the Roman superstition. Furthermore, he is a Deity who aids and abets the revolutionary activities of Anabaptists and prepares everlasting torments for their enemies, the landlord, the usurer, and the exploiter. One can rest assured that the appropriate deity, or aspect of Deity if there is but one God, will always be on the believer's side in all matters of profound emotion. Apart from factual considerations concerning the causal importance of economics in the erection of such symbolic structures as theology, the worst feature of Engels' perspective was that it led him to make opaque that which is transparent.

Under the heading of miscellaneous functions, I wish to dilate on only one topic. I called attention earlier to Marx's observation that religion was the "protest against real suffering" as well as the reflection of it. In addition, I noted his total failure to examine the implications of this atypical assertion. Whether or not Engels consciously took his cue from this failure, I cannot say. In any case, he expanded on the topic of religious protest as I have already shown in detail. Without repeating those details, three points can be made. First, when dealing with the role of religion in social protest, Engels was thinking neither of religion in general nor of the idiosyncratic religions of primitive and archaic peoples in particular. Second, he was thinking, on the contrary, of religion in the West at the time when it became universal, of Christianity (Judaism never having become universal and Islam being destined to slip back into oriental idiosyncrasy).[108] Third, it is clear that for Engels primitive Christianity was a revolutionary movement of social protest.[109] It is equally clear that to him the same radical spirit remained alive even after the institutionalization of Christianity in the fourth century and that it broke out repeatedly thereafter in instances of schism, heresy, and reform.[110] Thus, by his own admission, the dominant religion of the West often served as a vehicle of social protest. Marx could no more have been ignorant of this fact than Engels was, yet he persisted in explaining religious conceptions primarily in terms of ruling class interests and in emphasizing the conservative functions of orthodox religion to the exclusion of the radical roles of schismatic religion. If Marx had pursued his own point that religion is the protest against real suffering, he would perforce have come into close accord with Engels' views on the radical potential in Christianity if not in all religion. To have done this, however,

---

[108] Engels, "Bauer," MER, p. 203.
[109] Engels, "Revelation," MER, p. 207; "Early Christianity," MER, p. 316.
[110] Engels, "Early Christianity," MER, p. 317.

would have been for Marx to call in question some of his favorite opinions and to have modified his understanding of religion considerably.

THE UNITY OF ENGELS' CRITIQUE OF RELIGION

The word "unity" in this context is intended, first, to refer to the internal consistency of Engels' views on religion and, second, to refer to the external consistency of those views with the opinions of Marx on the same topic. When considering the internal consistency of Engels' critique of religion, it is important to remember that he attempted to establish a canon for at least some of his views on the subject. Less than five years before his death, he wrote that he had already said "what was most necessary" about religion in "the last section of Feuerbach."[111] Granted that Engels said all that was most necessary about the relationship of religious developments to different epochs of production, the larger question is whether or not he also said all that was necessary about religion in general in *Feuerbach* taken as a whole. At least three reasons indicate that he would have answered this question affirmatively. First, the work under consideration is a self-conscious attempt at continuing, if not completing, the task of self-clarification begun forty years earlier with Marx which resulted in *The German Ideology.*[112] Second, and more importantly, *Feuerbach* contains the most comprehensive statement on religion Engels ever gave. In this work he (a) applauds Feuerbach for his achievements in explaining religion and in overturning idealism and at the same time takes him to task for his failures;[113] (b) notes the conditions in nineteenth century Germany which made the criticism of religion the beginning of all criticism;[114] (c) acknowledges the significance of Strauss' *Life of Jesus* and of Bauer's pioneering work in New Testament criticism and touches on the intellectual battle between these two Young Hegelians;[115] (d) deals with the relationship between theism and philosophical idealism;[116] (e) presents an etiology of religion and sketches the development of monotheism out of polytheism;[117] (f) discusses tribal religion;[118] (g) utilizes the concepts of

---

[111] Letter, F. Engels to C. Schmidt, October 27, 1890, MESC, p. 507.
[112] Engels, *Feuerbach*, MESW, pp. 594-595.
[113] *Ibid.*, pp. 603, 613-617.
[114] *Ibid.*, p. 601.
[115] *Ibid.*, p. 602.
[116] *Ibid.*, p. 604.
[117] *Ibid.*, pp. 603-604.
[118] *Ibid.*, pp. 613, 628-629.

"spontaneous" and "artificial" religion, though not for the first time;[119] (h) contrasts Christian universalism with the particularism and vulnerability of national religions;[120] (i) recognizes the developmental nature of Christianity by contrasting Nicene theology with primitive Christianity taken as canonical;[121] (j) reaffirms the epiphenomenal nature of religion and notes the congruence between a given mode of production, such as feudalism, and its corresponding religious faith;[122] (k) develops the distinctive Marxist attitude toward agnosticism;[123] and (l) tolls the death knell for Christianity.[124] Third, the work under consideration is not only comprehensive but is also the last general statement he made on the subject.

Since *Feuerbach* preserves life-long themes common to Marx as well as to Engels, and since it neither rejects nor transcends these themes, it can be taken as a canon whereby Engels' various writings on religion can be measured and as a compendium of his more important views on the subject. Nevertheless, it was in *Feuerbach* that Engels first explicitly introjected animistic elements into his etiology of religion. This novelty broadened his understanding of religion but weakened the role of economics in determining it. The result was a major departure from his original position.

Although Engels wrote Marx in 1853 saying that "*every*" religious movement was "*formally a reaction*," he waxed enthusiastic in later life over primitive Christian progressivism.[125] Thus, while making harsh remarks about religion in general, Engels identified strongly with various forms of schismatic Christianity, particularly with various forms of plebeian heresy in the sixteenth century. The first indication of this is to be found in his work on the Peasant War (1850). Thus, consistent with himself or not, he maintained a cordial attitude toward religious radicalism throughout most of his adult life. Despite this cordiality, one is still but ill-prepared for the euphoric whimsy, cited earlier, in which he purposely confused Christians and socialists. Except for this change, which was one of degree, and the incorporation of animistic theory, which resulted in a change of

---

[119] *Ibid.*, p. 613.
[120] *Ibid.*, pp. 628-629.
[121] *Ibid.*, p. 629.
[122] *Ibid.*
[123] *Ibid.*, p. 605-606.
[124] *Ibid.*, p. 630.
[125] Letter, F. Engels to K. Marx, approx. May 24, 1853, MESC, p. 96.

kind, Engels' critique of religion remained largely unified throughout his life.

Turning now to external consistency, fourteen points can be made which will reveal that a high degree of unity exists between Engels' critique of religion and that of Marx. First, Engels, like Marx, developed a twofold etiology of religion. Second, Engels, following his mentor, exhibited relentless hostility toward orthodox, established religious beliefs, practices, and institutions, but neither of them favored the forcible destruction of religion.[126] Third, Engels agreed with Marx that no religious doctrine was true, and he, too, refused to distinguish between religion and superstition.[127] Fourth, both took religion to be epiphenomenal and assumed that each distinctive epoch in the history of economic development had produced a religion corresponding to and reflective of its interests, needs, and values.[128] Fifth, though Engels emphasized it less than Marx, he also assumed that the items of religious belief functioned as objects and forces external to man.[129] Sixth, both agreed that the kind of control religious objects exercise over man degrade and render him slavish.[130] Seventh, like Marx, Engels was aware of the close, if not identical, relationship between the interests of the propertied classes and those of ecclesiastical institutions.[131] Eighth, Engels was as cognizant as Marx of the longevity of religion and of its conservative functions in society.[132] Ninth, both contended that religious ethics were neither absolute nor universal.[133] Tenth, Engels concurred with Marx in thinking that there was an intimate relationship between Protestantism and political economy.[134] Eleventh, Engels, as Marx, identified the Jews with usury.[135] Twelfth, each regarded Catholicism as a remnant of feudalism which was beneath criticism. Thirteenth, like Marx, Engels regarded Protestantism as progressive when

---

[126] Engels, A-D, p. 435; "Flüchtlingsliteratur, Part II, Programm der blanquistischen Kommunelflüchtlinge," MEW, XVIII, 531-532.

[127] Engels, *Family, Property, and State*, p. 12; "Bauer," MER, 195; *Feuerbach*, MESW, pp. 604, 628; Letter to F. Mehring, July 14, 1893, MESC, pp. 540-541.

[128] Engels, "Juristic Socialism," MER, p. 272; *Family, Property, and State*, p. 15; Letter to J. Bloch, September 21-22, 1890, MESC, p. 498.

[129] Engels, DN, pp. 1-2; A-D, p. 434.

[130] Engels, A-D, pp. 433-434, 470.

[131] Engels, *Socialism*, pp. 27, 48-49; *Feuerbach*, MESW, p. 630; A-D, p. 434.

[132] Engels, *Socialism*, pp. 27, 48-50; *Feuerbach*, p. 631.

[133] Engels, A-D, p. 130-132.

[134] Engels, *Condition of Working Class*, p. 148; "Notes on Germany," *Peasant War*, p. 222.

[135] Engels, *Peasant War*, p. 82.

measured against earlier forms of orthodox Christianity.[136] Fourteenth and finally, both Engels and Marx wanted to transcend atheism understood and expressed merely as a negative faith in nondialectical opposition to theism.[137]

It goes without saying that Engels' adoption of animistic theory, his acceptance of primitive Christianity as a forerunner of socialism, and his partiality for radical sectarianism constitute significant departures from Marx's expressed position on religion. At the more trivial level, Engels did not emphasize analogical relationships between religious and economic thought entities, as Marx did, nor did he use theological concepts as heuristic tools for clarifying economic mysteries. To continue, he did not deal with religion quite so vehemently as Marx did, nor was he so sensitive as the latter to the servility allegedly engendered by religious belief and practice. Finally, whereas Marx ignored Calvin completely, Engels dealt with him and his movement at some length in connection with the rising bourgeoisie.[158] Despite the major departures and the minor divergencies, Marx's and Engels' critiques of religion reveal a high degree of like-mindedness.

---

[136] Engels, "Notes on Germany," *Peasant War*, p. 232.
[137] Engels, "Emigrant Literature," MER, p. 142.
[138] Engels, *Socialism*, pp. 30-31; *Feuerbach*, MESW, p. 630.

CHAPTER 3

LENIN'S CRITIQUE OF RELIGION

THE ORIGINS, DEVELOPMENT, SUBSTANCE, AND FUNCTIONS OF RELIGION

Introduction

Lenin's practical relationships to religion, church, and clergy as revolutionary leader and first Marxist Head of State have interested scholars far more than his critique of religion. In that which follows, I shall try to redress the balance of interest by focusing almost entirely on theoretical issues. But whether one is more interested in Lenin's theoretical treatment of religion or in his practical handling of it, it is important at the outset to assess its importance to him. Despite his assertion that religious questions ought not be advanced to first rank,[1] despite his repudiation of all purely intellectual approaches to religion,[2] and despite the few pages of his total literary output devoted to religion, some have warned correctly, I believe, against underestimating the enduring significance of his militant atheism, the abysmal depth of his anticlericalism, and the inexhaustible reservoirs of his animosity toward all things religious.[3] In the last analysis, religion was to him, as to Marx, just as important as conditions at different times and places made it. As long as it seemed to be expiring on schedule, it could be relegated to secondary and tertiary levels of concern, but should it show any signs of resurgence, Lenin was as quick to react to it as to any issue of primary importance.

The Etiology of Religion

Lenin observed that religions do not originate without cause.[4] "God,"

---

[1] Lenin, "Socialism and Religion," LCW, X, 87.

[2] *Ibid.*, p. 86.

[3] Bohdan R. Bociurkiw, "Lenin and Religion," *Lenin: The Man, the Theorist, the Leader,* ed. by Leonard Schapiro and Peter Reddaway (New York: Frederick A. Praeger, 1967), p. 108 (hereinafter referred to as *Lenin: Man, Theorist, Leader*).

[4] Lenin, *Materialism and Empirio-Criticism*, LCW, XIV, 125.

he said, "is . . . first of all the complex of ideas generated by the brutish subjection of man both by external nature and by the class yoke. . . ."[5] This twofold subjection of man is to Lenin the corollary of human impotence: first, the impotence of the "savage in his battle with nature"; second, of exploited peoples in their struggles with the ruling class.[6] The first type of impotence leads to belief in "gods, devils, miracles and the like" whereas the second conduces to faith in a heavenly reward for those who have lived on earth in meekness and humility. These views call to vivid recollection similar opinions expressed by Marx and Engels. Equally reminiscent is Lenin's relative disinterest in natural religion and his greater predilection for explaining religious phenomena in terms of class structure and exploitation. For him, as for Marx, economic slavery was ultimately "the true source of the religious humbugging of mankind" and the principal cause of religious belief among contemporary men.[7]

Despite obvious similarities, Lenin did not attribute his twofold etiology of religion to Marx and Engels, nor did he buttress his position by citing specific passages in their works. Although Lenin may have sensed some incompatibility between animistic theory and Marx's etiology of religion, and avoided it for that reason, it seems more likely that he rejected all additional etiologies, including Engels' animistic one, because he believed that Marx had already spoken definitively concerning the origins of religion.[8] Thus, to have said more would have been to indulge in redundancy and in unnecessary complication. This contention is borne out, I believe, by his highly selective reading of Feuerbach.

In his *Philosophical Notebooks* Lenin not only assembled numerous experts from Feuerbach's book, *Lectures on the Essence of Religion,* but also appended his own comments. Since there was much in Feuerbach which Lenin applauded, many of the notes he took contained points on which both agreed. My purpose is not to assemble a complete catalogue of these points but to focus exclusively on items relating to the etiology of religion. With respect to this topic, the notes Lenin took are as interesting for what they left out as for what they included.

The preeminence which Feuerbach assigned to feelings of dependency and fear and to primitive ignorance in the creation of religion reinforced

---

[5] Letter, V. I. Lenin to M. Gorky, second half of November, 1913, LCW, XXXV, 128.

[6] Lenin, "Socialism and Religion," LCW, X, 83.

[7] *Ibid.*, p. 87.

[8] Nikolay Valentinov (N. V. Volsky), *Encounters with Lenin*, trans. by Paul Rosta and Brian Pearce (London: Oxford University Press, 1968), p. 183.

Lenin's vision of savages quaking impotently before almighty nature. As might be expected, Lenin noted these pasages and called especial attention to Feuerbach's treatment of the role of human egoism in the creation of religion.[9] In addition, he wrote, "*Sehr gut!*" enthusiastically in the margin of his notebook opposite a passage in which Feuerbach discoursed on the part played by ignorance in religious projections.[10] Lenin also made the following note which I reproduce exactly as it appears in the English translation of his *Collected Works:*

Religion is innate in man ("this statement...simply means")=superstition is innate in man. (283)[11]

The number (283) refers to a page in Feuerbach's *Sämtliche Werke*, Band 8, (Leipzig, 1851). The same material can be found on page 219 of Manheim's translation of Feuerbach's *Lectures on the Essence of Religion.*[12] Said Feuerbach:

The above-mentioned observation that piety in the common sense of the word is often combined with diametrically opposed traits, has led many to suppose that man has a special organ of religion, a specific religious feeling. We should be more justified in assuming the existence of a specific organ of superstition. Religion, that is, the belief in gods, in spirits, in so-called higher invisible beings who rule over man, has been said to be as innate in man as his other senses. Translated into the language of honesty and reason, this would only mean that, as Spinoza has already maintained, superstition is innate in man.[13]

Lenin doubtless found this passage worthy of note because he, like Feuerbach, did not believe that man possessed a special organ of religious feeling and because he approved of the way in which Feuerbach had assimilated religion to superstition à la Spinoza.

In the context of what I am trying to show, however, it is irrelevant whether or not religion and superstition are to be taken as identical. The point is that Feuerbach argued in the same book that religion "is indeed essential to or innate in man" provided that one means by this "nothing

---

[9] Lenin, "Conspectus of Feuerbach's Book: *Lectures on the Essence of Religion,*" LCW, XXXVIII, 65 (hereinafter referred to as "Conspectus on Religion").

[10] *Ibid.*, p. 78.

[11] *Ibid.*, p. 74.

[12] Ludwig Feuerbach, *Lectures on the Essence of Religion*, trans. by Ralph Manheim (New York: Harper and Row, Publishers, 1967), p. 219 (hereinafter referred to as *Lectures on Religion*).

[13] *Ibid.*

other than man's feeling of finiteness and dependency on nature."[14] Lenin ignored this aspect of Feuerbach's thought altogether. The reason why Lenin picked and chose as he did is that he, like Marx and Engels, needed an etiology of religion which was consistent with the eventual abolition of religion. It would never do for an orthodox Marxist to entertain a concept of religion which enabled it, like hope, to spring eternal from the human breast. Since science and education could be relied on to banish superstition, since the proletarian revolution could equally be depended on to abolish class rule, religion could be expected to disappear in a society containing no resources for its resurrection and renewal.[15] But to envision future conditions in which religion was impossible was to contradict Feuerbach who said:

Though I myself am an atheist, I openly profess religion in the sense just mentioned, that is, nature religion. I hate the idealism which wrenches man out of nature; I am not ashamed of my dependency on nature; I openly confess that the workings of nature affect not only my surface, my skin, my body, but also my core, my innermost being, that the air I breath in bright weather has a salutary effect not only on my lungs but also on my mind, that the light of the sun illumines not only my eyes but also my spirit and my heart.[16]

One need not adopt Feuerbach's etiological position concerning the continuing relationship between religion and the elements of finitude and dependency innate to the human condition to recognize that Lenin, far from refuting this position, simply ignored it.

This line of reasoning may also explain why Marx, Engels, and Lenin minimized the part played by death in the creation and maintenance of religion. Although one may assume that dread of the grave periodically convulsed the minds of the savages they postulated standing before almighty nature, still Marx, Engels, and Lenin minimized death and dismissed completely from their etiology of religion the other rites of passage along with their accompanying vicissitudes. Certainly, they had very much less to say about the tomb than did Feuerbach who wished to emphasize the role played by this kind of fear in the development of religion.[17] Engels considered death and immortality, but only in the rather abstract explanatory terms of animistic theory.

---

[14] *Ibid.*, p. 34.

[15] Lenin, "Political Agitation and 'The Class Point of View'," LCW, V, 338 (hereinafter referred to as "Political Agitation").

[16] Feuerbach, *Lectures on Religion*, pp. 35-36.

[17] *Ibid.*, p. 33.

Marx, Engels, and Lenin appear to have reasoned somewhat as follows: The degree to which religion is based on human impotence is the degree to which it will disappear when classless man takes complete rational control in producing his own subsistence; the degree to which religion is based on exploitation is the degree to which it will vanish in the post-revolutionary society; and the degree to which it is based on ignorance is the degree to which it will wither away when all education becomes scientific. Therefore, when these conditions are met in the coming classless society, religion will be no more. But, even if exploitation were to be abolished and education were to become scientific, what of the so-called vicissitudes of life which may be expected from time to time to confront even those who live in the classless society? Regrettably, Marx, Engels, and Lenin dealt with this question by ignoring it or by shoving its relevance into the distant past. Their position on the withering away of religion would have been more convincing, if, instead of ignoring the problem, they had sought to show empirically why the kinds of crises which have evoked religious responses in the past could and would no longer do so in the future. If as Feuerbach said, and Lenin duly noted, "the foundation of religion is the feeling of dependency," why is that foundation to be totally absent in the coming classless society?[18] Are Marxian communists to become thoroughly self-sufficient?

Despite the importance Feuerbach accorded to human finitude and fear in the production of religion, he knew that no single cause could explain its manifold expressions. Accordingly, he called attention to other elements productive of religious behavior, some of which Lenin noted while ignoring others. Among the causal elements he noted but failed to develop were the transference of human purposiveness to nature,[19] the desire to be happy,[20] and the permanent need to have an ideal, "a goal, a model to emulate."[21] Among the points which Lenin chose to ignore were Feuerbach's convictions that the anthropological in general and the pathological in particular had causal significance for religion and that joy and delight, as well as fear and trembling, contributed to it. Indeed, Feuerbach believed

---

[18] *Ibid.*, p. 25.

[19] Lenin, "Conspectus on Religion," LCW, XXXVIII, 71; Feuerbach, *Lectures on Religion*, p. 125.

[20] Lenin, "Conspectus on Religion," LCW, XXXVIII, 73; Feuerbach, *Lectures on Religion*, pp. 196, 199.

[21] Lenin, "Conspectus on Religion" LCW, XXXVIII, 75; Feuerbach, *Lectures on Religion*, p. 256.

that the gratitude and rejoicing occasioned by the benevolent aspects of nature led to their deification.[22]

Implacable hostility toward religion, tactical considerations designed to facilitate its extirpation, and the desire to remain consistent with Marx and Engels prompted Lenin to ignore, reject, or revile all data which might have exonerated it by indicating that it had some benign dimensions useful to individuals and social groups. "Never," said Lenin, "has the idea of God 'linked the individual with society': It has always *tied* the oppressed *classes hand and foot* with faith in the divinity of the oppressors."[23] Thus, he brushed aside all evidence in support of the view, shared by the god-builders, that God is the complex of those ideas which awaken and organize social feelings.[24]

Lenin did not directly assess the continuing influence of man's subjection to nature on contemporary religion. He did, however, explicitly reject as superficial the view that ignorance alone was the cause of it among the "backward sections of the town proletariat" and the "mass of the peasantry"—a view which he attributed to "the bourgeois progressist, the radical or the bourgeois materialist."[25] To him the superficiality of this view lay in its failure to recognize that the roots of religion were mainly social in modern capitalistic countries:

The deepest root of religion today is the socially downtrodden condition of the working masses and their apparently complete helplessness in the face of the blind forces of capitalism, which every day and every hour inflicts upon ordinary working people the most horrible suffering and the most savage torment, a thousand times more severe than those inflicted by extraordinary events, such as wars, earthquakes, etc. "Fear made the gods." Fear of the blind force of capital—blind because it cannot be foreseen by the masses of the people—a force which at every step in the life of the prolatarian and small proprietor threatens to inflict, and does inflict "sudden", "unexpected", "accidental" ruin, destruction, pauperism, prostitution, death from starvation—such is *the root* of modern religion. . . .[26]

Even if one discounts as bombast Lenin's point that the torments of capitalism are a thousand times worse for the proletariat than natural disasters, still the foregoing is a most unsatisfactory account of the cause of modern religion for at least three reasons.

[22] Feuerbach, *Lectures on Religion*, pp. 29-31, 188, 199, 211.
[23] Letter, V. I. Lenin to M. Gorky, last half of November, 1913, LCW, XXXV, 129.
[24] *Ibid.*, p. 127.
[25] Lenin, "The Attitude of the Workers' Party to Religion," LCW, XV, 405 (hereinafter referred to as "Attitude of Workers to Religion").
[26] Lenin, "Attitude of Workers to Religion," LCW, XV, 405-406.

In the first place, how did Lenin know that the deepest root of contemporary religion was the socially downtrodden condition of the proletariat? What empirical data served as the basis for this conclusion; what method did he utilize in discerning this data; what instrument did he use in measuring it? Granted that misery, privation, and insecurity are effective in developing and sustaining types of religious response, a question still remains as to what extent these evils are social and to what extent natural. Moreover, one must always take account of the degree of interaction between the two at various times in different places. There is no doubt, for example, that industrial requirements in the nineteenth and early twentieth centuries led to the concentration of workers near factory sites which resulted in fetid slums that in turn incubated microorganisms eventuating in epidemics of dire consequence for whole populations. But the bacteria which sometimes lead to pathology and death exist independently of socio-economic structures even though they may be related to the latter.

Lenin's doctrinaire position exemplifies one of the most disappointing aspects of the Marxist etiology of religion: the dogged refusal to recognize that some of the causes or conditions of religion among primitive men persist among modern men and that these factors, such as disease, disorder, and death, interact with contemporary social and cultural realities. In addition to restoring the natural root to the social or exploitive root of religion, to say nothing of the psychological root, it is also necessary to discover whether or not there is a social root which does not relate primarily to economic structures. There is, in fact, such a root: It consists of ethnic, racial, nationalistic, and cultural elements which are duly exemplified, celebrated, and enshrined in religion. To retain Lenin's metaphor, the question is not so much which root is the deepest but how deep it is in comparison with other roots and how they function together in supplying the nutrients of religion.

In the second place, even if Lenin had been entirely correct in contending that fear created the gods originally, it was quixotic of him to have implied that proletarian fear of the "blind force of capital" continued to create deities in modern times.[27] Since the Judeo-Christian God of the West is of ancient fabrication, the most accurate, if prosaic, way for him to have made his point would have been to assert that proletarian privation sustained the traditional deity more than any other source. Although this may have been true at various times and places, it was not

---

[27] *Ibid.*, p. 406.

universally true if Engels is to be believed. Speaking of the English proletariat during the middle of the nineteenth century, Engels said:

It is all very pretty and very agreeable to the ear of the bourgeois to hear the "sacredness of property" asserted; but for him who has none, the sacredness of property dies out of itself. Money is the god of this world; the bourgeois takes the proletarian's money from him and so makes a practical atheist of him. No wonder, then, if the proletarian retains his atheism and no longer respects the sacredness and power of the earthly God.[28]

Furthermore:

His faulty education saves him from religious prepossessions, he does not understand religious questions, does not trouble himself about them, knows nothing of the fanaticism that holds the bourgeoisie bound; and if he chances to have any religion, he has it only in name, not even in theory. Practically he lives for this world, and strives to make himself at home in it. All the writers of the bourgeoisie are unanimous on this point, that the workers are not religious, and do not attend church.[29]

Finally:

English Socialism affords the most pronounced expression of the prevailing absence of religion among the working-men, an expression so pronounced indeed that the mass of the working-men, being unconsciously and merely practically irreligious, often draw back before it.[30]

Engels is not to be believed without qualification, but this in no way exonerates Lenin's slapdash conclusion that proletarian fear constituted the deepest root of modern religion. Chadwick has shown that only about ten percent of the urban proletariat attended church or chapel at mid-century,[31] that slum chapels, never very numerous, were, according to the religious census of 1854, only half full on Sundays;[32] and that apathy, infidelity, and hostility all played a role in the religious, or irreligious, ambience of the urban poor.[33] But he also reveals that the English proletariat did not become irrevocably secular in the nineteenth century;[34] that it remained vaguely Christian in a nonconformist way;[35] that it

---

[28] Engels, *Condition of Working-Class*, MEB, p. 148.

[29] *Ibid.*, pp. 158-159.

[30] *Ibid.*, p. 274.

[31] Owen Chadwick, *The Victorian Church* (2 vols.; New York: Oxford University Press, 1966-70), I, 332.

[32] *Ibid.*, p. 367.

[33] *Ibid.*, p. 333.

[34] Chadwick, *The Victorian Church*, II, 263.

[35] *Ibid.*, pp. 263, 267.

assimilated socialism to true Christianity, or vice versa, in varying degrees[36] and that it was only more or less hostile to religion, church, and chapel at different times.[37] Since the data is confusing and contradictory and since there were no reliable instruments of social research available for measuring nineteenth century British religiosity beyond mere census taking and individual observation, it is difficult to arrive at any conclusion except that Lenin could not have inferred validly that proletarian fear was the deepest root of modern religion. In fact he contradicted his earlier assertion about this fear when he said:

In Britain, religious sects have their stronghold in the middle classes, and partly in the *upper stratum of the workers*, whereas the broad middle strata of workers, especially those in the big towns, are in general little susceptible to religious influences.[38]

Those who would make sweeping generalizations concerning relationships between two such complicated social entities as the international proletariat and religion must be prepared to utilize sophisticated instruments for analyzing times, places, traditions, social structures, cultural interaction and the like, tasks to which Lenin never seriously put his mind.

In the third place, had Lenin been thorough in his analysis of the etiology of modern religion, he would have examined the vigorous religion of the bourgeoisie more with an eye to discovering its sanctioning functions than to excoriating its devotees. Those who have succeeded in the world, having gained much to conserve in the process, but who would also fare well in the next world must, if they are Christians, justify their style of life and sanctify the interests of their class. After all, despite Jesus' injunctions to the contrary, the bourgeoisie do take thought of the morrow, but not so as to give the proceeds thereof to the poor nor to give up a coat on a cloak's demand. Unlike the lilies of the field, they do most assiduously spin, and unlike their Lord do indeed have a place to lay their heads. The mistake in Lenin's assessment is that he perceived only shameless hypocrisy when he noticed that the ruling class approved of the religion that taught others to shoulder their burdens without protest,[39] and adjured the masses to love everyone including factory owners.[40] What he failed to discern was that the middle and upper classes

---

[36] *Ibid.,* p. 264.

[37] Chadwick, *The Victorian Church*, I, 331-332: II, 264, 266-269.

[38] Lenin, "Notebook Lambda." LCW. XXXIX. 446.

[39] Lenin, "Political Agitation." LCW. V. 337-338.

[40] Lenin, "Draft and Explanation of Programme for the Social Democratic Party," LCW, II, 116.

were not only hypocritically calling upon the masses to obey what their betters regarded as the strictures of the Lord but were also unconsciously and even innocently using suitable elements within Christianity to applaud and to uphold their own felt values. If there is to be any religion at all, it must function in such a way as to sacralize whatever is perceived as good. Accordingly, if Lenin had been genuinely scientific in seeking the roots of modern religion, he would have had to examine bourgeois economic and political success and the religious needs generated by that good fortune in the context of Christianity.

The Development of Religion

The history of religion, which was but an episode in the childhood of mankind to Lenin, held even less allure for him than did its etiology. With the exception of a few remarks on the evolution of Christianity, he said nothing concerning the history of any religion in particular.[41] After all, if one were to conclude, with Marx and Engels that ecclesiastical institutions and hieratical structures invariably exist to serve and justify ruling class interests, then nothing could be gained by scribbling redundant histories of these phenomena. The same is true of the constant functions of religious palliation and consolation designed to assuage the grief of the downtrodden. Finally, in view of the falsity and relativity of all ideological reflections, it would have been puerile of Lenin to have devoted time to the history of religious thought. It might also be noted that he neither adopted nor developed the analytic niceties of "spontaneous" and "artificial" religion which Engels introduced, although on one occasion he compared "the primitive, unconscious, matter-of-fact religiousness of the peasant" with what he regarded as the Cadets' "hypocritical, deliberately reactionary defence of religion."[42] If pressed to develop this point, he might well have done so in the manner of Engels.

When Lenin contended that the "struggle of democracy and of the proletariat" had once taken the form of a struggle between religious conceptions,[43] when he asserted that the church forgot the "democratic revolutionary spirit" of primitive Christianity upon becoming the state religion,[44] and when he agreed with Paul Golay that Christianity lost

---

[41] Lenin, "Conspectus on Religion." LCW, XXXVIII. 73.

[42] Lenin, "Classes and Parties in their Attitude to Religion and Churches." LCW, XV, 422 (hereinafter referred to as "Classes and Parties").

[43] Letter, V. I. Lenin to M. Gorky, latter half of November, 1913, LCW, XXXV. 128.

[44] Lenin, "The State and Revolution," LCW, XXV. 420.

value on the day when Constantine promised it revenue and a place at court, he appears to have been echoing Engels.[45] Unless it can be shown that Lenin did not know Engels' work on the Peasant War and his article, "On the History of Early Christianity," then it must be concluded that he read Engels with same selectivity which characterized his use of Feuerbach.

The attention which Engels drew to the radical socialism of primitive Christianity, to the revolutionary characteristics of such schismatics as the Waldenses, and to the corollation between Anabaptist heresy and proletarian economic interest went far towards laying the basis for a conflict theory of religion at the sectarian level. While trying to show how socialism had been nurtured throughout the centuries in the expendable womb of revolutionary Christianity, Engels succeeded more fully in revealing that religon can, on occasion, assist in unfurling the flags of class war quite as well as it can dose the peasantry with social sedatives and that it can support lower class interests, now and again, as aptly as it can justify those of the upper classes. In order to extricate himself from the non-Marxian implications of this misconceived display, Engels resorted to his theory of the masks and disguises of religion whereby economic realities were made to lurk behind religious appearances.

Since Lenin had no stomach for drawing conclusions uncongenial to Marxism and no enthusiasm at all for rhapsodizing Christianity as the virgin-mother of socialism, he ignored Engels' offensive opinions and relegated the revolutionary aspects of Christianity to those ancient days before Constantine spoiled it. Perfidious disregard alone could enable a Marxist to ignore Engels' assessment of plebeian religious radicalism in the sixteenth century and then to announce, as Lenin did, "The idea of God *always* put to sleep and blunted the 'social feelings,',[46] and "Marxism has always regarded all modern religions and churches and each and every religious organization, as instruments of bourgeois reaction that serve to defend exploitation and to befuddle the working class."[47]

The Substance and Functions of Religion

Since to the Marxist religion is very largely what it does, or what he assumes it does, there is very little he can say about it substantively.

---

[45] Lenin, "The Voice of an Honest French Socialist." LCW. XXI. 353.

[46] Letter, V. I. Lenin to M. Gorky, last half of November, 1913, LCW, XXXV, 129.

[47] Lenin, "Attitude of Workers to Religion," LCW. XV. 403.

Accordingly, not much can be reported on what Lenin took religion to be, although he did, in one context or another, reiterate most of Marx's and Engels' opinions on the subject. Among these were the oft repeated contentions that religion was a reflection of socio-economic conditions,[48] a set of mental projections corresponding to no realities in the external world,[49] and a manifestation of ideology.[50] Lenin characterized the epiphenomenal nature of religion picturesquely when he referred to its modern expressions as "medieval mildew."[51] But, epiphenomenal or not, it did constitute a juggernaut of spiritual oppression and a terrible vehicle of self-humiliation.[52] In short, religion was to Lenin "one of the most odious things on earth," the idea of God, a concept of "inexpressible foulness."[53]

Lenin never produced a scientifically respectable account of the functions of religion, but from time to time he mouthed the familiar Marxist themes of religious consolation and justification. Most especially, he enjoyed emphasizing the narcotic aspects of religion. He did not stop with its analgesic capacities but also pointed with scorn at its intoxicating effects. He called religion "a sort of spiritual booze" and said in a speech, "As for icons, someone has just given a reminder that the peasants are asking for icons. I think [he continued] that we should not follow the example of the capitalist countries and put vodka or other intoxicants on the market. . . ."[54] To Lenin, a befuddled brain was the price one paid for religious palliation.

Remembering the sympathetic context in which Marx had opined that religion was the opium of the people, Conquest has judged Lenin's treatment of the same theme to be far more severe and inimical.[55] Although this judgment is true from the standpoint of the contexts in

---

[48] Lenin, "Socialism and Religion," LCW. X. 86.

[49] Lenin, *Materialism and Empirio-Criticism*, LCW. XIV. 78. 186.

[50] Lenin, "What the Friends of the People Are," LCW, I, 139 (hereinafter referred to as "Friends of People").

[51] Lenin, "Socialism and Religion," LCW. X. 87.

[52] Lenin, "Socialism and Religion," LCW, X, 83; Letter, V, I, Lenin to M. Gorky, November 13 or 14, 1913, LCW, XXXV, 122.

[53] Lenin. "Leo Tolstoy as the Mirror of the Russian Revolution," LCW. XV. 205: Letter, V. I. Lenin to M. Gorky, November 13 or 14, 1913, LCW, XXXV, 122.

[54] Lenin, "Socialism and Religion," LCW, X, 84: "Attitude of Workers to Religion," LCW, XV, 402; "Classes and Parties," LCW, XV, 420, 422-423; "Tenth All-Russian Conference of the R. C. P. (B.)", LCW, XXXII, 426.

[55] Robert Conquest (ed.), *Religion in the U. S. S. R.* (New York: Frederick A. Praeger, 1968), p. 7.

which each used the term opium, Marx was, theoretically, quite as capable of decrying the stupefying effects of religion as Lenin. The difference, if any, lies primarily in the fact that Lenin found religion's dogged persistence more vexing than did Marx.

Lenin discerned an intimate relationship between the consolatory-palliative functions of religion and its sanctioning activities:

What a profitable faith it is indeed for the governing classes! In a society so organized that an insignificant minority enjoys wealth and power, while the masses constantly suffer "privations" and bear "severe obligations," it is quite natural for the exploiters to sympathize with a religion that teaches people to bear "uncomplainingly" the hell on earth for the sake of the alleged celestial paradise.[56]

Thus, while the impotent and exploited of earth drowned their misery in spiritual moonshine and envisioned the delights of paradise in the ensuing delirium, the powerful and parasitic of the earth busied themselves stabilizing the conditions which insured their continued profit. In order to make existing conditions palatable, priests were dispatched to identify God with the authorities, to sacralize ruling class policies, and to prove that serfdom was approved by the Most High and duly ratified by Holy Writ.[57] Should the priest fail in his sanctifying endeavors, the hangman appeared to ply his trade, whereupon the priest, that gendarme of Christ, that encassocked official, retired to change hats, so to speak, and then reemerged to give the final consolations of religion.[58] Should the exploiter feel the prickings of conscience, should "religious delusions" not permit peaceful sleep, he could always resort to Christian charity, a cheap way to justify his existence.[59] Since the stupor of spiritual consolation led to proletarian passivity and since the delusions of faith reinforced the status quo, Lenin quite rightly perceived in religion a conservative force of enormous potential.

In addition to its sanctioning activities on behalf of ruling class interests, Lenin also knew that at least one religious idea, that of God, carried out explanatory functions. The peasant, for instance, viewed natural disasters as the will of God.[60] Furthermore, ordinary ideologists, untouched by the

[56] Lenin, "Political Agitation," LCW, V, 338.

[57] Lenin, "Friends of People," LCW, I, 262; "First Draft: Thesis for an Appeal to the International Socialist Committee and All Socialist Parties," LCW, XXIII, 208; "To the Rural Poor," LCW, VI, 424.

[58] Lenin, "The Collapse of the Second International," LCW, XXI, 231-232.

[59] Lenin, "Socialism and Religion," LCW, V, 83.

[60] Lenin, "Review of Home Affairs," LCW, V, 275, 77.

likes of Darwin, continued to hold that different species of plants and animals were created immutable by God.[61] Finally, philosophical sophisticates, such as idealists, theists, teleologists and the like, resorted to God regularly in the futile hope of completing their fantastic systems and in the vain attempt at refuting materialism.[62] Furthermore, despite his lack of intention and perception, the ideologist who relies on religious fabrications for explanatory purposes also produces systems reflective of actual conditions. To illustrate, Lenin pointed at Tolstoy who, thinking he was upholding "the eternal principles of religion," was in reality merely maintaining "the old . . . feudal order, the way of life of the oriental peoples," the "religious yoke" being in the last analysis nothing but the reflection of the "economic yoke."[63]

Except for some frights and irritations, to be dealt with later, Lenin was theoretically confident that the apparently vigorous and manifold functions of religion would eventually disappear altogether. As he saw it, nearly everything was against its continuation. The coming proletarian revolution would deprive the established church of political power, police protection, and sanctuary and would abolish all class structures conducive to the sanctioning and consolatory functions of religion. Thus, with nowhere to go and nothing to do, religion would fade away. To continue, since religion had already been explained materialistically, it would be exposed as fraudulent and repudiated. Moreover, the continued advance of science and the extension of education would surely produce a non-religious consciousness in people.[64] Finally, and ironically, even capitalism no longer left any room for God.[65] Still and all, religion was damnably tenacious and might rise, phoenix-like, even from the ashes of revolution unless precautions were taken. Accordingly, Lenin did not rely on proletarian revolution, dialectical materialism, and secular socialism to confirm the masses in atheism but also depended on propaganda, agitation, and various directives on church-state and church-party relationships to guarantee the extirpation of religion.

---

[61] Lenin, "Friends of People," LCW, I, 142.

[62] Lenin, "Conspectus of Hegel's Book *Lectures on the History of Philosophy*," LCW, XXXVIII, 283.

[63] Lenin, "Leo Tolstoi and His Epoch," LCW, XVII, 50; "Socialism and Religion," LCW, X, 86.

[64] Lenin, "Socialism and Religion," LCW, X, 84, 86.

[65] Lenin, "Friends of People," LCW, I, 142, 176.

RELIGION AND THE UNITY OF MARX, ENGELS, AND LENIN

Bociurkiw contends that Lenin's writings on religion fall into three periods. During the earliest period, lasting until 1905, he examined religion in the context of political agitation. During the final period, beginning in 1917, Lenin, as a policy maker, sought to adjust his program on religion to existing conditions without modifying his long-range goals. During the middle and most important period from 1905 to 1917, Lenin, as revolutionary theorist and tactician, polemicist and defender of orthodox Marxism, made his major contributions to religious topics.[66] A survey of the works cited in the preceding section, along with their dates of authorship and publication, will bear this out. Foremost among these works are "Socialism and Religion," written in 1905, "The Attitude of the Workers Party to Religion," and "Classes and Parties in Their Attitude to Religion and the Church," both written in 1909. To this list, one might add *Materialism and Empirio-Criticism*, written in 1908, some illuminating comments made on Feuerbach in 1909, and two letters written to Gorky in 1913.[67] Although it is possible to show that Lenin changed his tactics respecting religion from time to time, there is neither alteration nor development in his critique of religion expressed in the important works mentioned above and scattered elsewhere throughout his writings.[68] Since he was convinced that Marx and Engels had said everything necessary concerning religion, he could not have been expected to modify what he took to be their final pronouncements. Accordingly, he failed to improve their critique of religion, perpetuated its errors, and preserved its integrity by seeing only what he wanted to see in others, such as Feuerbach, and by closing his eyes to non-Marxian investigations of religion. He also averted his eyes from Engels whenever the latter was wont to stray from the master's dictates.

It is commonplace to assert that Lenin was not only profoundly influenced by Marxism but also by nineteenth century Russian radicalism:

In Lenin's concern with spiritual slavery, in his equation of atheism with freedom and progress, and in his vehement anticlerical bent, one cannot fail to detect the influence of nineteenth-century Russian radical thought, in particular of

---

[66] Bociurkiw, "Lenin and Religion," p. 107.

[67] Letter, V. I. Lenin to M. Gorky, November 13 or 14, 1913, LCW, XXXV, 121-124;Letter, V. I. Lenin to M. Gorky, second half of November, 1913, LCW, XXXV, 127-129.

[68] Bociurkiw. "Lenin and Religion," p. 126.

Belinsky, Herzen, Pisarev and Bakunin, whose mood and phraseology are clearly apparent in Lenin's utterances on religion.[69]

Lenin's anticlericalism and hostility to Russian Orthodoxy, more vitriolic than Marx and Engels at their scathing best, may indeed have been influenced by Russian radicalism, but the personal foundation for it appears to have been laid early in his life.[70] At the very least, one may opine that radical thought reinforced Lenin's precocious atheism and anticlericalism. It may also be true that Russian radical sources prompted him to identify religion with spiritual slavery and to equate atheism with freedom and progress, but these are themes common to Marx and Engels. Whatever the role of radicalism may have been in influencing or in reinforcing Lenin's views on religion, his theoretical position is consistent with Marx's critique of religion and generally in harmony with that of Engels.

The following six points should establish this beyond doubt. First, Lenin adopted without reservation the twofold etiology of religion distinctive of Marx and Engels. Refusing to believe in any religious faculty of man or in any permanent condition in his social life productive of faith, he descried the fear of nature as the principal cause of religion among the first men and the fear of capital as the deepest root of religion among modern men. Focusing on the social sources of religion, he ignored the continuing influences of natural religion and of all nonsocial fear in contemporary faith. Second, Lenin equated religion and superstition, denied objectivity to all the powers and principalities of the air, took no religious doctrine to be true, and refused universality to all religious ethics.[71] Third, he believed that the figments of faith, projected into bogus objectivity, were ultimately caused by, and were reflective of, economic conditions, that religion was, in short, epiphenomenal. Fourth, Lenin held that the functions of religion were primarily twofold in that it sanctioned the status quo on behalf of the ruling class and also provided consolation for the downtrodden. Fifth, he believed that the consequences of religious belief and ecclesiastical power were intellectual stultification, economic exploitation, and social enslavement; in short, that religion was a most

---

[69] *Ibid.*, p. 110.

[70] Bociurkiw, "Lenin and Religion," p. 110; Lewis Feuer, "Lenin's Fantasy," *Encounter*, vol. XXXV (December, 1970), 29; N. K. Krupskaya, *Reminiscences of Lenin* (Moscow: Foreign Languages Publishing House, 1959), p. 196; Louis Fischer, *The Life of Lenin* (New York: Harper and Row, Publishers, 1964), p. 9.

[71] Lenin, "Leo Lolstoi and His Epoch," LCW, XVII, 50.

serious obstacle to human progress and freedom.[72] Sixth, he professed confidence in proletarian revolution and in the subsequent abolition of all religion.[73]

In addition to these points of intellectual congruence with Marx and Engels, Lenin personified two attitudes which reinforced his unity with the founders of Marxism. First, he was as hostile theoretically to all religious doctrines, priestcraft, and ecclesiastical power as Marx and Engels. Second, convinced that the Marxist critique of religion was irrefrangible and could only be developed, if at all, in the spirit of Marx, Lenin set his mind steadfastly against any alien hypothesis or unpalatable data which might criticize, contradict, or modify that critique.[74] To him, the results of such treacherous tampering could lead only to revisionism.

Despite the high degree of unity between Marx, Engels, and Lenin on the topic of religion, divergencies did occur between him and his mentors. In addition to Lenin's failure or refusal to entertain animistic theories respecting religious origins, he was less sensitive to the complexities of religion and less well informed than Engels. Had his dogmatism not precluded it, Lenin could have drawn upon a whole generation of anthropological and ethnographic research, subsequent to Engels' death, for further information about the origin, nature, and functions of religion, but he spurned this material.

Hostile to all established churches and orthodox doctrines, Engels was, nonetheless, appreciative of Christianity insofar as it had originally been a mass protest with univerval characteristics and appeals and insofar as it had preserved the possibility of continued protest in the form of sectarian movements. Although Lenin paid his respects to primitive Christianity by observing that it had once possessed a "democratic revolutionary spirit," he lost no love on any form of faith and, following Marx, paid no attention to the schismatic movements which excited Engels' admiration.[75] This is all the more striking in that Lenin knew of religious protest in Russia,[76] collaborated with the progressive clergy on occa-

---

[72] Lenin, "The Tasks of the Youth Leagues," LCW, XXXI, 291; "On the Significance of Militant Materialism," LCW, XXXIII, 232; "Socialism and Religion," LCW, X, 83.

[73] Lenin, "Socialism and Religion," LCW, X, 84; "Draft Program of R. C. P. (B)," LCW, XXIX, 111, 134.

[74] Valentinov (Volsky), *Encounters with Lenin*, pp. 182-183.

[75] Lenin, "The State and Revolution," LCW, XXV, 420.

[76] Lenin, "The Third Congress," LCW, VIII, 448.

sion,[77] and tried to take advantage of the favorable conditions for agitation created by religious dissent.[78] Nor was the protest limited to reformative, if not revolutionary, clergymen like Gapon.[79] Indeed, according to Lenin, even ignorant Orthodox functionaries were "joining in the demand for freedom" and were "protesting against bureaucratic practices and officialism," and "against the spying for the police imposed on 'the servants of God'."[80] Nevertheless, Lenin was not about to pay any unnecessary respects to Christianity, sectarian or otherwise, to develop a protest model of religion, nor to admit that faith can sometimes stimulate as well as intoxicate and narcotize its devotees.

Lenin's failure to follow Engels into animistic theorizing and into postulating an affinity between socialism and radical Christianity, his failure to take into account any scientifically founded, but non-Marxist, approach to religion, and his failure to develop Marx's critique of religion makes him closer to Marx on the religious question than to Engels. Nevertheless, there were some differences, four of which deserve attention. The first and most trivial difference lies in the way each dealt with the Jewish Question. Lenin felt no need to reproduce this aspect of Marx's treatment of religion, had not the slightest interest in Judaism as a religion, did not equate Jehovah with capital, and thought that some Jewish merchants were less exploitive than their critics.[81] Apart from his general intention that religious conservatism and obscurantism should not impede social progress, Lenin's concern with Jews was that they not claim separate national existence and that Jewish Marxists not be divisive in thinking that their Bund was the sole representative of the Jewish proletariat.[82]

The second difference between Marx and Lenin lies in their respective antipathies to religion. Although they were in complete, or almost complete, theoretical agreement, Lenin was more actively hostile than Marx toward religious institutions. If theoretical considerations are not at issue and if one ignores personal psychology as I intend to do, then there is but one explanation for this divergency, and that lies in the differing

[77] Bociurkiw, "Lenin and Religion," p. 126.

[78] *Ibid.*, p. 112.

[79] Lenin, "Revolutionary Days," LCW, VIII, 106, 112-113: "On the 'Nature' of the Russian Revolution," LCW, XV, 27.

[80] Lenin, "Socialism and Religion," LCW, X, 85.

[81] Lenin, "Draft for a Speech on the Agrarian Question in the Second Duma," LCW, XII, 273.

[82] Lenin, "To the Jewish Workers," LCW, VIII, 496; "Draft Resolution on the Place of the Bund in the Party," LCW, VI, 470; "Critical Remarks on the National Question," LCW, XX, 26.

conditions Marx and Lenin faced. Whereas Marx faced a progressive church allied with the bourgeoisie against feudalism, Lenin encountered a medieval church, untouched by Reformation or Enlightenment, allied with the aristocracy; whereas Marx faced a divided church growing weaker yearly, Lenin encountered an autocratic institution of enormous repressive power; and whereas Marx faced the rise of atheism and agnosticism in the West, Lenin encountered in the East masses of peasants "too passively Christian" for any good use.[83] Thus Lenin, unlike Marx, could not be particularly sanguine about the withering away of religion. Accordingly, he could not and did not emphasize this point. Impatient over the death agonies of religion and eager to get on with the business of revolution, Lenin determined to smite the hateful thing in the hope of hastening its end.

The third difference between Marx and Lenin can be seen in their verbal attacks on religion. Although Marx and Lenin were equally trenchant theoretically, Marx was able to be both incisive and serene in his critique of religion. Lenin, on the contrary, was shrill and strident, heaping epithet upon epithet, in the hope that this loathing of religion would be infectious and would accomplish in others what Marxist fact and logic alone might not do.[84]

The fourth difference between Marx and Lenin lies in their partiality for different brands of Christendom. Whereas Marx favored Lutheranism for its progressive position vis-à-vis Catholicism, and whereas Engels was partial to radical sectarianism, Lenin preferred Orthodoxy in all its corruption to any more benign or progressive faith. So singular was he in this respect that I shall return to it later.

Bociurkiw has suggested that Lenin modified Marx by upgrading the importance of "the active struggle against religious ideology as a means, if not a condition, of a successful struggle against political and economic oppression."[85] Without denying that the conditions were different, it must not be forgotten that Marx himself used the criticism of religion to attack existing conditions in "theoretical Germany." The modification in question

---

[83] Lenin, "The New Factory Law," LCW, II, 292; "Two Speeches by Marshalls of the Nobility," LCW, V, 291-292; "Political Agitation," LCW, V, 341; "Classes and Parties," LCW, XV, 416; "L. N. Tolstoy," LCW, XVI, 326; "Liberals and Clericals," LCW, XVIII, 228; "The Priesthood in Politics," LCW, XVIII, 310; "Lecture on the 1905 Revolution," LCW, XXIII, 245.

[84] Letter, V. I. Lenin to M. Gorky, November 13 or 14, 1913, LCW, XXXV, 121-124; Valentinov (Volsky), Encounters with Lenin, p. 215.

[85] Bociurkiw, "Lenin and Religion," pp. 109-110.

was not so much theoretical as tactical. Religion had not only failed to decay as rapidly as Marx had expected, but also Lenin was up against a deeply entrenched ecclesiastical institution which, having the power to counterattack, used it.[86] I am not denying that from a practical standpoint Lenin delivered blows to religion which Marx had neither anticipated nor counseled; what I am suggesting is that there was very little, if any, theoretical divergency between their views on the origin, history, and functions of religion. It was the circumstances, plus whatever psychological variables one might legitimately include, that made the difference.

One might also discern a theoretical difference between Marx and Lenin in the latter's failure either to reiterate Marx's analysis of alienation or to give his own. Theoretically, religion was for Marx primarily a product of alienation and then secondarily a source of it. But the further in time and thought Marx moved from Hegelian concepts and terminology and the more he focused on economics, the less he said of alienation and the more he spoke of exploitation. These changes of focus and nomenclature did not, however, result in any substantial changes in his critique of religion. Since the mature Marx did not modify the young Marx on religion, Lenin's greater affinity for the later Marx does not imply any theoretical criticism or repudiation of the younger Marx. Moreover, since neither an emphatic reiteration of Marx's concept of alienation nor a newly-phrased analysis had any great tactical significance for the Russian proletariat, Lenin left the topic alone. The absence of alienation in his critique of religion is, I should judge, a relatively unimportant omission.

There is some evidence that Lenin, late in life, changed his mind on certain points. Payne notes in his biography that Lenin confessed to being "strongly guilty before the workers of Russia,"[87] and Volsky finds enormous significance in Lenin's very late statement, "The worst thing of all would be to rely on the assumption that we know anything.[88] More to the point, Bociurkiw has written:

As he was approaching the end of his politicial career, Lenin seems to have become more aware of the emotional and aesthetic dimensions of religion, though characteristically he reduced the latter to its external forms, the ritual. On one occasion, according to Kalinin, he reflected on the need to provide the 'masses' with a substitute for religion, ascribing this role to the theatre. Reportedly, he also

---

[86] Lenin, "Classes and Parties," LCW, XV, 416-418.

[87] Robert Payne, *The Life and Death of Lenin* (New York: The Hearst Corporation, 1967), p. 662.

[88] Valentinov (Volsky), *Encounters with Lenin*, pp. 264-265.

welcomed bolshevik attempts to devise new secular 'Soviet rites' as substitutes for religious ceremonies marking the momentous occasions in a man's life.[89]

If Lenin did indeed change his mind about religion, it was already too late for him to rectify the belief, so innocently mouthed by Krupskaya, that he "had dealt with religion in all its complexity."[90]

SHAMEFACED IDEALISM, GOD-BUILDING, AND THE DISADVANTAGES OF IMPROVED RELIGION

Shamefaced Idealism

When Santayana defined the fanatic as one who upon forgetting his aims redoubles his efforts, he might well have had the author of *Materialism and Empirio-Criticism* in mind. Begging the epistemological question throughout by delivering apodictic assertions on ontology,[91] handling the truth about Mach, Avenarius and Company most carelessly,[92] and quoting Marx and Engels in the proof-text manner made infamous by divines, Lenin struggled to defend materialism against its enemies, real and imaginary.[93] It goes beyond the scope of this study to examine *Materialism and Empirio-Criticism* in detail. The first of two fairly obvious reasons for this is that Lenin's only major foray into philosophy makes but minor contributions to his critique of religion; the second, that a number of studies have already been done, rendering yet another one superfluous.[94] The importance of *Materialism and Empirio-Criticism* for this study lies in an examination of the dire consequences to proletarian truth which,

---

[89] Bociurkiw, "Lenin and Religion," p. 128; Max Eastman, *Artists in Uniform* (New York: Alfred A. Knopf, 1934), p. 224.

[90] Krupskaya, *Reminiscences of Lenin*, p. 196.

[91] Lenin, *Materialism and Empirio-Criticism*, LCW, XIV, 227-228.

[92] Valentinov (Volsky), *Encounters with Lenin*, pp. 209-210; Lenin, *Materialism and Empirio-Criticism*, LCW, XIV, 192-193, 341, 346, 348; George Katkov, "Lenin as Philosopher," in *Lenin, Man, Theorist, Leader*, p. 81; Albert William Levi, *Philosophy and the Modern World* (Bloomington: Indiana University Press, 1959), pp. 342-343.

[93] Lenin, *Materialism and Empirio-Criticism*, LCW, XVI, 107-115, 138, 156, 336-339.

[94] A. James Gregor, *A Survey of Marxism* (New York: Random House, 1965, Chapter Three; Katkov, "Lenin as Philosopher" in *Lenin, Man, Theorist, Leader*, Chapter Four; Gustaf Wetter, *Dialectical Materialism*, pp. 116-125; Levi, *Philosophy and the Modern World*, pp. 212-219; Louis Althusser, *Lénine et la philosophie* (Paris: François Maspero, 1969), especially pp. 11-19, 33-57; G. A. Paul, "Lenin's Theory of Perception," *Analysis*, V (August, 1938), 65-73.

Lenin thought, any alternatives to, backsliding from, or revision of Marxist ontology and epistemology would entail. The career of agnosticism in the thought of Engels and Lenin will illustrate what I mean.

Engels observed that the English became civilized in 1851 in connection with their great industrial exhibition. During that year both salad oil and Continental skepticism were introduced to those insular folk. Since then, Engels noted, agnosticism had already surpassed the Salvation Army in respectability and had achieved parity with Baptism. Even if it had not yet become quite as much "the thing" as the Church of England, he remained optimistic that it would soon become as respectable as Anglicanism. The chief difficulty with agnosticism was that its devotees were less than candid. "What, indeed, is agnosticism but, to use an expressive Lancashire term, 'shamefaced' materialism?" Engels asked.[95] Moreover, even if the agnostic "admits the possibility of spiritualism *in abstracto,* he will have none of it *in concreto.*" Epistemological quibbles and qualifications, notwithstanding, the agnostic is, according to Engels, really a rank materialist.[96] These convictions appeared in print in 1892, but by 1908, when *Materialism and Empirio-Criticism* was published, agnostics had become shamefaced idealists. Herein lies a saga, which deserves attention.

To the extent to which Hume had discomfited the pious with his agnosticism and wit, and Kant had delivered consternation to the faithful through his agnosticism and sobriety, Engels applauded them. He was, of course, vexed that most, if not all, of their philosophic descendants were phenomenalistic and subjectivistic in epistemology, were, accordingly, still disposed to place limits on human knowledge, and were willing to consider unknowable dimensions of reality, if not to posit the thing-in-itself. Still Engels did not worry over the epistemological niceties of agnosticism, for had not Darwin rendered a nonnatural reality impossible, had not Hegel clearly denied the thing-in-itself, and, if that were not enough, had not Marx and he prescribed practice as the way to resolve the logical problems of naive realism?[97] Yet that which seemed but a quibble to Engels appeared to be a potential catastrophe to Lenin.

Although Lenin continued from time to time to use the term "shame-faced materialists" in reference to agnostics, it is clear that on most occasions he did not have in mind crypto-materialists, too cautious to speak

---

[95] Engels, *Socialism: Utopian and Scientific,* p. 20.

[96] *Ibid.,* p. 25.

[97] *Ibid.,* pp. 21-24.

their real opinions.[98] On the contrary, he was thinking of those whose agnosticism was in fact concealing materialism,[99] or worse yet of those for whom agnosticism was a vacillation between materialistic science and clericalism,[100] or worst of all of those for whom agnosticism was the abandonment of materialism.[101] Ever zealous to do battle with idealism in order to preclude all further possibilities of mysticism, fideism, and priestcraft, Lenin discerned in agnosticism a more insidious threat than the philosophic enemy he was openly attacking. With venomous clarity he observed that philosophic idealism leading directly to God was more honest than agnosticism "with its hypocrisy and cowardice."[102] To Lenin, those who were neither avowed materialists nor idealists were "all a wretched mush," a "contemptible *middle party* in philosophy."[103]

In short, the door which materialism had closed on fideism had been slyly opened again by Hume and Kant, by their epistemological disciples Mach and Avenarius, and by such traitors to Marxism as Bogdanov and Valentinov. If lunatics such as Mach and Company deny objectivity to time and space, what kind of defense can there be against theologians, Lenin wondered, and if simpletons such as Hume and Kant deny objective truth, what will prevent "philistine, cowardly tolerance" from being extended to "dogmas regarding sprites, hobgoblins, Catholic saints and the like?"[104] "Once you deny objective reality, given us in sensation," said he, "you have already lost every weapon against fideism, for you have slipped into agnosticism or subjectivism—and that is all fideism requires."[105] In such circumstances, even materialist epistemology, the most "universal weapon against religious belief," avails naught.[106]

Even if agnosticism is not so broad and easy a gate to idealism and religious belief as Lenin supposed, his strategic concern with it was justified, given his premises. Theology in the West, if not everywhere, involves the concept of God subsisting in an elusive region of conceivability

---

[98] Lenin, *Materialism and Empirio-Criticism*, LCW, XIV, 184; "Notes on Rey's *Modern Philosophy*," LCW, XXXVIII, 436, 461, 464, 467.

[99] Lenin, *Materialism and Empirio-Criticism*, LCW, XIV, 92.

[100] Lenin, "Twenty-Fifth Anniversary of the Death of Joseph Dietzgen," LCW, XIX, 80.

[101] Letter, V. I. Lenin to N. Y. Vilanov, April 7, 1910, LCW, XXXIV, 418.

[102] Lenin, "Conspectus of Hegel's Book *Lectures on the History of Philosophy*," LCW, XXXVIII, 303.

[103] Lenin, *Materialism and Empirio-Criticism*, LCW, XIV, 340.

[104] *Ibid.*, p. 128.

[105] *Ibid.*, p. 344.

[106] *Ibid.*, pp. 340-341.

beyond definitive verification or refutation. Depending on the development of thought at a given time and place, this region is larger or smaller, closer at hand or farther afield. Granted that every advance in human technical competence denies to God one more direct function and that every scientific advance robs the world of one more opportunity for mystery and myth, still God remains elusive, employed, and content with his lot. If, for example, a Darwin denies him the rights to create every living species by fiat within six days, he is perfectly willing to create the whole evolutionary process and put it to work throughout eons of time. Since the only limit to the concept of God is human ingenuity and since man's mind is wondrously fanciful metaphysically, there is no definite end to the number of modifications the concept of God can suffer and no precise limit to the subtlety with which these modifications can be made. Lenin, however, thought that with materialism, realism, and Marxian epistemology, the elusive region of conceivability wherein God dwells could be abolished once and for all, the door being closed forever to fideism. Finding the door ajar when he thought it had been hermetically sealed, Lenin, understandably, lashed out at those who had, according to him, reopened it through their pernicious skepticism.

Although agnosticism has little, if anything, to do with opening or reopening the door to religious belief, sophisticated fideists can and do plague their atheistic opponents by using agnosticism as a permanent obstacle to sealing the door. Accordingly, Lenin was equally aggrieved by the open door because it permitted traffic in evil spirits and priestcraft and also prevented Marxism from becoming definitive ontologically and epistemologically. Whether or not the Machian position really implied the resurrection of God, spirits, and immortal souls, it was clear that Machians had accused Marx of metaphysics,[107] had made light of Marxian epistemology,[108] and had even accused materialists of making a fetish of matter.[109] Lenin realized that if scientific agnosticism and epistemological skepticism were to prevail, dialectical materialism might cease to represent the most obvious of realities and become a mere concept destined to dwell cheek by jowl with the Heavenly Father.

Whatever the final assessment of *Materialism and Empirio-Criticism* may be, Lenin illustrated the important truth that religious concepts

---

[107] Lenin, *Materialism and Empirio-Criticism,* LCW, XIV, 318; Letter, V. I. Lenin to M. Gorky, written between February 15 and 25, 1913, LCW, XXXV, 84.

[108] Lenin, *Materialism and Empirio-Criticism,* LCW, XIV, 317-318.

[109] *Ibid.,* p. 23.

require but the slightest leeway in which to function. Granted only the remotest possibility of truth by agnosticism, idealism continues to flourish. To make matters worse, as "a subtle, refined form of fideism," it "stands fully armed, commands vast organizations and steadily continues to exercise influence on the masses, turning the slightest vacillation in philosophical thought to its own advantage."[110]

God-Building

Confronted by the problem of whether or not Social-Democrats could profess socialism as their religion, Lenin concluded on tactical grounds that this was permissible. Agitators, for instance, who lapsed into religious jargon the better to communicate with the backward masses could be tolerated, for in calling socialism their religion, they had but used a rhetorical device. However, there were others who, in making the same claim, were deviating from Marxism treacherously. Unwilling to tolerate heterodoxy, Lenin wrote:

It is another thing when a writer begins to preach 'god-building,' or god-building socialism (in the spirit, for example, of our Lunacharsky and Co.). While in the first case censure would be mere carping, or even inappropriate restriction of the freedom of the agitator, of his freedom in choosing 'pedagogical' methods, in the second case party censure is necessary and essential. For some the statement 'socialism is a religion' is a form of transition from religion to socialism; for others, it is a form of transition *from* socialism to religion.[111]

Those whom Lenin described moving illegitimately from socialism to religion were, of course, the god-builders, such as Gorky, Lunacharsky, and Bogdanov. Desirous of filling the emotional and aesthetic abyss left in communist society by the expulsion of religion, they sought to sacralize and celebrate the values and goals of scientific socialism. As Kline has put it, "Gorky and Lunacharsky preached not the ideal *in* man, with the ethical culturists and humanists, or the ideal *above* man, with the theists, but the ideal *ahead* of man in history."[112] Indeed, to Gorky, the new man and the collectivist society then being created by communism were so ideal and eminently desirable when compared with existing man and society that they might well be taken as divine.[113] Lunacharsky, agreeing com-

---

[110] *Ibid.*, p. 358.

[111] Lenin, "Attitude of Workers to Religion," LCW, XV, 409.

[112] George L. Kline, *Religious and Anti-Religious Thought in Russia* (Chicago: University of Chicago Press, 1968), pp. 104-105.

[113] *Ibid.*

pletely, went even further by identifying socialist realities with Christian symbols, by classifying Marxism as a religion, and by elevating Marx to the rank of Hebrew prophet.[114] Despite what may be excessive naivete in assimilating socialism to religion so easily, the god-builders remained atheists and stoutly resisted classification with all theists including such god-seekers as Berdyaev and Bulgakov.[115] After all, as Gorky said, "Gods are not sought—*they are created*."[116]

Degrading the distinction between god-building and god-seeking to that of a dispute over the difference between blue and yellow devils, Lenin "stuck the convicts badge" on all who sought to make socialism a religion or to reconcile Marxism with it.[117] Such people were hostile to scientific socialism and reactionary.[118] Whatever their intentions, their activities served only the counterrevolutionary aims of the bourgeoisie. Accordingly, in 1909, the god-builders were cast into outer darkness where all religionists weep and wail and gnash their teeth.[119]

The purpose here is neither to analyze god-building further nor to catalogue the practical problems it raised for Lenin. Nor need there be continued concern over the ways in which he responded to these problems. The purpose, rather, is to observe that the most unlikely concepts can become grist for the religious mill.

The Disadvantages of Improved Religion

The title of this subdivision is intended neither to be playful nor self-contradictory. It is rather a sober assertion of one of Lenin's convictions. He had nothing but loathing for those religious manifestations which most observers would applaud as liberal, progressive, and humane when measured, for instance, against Russian Orthodoxy. Tactically, it was far easier to destroy an obviously malignant religion than one which appeared benign. Thus, Lenin preferred that Orthodoxy remain autocratic and repressive, medieval and absurd. By the same token, he feared and resisted

---

[114] Wetter, *Dialectical Materialism,* p. 91; Bociurkiw, *Lenin and Religion,*" p. 122; Kline, *Religious and Anti-Religious Thought in Russia,* p. 118.

[115] Kline, *Religious and Anti-Religious Thought in Russia,* pp. 119, 123; Bociurkiw, "Lenin and Religion," p. 122.

[116] Letter, V. I. Lenin to M. Gorky, November 13 or 14, 1913, LCW, XXXV, 121.

[117] Letter, V. I. Lenin to M. Gorky, November 13 or 14, 1913, LCW, XXXV, 121; Valentinov (Volsky), *Encounters with Lenin,* p. 182.

[118] Letter, V. I. Lenin to A. I. Lyubinov, written in early September, 1909, LCW, XXXIV, 401-402.

[119] Lenin, LCW, XXXIV, 509, n. 400.

any attempt at refurbishing religion, at making it less preposterous and slavish.[120] A new refined religion could only be a "new, refined [and more] subtle poison for the oppressed masses," a more insidious narcotic, a more cunning deception, a more reactionary ploy.[121] Nothing can be gained by expatiating further on these points. It suffices to remember in this connection that Lenin knew perfectly well that there were radical clergymen afoot, that a liberal reform movement had begun in the bosom of the church and that even some of the most benighted priests had begun demanding freedom and the redress of grievances. Thus, whether or not one wishes to think of it as progressing or regressing, improving or degenerating, religion is manifestly neither a monolithic nor a homogeneous entity. The devotees of a complex religion, such as Christianity, can be more or less autocratic, more or less conservative, and more or less orthodox without losing their faith. Put differently, any highly developed religion, drawing nourishment from a rich, extensive, and manifold tradition, can be adapted extensively in upholding the most diverse values and goals.

I have already concluded that religious concepts require but the slightest leeway in which to function, that the most unlikely concepts can become grist for the religious mill, and that a complex religion can be adapted extensively in upholding the most diverse values and goals. The question is, "Did Lenin take these empirical generalizations into account?" The answer is, "Yes and No." As a practical man, he was forced to take them into consideration, but only grudgingly and never with any willingness to be scientifically thorough and dispassionate in trying to comprehend them in his critique. Lenin the dialectical materialist knew that religion always served ruling class interests and that it never failed to deaden genuine human feelings, but the tactician in him took advantage of religious dissent among the proletariat and witnessed attempts at sacralizing socialist values. Lenin the theorist knew that religion was a narcotic resulting in social quiescence, but the man of affairs witnessed it as a stimulant in the progressive, if not radical, clergy. Lenin the scientific socialist knew that an atheistic and totally secular consciousness was in the making which would provide no nourishment for religion, but the propagandist recognized that even the merest hint of agnosticism could open the floodgates to faith. Lenin the Marxist knew that the objects of religious

---

[120] Lenin, "Attitude of Workers to Religion," LCW, XV, 411; Krupskaya, *Reminiscences of Lenin*, p. 196; Louis Fischer, *The Life of Lenin*, p. 26.
[121] Lenin, "L. N. Tolstoy," LCW, XVI, 325; "Classes and Parties," LCW, XV, 419.

belief were invariably supernatural, but the man of affairs beheld with loathing attempts at the apotheosis of naturalistic Marxism. If the realities of religion, in all their complexity, cast doubt on the adequacy of Lenin's critique, so much the worse for the realities.

CHAPTER 4

KAUTSKY'S CRITIQUE OF RELIGION

TOWARD A DEVELOPED MATERIALIST THEORY OF RELIGION

Introduction

"Up to the 1914-16 war," said Lenin, "Karl Kautsky was a Marxist, and many of his major writings and statements will always remain models of Marxism."[1] But from that time forward, Lenin vehemently attacked "The Renegade Kautsky."[2] His "disgraceful rubbish, childish babble and shallowest opportunism impel me to ask: Why do we do nothing to fight the theoretical vulgarisation of Marxism by Kautsky?" Furthermore, and I reproduce Lenin's comments exactly:

Kautsky has absolutely failed to understand and has distorted in a purely opportunist way

> the teaching of Marx on the state
> the teaching of Marx *on the dictatorship* of the proletariat
> the teaching of Marx on bourgeois democracy
> the teaching of Marx on parliamentarism
> the teaching of Marx on the role and significance of the Commune, etc.[3]

Lenin was also wroth over the counsel Kautsky had given the German Social Democrats concerning the relationship of the party to religion. He quoted as follows a fragment of that advice taken from the second of two articles on religion which Kautsky wrote in 1913:

---

[1] Lenin, "A Caricature of Marxism and Imperialist Economism," LCW, XXIII, 35.

[2] Lenin, "The Proletarian Revolution and the Renegade Kautsky," LCW, XXVIII, 105-108; Letter to A. G. Shylapnikov, October 17, 1914, LCW, XXXV, 162; "The State and Revolution," LCW, XXV, 412; "Under a False Flag," LCW, XXI, 147, 149.

[3] Letter, V. I. Lenin to Y. A. Bergin, V. V. Varonsky and A. A. Joffe, September 20, 1918, LCW, XXXV, 362.

K. Kautsky on religion. Inter-
alia, p. 353: On the question of religion our propagandists must state
that this question is neither raised
nor answered at our party meetings,
because we want to make religion,
a private matter of the individual, *and*
we demand of the state that it *too* should
treat it as such" . . .
[vulgarian!]⁴

!!??
Kautsky
on
religion

Lenin might easily have pointed to further evidences of "treachery" to Marxism in each of these articles. For example, in the first one (herein-after referred to as "Religion I"), Kautsky not only revised his position on the origin and development of religion but also announced that Marx and Engels had held an untenable position on the topic.[5] Continuing the revision of Marx's etiology of religion in his second article ("Religion II"), he ended by introducing views more at variance with it than Engels' animism.[6]

In 1913 Kautsky wrote, "Ich gestehe gern, das auch ich jetzt manche früher von mir geäusserten Anschauungen über religiöse Anfänge zu revi-dieren habe."[7] The immediate cause of his revision was Henrich Cunow (1862-1936) sociologist, political scientist, and ethnologist who at one time or another served as the editor of *Die Neue Zeit*, as professor of political theory at Berlin, and as the director of a German ethnological museum. In 1913 Cunow published a book entitled, *Der Ursprung der Religion und das Gottesglaubens*.[8] Readers of *Die Neue Zeit* had already seen a preview of this work in a series of articles entitled, "Religionsgeschichtliche Streif-züge," published in it two years earlier.[9] So forcefully did these writings strike Kautsky that he wrote, "Aber den Revisionismus, zu dem uns Cunow veranlasst, kann man sich wohl gefallen lassen. Es ist ein Revisionismus,

---

⁴ Lenin, *Notebook "Omicron,"* LCW, XXXIX, 590. The first of Kautsky's two 1913 articles (referred to as hereinafter as "Religion I") appeared in *Die Neue Zeit*, Vol. I, No. 6 (November 7, 1913), pp. 182-188. The second one (to be referred to hereinafter as "Religion II") appeared in *Die Neue Zeit*, Vol. I, No. 10 (December 5, 1913), pp. 352-360.

⁵ Kautsky, "Religion I," pp. 183-185.

⁶ Kautsky, "Religion II," pp. 354-355.

⁷ Kautsky, "Religion I," p. 184.

⁸ Heinrich Cunow, *Ursprung der Religion und des Gottesglaubens* (Berlin: Verlag: Buchhandlung Vorwärts Paul Singer G. m. b. H., 1913), especially Chapters One through Three, and Eight.

⁹ Kautsky, "Religion I," p. 183.

der die Einheitlichkeit und Geschlossenheit unserer theoretischen Grund-
lage verstärkte."[10] Aware that the opprobrious label of "revisionist" might
be tacked on him, Kautsky announced that only "eclectic" revisionism was
objectionable.

Admittedly relying on the work of Tylor, Baldwin Spencer, and Lippert,
Cunow might have seemed revisionistic in theory had he not clung fast to
Marx's methodology and thus escaped objectionable eclecticism. In so
doing, he succeeded, according to Kautsky, in giving the first materialist
history of religious origins.[11] He also revealed the manner in which man's
earliest religion, based on animism, developed into the nature cults of
primitive peoples, something which Kautsky thought no other
anthropologist had been able to do. In "Religion I," Kautsky summarized
Cunow's conclusions and adopted them as his own. Within the context of
the etiology of religion, I should now like, first, to give an exposition of
these conclusions, second, to examine the original position on religion
which Kautsky revised in 1913, third, to bring to light those portions of
"Religion II" which are relevant to the origin of religion, fourth, to pursue
the etiological themes introduced in "Religion I" and "Religion II" to their
conclusion in Kautsky's *Die Materialistische Geschichtsauffassung*, and
fifth, to criticize and to assess his contribution to this topic.

The Etiology of Religion

Kautsky noted that as late as the publication of his two articles on
religion many scholars had assumed that religion was the product of
man's fear of nature. Marx and Engels had clearly expressed this view,
but Tylor's work on animism had rendered it untenable. Having made
these two general points, Kautsky criticized Engels in detail on three
further points.

First, when Engels asserted in *Anti-Dühring* that all religion was nothing
but the fantastic reflection in men's minds of those external forces which
control their daily lives, he erred by assuming that primitives had a
higher capacity for thought than was the case. To personify the powers of
nature, argued Kautsky, is to have knowledge of the external forces which
govern man, but to have such knowledge is to possess powers of abstraction beyond any that primitive man may reasonably be supposed to have
had at the point of his emergence from the animal kingdom. "Der Wilde

[10] *Ibid.*, p. 184.
[11] *Ibid.*

ist ein ungemein scharfer Beobachter, aber kein Denker über das Nächstliegende hinaus."[12]

Second, Engels had blithely stated in *Anti-Dühring* that it was not long before social forces, "side by side with natural forces," became active in the production of religion. According to Kautsky, a similar bifurcation occurred in the preface to the first edition of *The Origin of the Family, Private Property and the State*, for there Engels had written:

According to the materialist conception, the determining factor in history is, in the last resort, the production and reproduction of immediate life. But this itself is of a twofold character. On the one hand, the production of the means of subsistence, of food, clothing and shelter and the tools requisite therefor; on the other, the production of human beings themselves, the propagation of the species. The social institutions under which men of a definite historical epoch and of a definite country live are conditioned by both kinds of production: by the stage of development of labour, on the one hand, and of the family, on the other. The less the development of labour, and the more limited its volume of production and, therefore, the wealth of society, the more preponderatingly does the social order appear to be dominated by ties of sex.[13]

Rightly or wrongly, Kautsky took this to mean that history was determined first by the production of people and later by the production of food: "Danach wäre also anfangs das bestimmende Moment der Geschichte die Produktion von Menschen, später die von Lebensmitteln."[14] To him this was a departure from the materialist method. Since the production and reproduction of people had always remained the same, it could not be called a "determining moment" in history nor used as a means of explaining why history had developed as it had. Kautsky noted that Engels, perhaps dimly aware of the problem, had quietly discarded his idea of the reproduction of people and had drawn his concept of the family onstage as a *deus ex machina* to explain history. As Kautsky saw it, this ploy failed, because it postulated the family as a viable unit existing prior to the influence of work. Historically, the family as well as the tribe were nothing more than special types of social order developed concurrently with the development of socially necessary work. The family and its work, when taken together, explain social development and history from the beginning.

Third, Engels was mistaken in understanding religion to be first a reaction to the forces of nature and later a reaction to social forces. Since

[12] *Ibid.*, p. 186.
[13] Engels, *Family, Property, and State*, p. 6.
[14] Kautsky, "Religion I," p. 185.

the development of religion went hand in hand with the development of society, it was mistaken to place its origin in a presocial context. Although Kautsky supposed, naively, that Marx's and Engels' knowledge of Morgan gave them access to prehistory, they did not exploit this opportunity and thus bequeathed it by default to their followers, particularly to Cunow.[15]

According to Kautsky, it was Tylor who initially discovered the beginnings of religion and laid bare the real origins of religious thought.[16] The crucial type of experience which underlay this primordial religion was dreaming. As a result of it, men came not only to regard themselves as possessing both a body and a separable soul but also to believe in the hereafter as the abode of departed spirits who dwelt there for an indefinite time, if not forever. Moreover, just as one was obligated in numerous ways to his living kith and kin, so also one had duties to perform on behalf of his ancestral spirits. Given these beliefs, all elements necessary to religion were present according to Kautsky.[17]

In order for monotheism to develop, it was necessary that one spirit receive greater respect than the others, become the center of a cult elevating his reputation above that enjoyed by his former peers, and achieve a more durable place in the tribal memory than that shared by his rivals:

Die Bedingungen dafür wurden durch die soziale Entwicklung geschaffen, vor allem durch die wachsende Geschlossenheit der Horden- oder Stammesorganisation. Einzelne Individuen wurden jetzt zu Häuptlingen und als solche dauernd über ihre Genossen erhoben, gleichzeitig erhielten aber auch die Blutbande zunehmende Bedeutung. Die Stellung des einzelnen in der Gesellschaft hing immer mehr von seinin verwandtschaftlichen Beziehungen ab; diese jederzeit genau zu überblicken, wurde von der äussersten Wichtigkeit für jederman. Die genaue Kenntnis des Stammbaums war damals nicht wie bei modernen Aristokraten eine lächerliche Schrulle, sondern eine Lebensfrage. Der Name der Ahnherrn erheilt sich von Geschlect zu Geschlect.[18]

Cunow completed his study of religious origins with the point at which tribal groups forsook the nomadic life in favor of settled agricultural ways. When that occurred their original gods, having been war gods, had to assume responsibility for the functions of nature imperative to successful farming. The preexisting gods capable of the transition became nature gods set to the task of assisting men meet their economic needs.

On the basis of the foregoing analysis, Kautsky concluded that all belief in God, even the most sophisticated and sublime, had its origin in the

---

[15] *Ibid.*, p. 186.
[16] *Ibid.*, p. 183.
[17] *Ibid.*, p. 187.
[18] *Ibid.*

phantasms of the dreaming savage.[19] From this perspective it is not surprising that he should have taken Marx and Engels to task for having based religion, first, on the fear of natural forces and, second, on the fear of social forces. It is surprising, however, that he should have singled out Engels for detailed refutation since it was Engels who first imported animism into Marxism. Since it is unthinkable that Kautsky did not know the contents of *Feuerbach,* the mystery remains unsolved. Perhaps a clue lies in Engels' failure to acknowledge the need to revise, if not to repudiate, his comments on the origin of religion in *Anti-Dühring* after he had already modified them in *Feuerbach.*

Kautsky's admission that he was revising his views on religion arouses curiosity concerning the opinions he held prior to 1913. A sample of those views can be found in his book, *Thomas More and His Utopia* (hereinafter referred to as *More*):

The intellectual roots of religion, the causes of religious thought and feeling lie in the existence of superhuman and incomprehensible forces, in face of which man is helpless, whose operations he can neither control nor foresee, and which exert such a decisive influence upon his weal and woe that he feels the need of propitiating them.

These forces are either natural or social forces.[20]

Up to this point (1888) Kautsky's comments were consistent with the views expressed by Marx and Engels in *The German Ideology* and with those of Engels in *Anti-Dühring.* Furthermore, there was no hint as yet of any animistic reinterpretation of religious origins. But, having made these orthodox points, Kautsky became heterodox:

Under primitive communism the social forces play no part. There the fate of mankind is settled by economic conditions, so far as they depend upon social co-operation. At this primitive stage man is all the more dependent upon nature. He still feels himself to be part of nature, like an animal, he has not yet broken away from nature's umbilical cord, and so dreams his days away. Of religion there is as yet little mention.[21]

He continued by insisting that it was not until the "rise of commodity production" that social forces became efficacious in producing religion. Thus, "In the small communities of Antiquity and the Middle Ages this second root [the social root] remains quiescent."[22] By More's time, how-

---

[19] *Ibid.,* p. 188.

[20] Karl Kautsky, *Thomas More and His Utopia* (New York: Russell and Russell, 1959), p. 72 (hereinafter referred to as *More*).

[21] *Ibid.*

[22] *Ibid.,* p. 73.

ever, the first root [the natural root] had withered, but the social root had "sprouted luxurious shoots."[23] In addition to this he wrote:

Social phenomena must become mass phenomena before men become aware of the social forces and realize their impotence in face of them, before the social forces can captivate the imagination and the reason and exercise a decisive influence on the character of religion.[24]

Although the treatment of religion in *The German Ideology* is less than pellucid, there is little doubt that Marx believed that the social root of religion reached nearly as far back as the natural root, and there can be no doubt that Engels held this position in *Anti-Dühring*. At least, the social root was interpreted as having been effective before the disappearance of primitive communism. Thus, in denying efficacy to this root until the mass phenomena of commodity production emerged, Kautsky clearly parted company with his mentors. His position on religion in *More* was also quite different in one further respect from the one he adopted in 1913. In *More* Kautsky, like Marx and Engels, had assumed that natural religion was the earliest manifestation of religious phenomena, but by 1913 he had explicitly repudiated this position, had accepted the soul-cult as the earliest form, and had reinterpreted the cult of nature as a phase in the evolution of religion.

To digress for a moment, "Religion I" contains materials concerning the importance to religion of the family, of ethical obligations to the living and the dead, of the growing importance of tribal organization (*die Gentil-verfassung*), of the emergence of elitist leadership, and of the increased significance of the endogamous group.[25] The reader may view these as social forces and wonder how Kautsky could have been so naive as to think, in *More*, that natural religion, apparently minus social forces, could have persisted until the end of the Middle Ages. Although Kautsky took the phenomena itemized above to be social relations, exercising more or less power over the individual, he did not confuse them with the "social forces" of commodity production which he thought eventually became efficacious in producing modern religion. The upshot is that, whereas in 1888 Kautsky utilized only "natural forces" and "social forces" as categories explanatory of religion at different times and places, by 1913 he could enrich his explanation with the concept of social relations in addition to Tylor's animism. He had probably been moving in this direction for

---

[23] *Ibid.*, p. 72.
[24] *Ibid.*, p. 73.
[25] Kautsky, "Religion I," p. 187.

some time. By 1906 in *Ethics and the Materialist Conception of History* (hereinafter referred to as *Ethics*) he had already emphasized the social nature of the human species,[26] and by 1908 in the *Foundations of Christianity* (hereinafter referred to as *Christianity*) he had already begun to incorporate animism in his thought.[27]

Lest it should seem that Kautsky's interpretation of religion became less and less orthodox from 1888 to 1913, I present one example in which the trend was reversed. In *More* he wrote, "Religion becomes a human need from the moment man begins to ponder upon nature until the rise of the natural sciences."[28] The problem which this poses for Marxism is not so much one of fixing the date when man began to ponder upon nature as it is one of determining whether or not all prescientific pondering productive of religion is dependent on economic forces. If not, then an independent variable involving some psychological or epistemological need or other must be taken into account, but to do this is to weaken, if not deny, the preeminence which Marx and Engels accorded to economic forces in determining religion. By 1913 Kautsky had very clearly changed his mind on this point in favour of orthodoxy. Referring to the time by which men had already become settled agriculturalists and had produced nature cults, he wrote:

Das Eingreifen in die Natur wurde jetzt zur wichtigsten Aufgabe des Gottes. Aber auch da finden wir noch kein *philosophisches* Bedürfnis, das Walten der Natur-mächte durch eine phantastische Vorstelling zu *erklären*, sondern nur das ökono-mische Bedürfnis, die Natur dem Produktionsprozess *deinstbar zu machen*. Und nur soweit die Götter dazu helfen sollen, werden sie zunächst *Naturgötter*.[29]

He had made a similar point seven years earlier in *Christianity* by asserting that belief in a shadowy after-life was a "naive hypothesis arrived at explaining certain dream phenomena." "It did not," he added, "arise from a need of the soul."[30] He reinforced this position by contending that religion springs from the notion that there exist spirits, more powerful than men, who can either aid or harm society, the implication being that religion is purely a practical affair.[31]

---

[26] Karl Kautsky, *Ethics and the Materialist Conception of History*, trans. by J. B. Askew (London: The Twentieth Century Press, Ltd., 1906), p. 73 (hereinafter referred to as *Ethics*).

[27] Karl Kautsky, *Foundations of Christianity*, trans. by Henry F. Mins (New York: Russell and Russell, 1953), p. 90 (hereinafter referred to as *Christianity*).

[28] Kautsky, *More*, p. 73.

[29] Kautsky, "Religion I," p. 188.

[30] Kautsky, *Christianity*, p. 90.

[31] Kautsky, "Religion II," p. 354.

To recapitulate, Marx and Engels began by contending that religion was produced first by man's fear of almighty nature. To this they added the notion that the fear of overwhelming social forces also produced religion. Lenin agreed and let the matter drop. But, falling under the influence of Tylor toward the end of his life, Engels introjected animistic elements into the Marxist position. For whatever reason, Lenin failed to come to grips with this novelty. Kautsky began as Marx and Engels had but denied that social forces were productive of religion until they became mass phenomena. As silent as Lenin had been concerning Engels' unselfconscious appropriation of animism, Kautsky, nevertheless, adopted it explicitly and sought to show how the fear of nature and the resulting nature cults were based on the dream life and the cult of souls. But just as animism arrived unannounced and unheralded in Engels' later thought, so still another explanation respecting the origin of religion appeared without fanfare in Kautsky's thought from 1913 onward.

In a digression above, I called attention to the fact that in "Religion I" Kautsky noted the importance to religion of such items as ethical obligation, tribal organization, and endogamous concerns. Nor were these items limited to the terrestrial sphere: "Wie seine Pflichten gegenüber den lebenden Hordengenossen, muss er auch die gegenüber den Seelen der verstorbenen erfüllen."[32] Emphasizing repeatedly in "Religion II" that religion is not a private metaphysical solution and that it does not stem from the inspiration of the individual, Kautsky contended that it is a phenomenon of the many and that it arises from the common experience of the group. Moreover, it becomes the means of social unity and of social struggle against threatening forces.[33] As noted above, religion springs from belief in potentially dangerous spirits whose favor is important to the group and can be curried by them. It is from belief in spirits such as these that the ancestral deities of a group emerge. These deities are of paramount importance, because they constitute the bond that unites a tribal group into a society. Since their function is not to solve metaphysical puzzles nor to meet the so-called needs of the individual soul, but rather to meet communal needs, their cult is social and public and by no means an issue to be decided by private belief or disbelief. "*Diese soziale Verpflichtung zum Gottesglauben und zum Gottesdienst*, sie bildet das wesentlichste Kennzeichen der Religion und des wahrhaft religiösen

---

[32] Kautsky, "Religion I," p. 187.
[33] Kautsky, "Religion II," p. 354.

Menschen."[34] To this Kautsky added, "Nichts also verkehrter, als in der Religion die Wurzel der Moral zu sehen. Vielmehr ist es ein starkes ethisches Empfinden, aus dem die Religion ihre Kraft zieht."[35]

Kautsky did not cease thinking about religion after his revisions of 1913. Throughout both volumes of *Die Materialistische Geschichtsauffassung* (referred to hereinafter in the text as *Geschichtsauffassung*) he scattered his opinions on such topics as the etiology of religion, ancient religions, biblical and postbiblical Judaism, primitive Christianity (particularly in relation to revolution), post-Constantinian Catholicism, and Protestantism.[36] Moreover, he continued to develop his thought concerning the relationship between morality and religion. Entirely in keeping with the contents of "Religion II." in which he had said that religion draws its power from strong ethical feelings, Kautsky wrote:

Die enge Verquickung zwischen Moral und Religion, auf die wir in einem anderen Zusammenhange schon im Anfang des ersten Buches hinwiesen, wird gefördert dadurch, dass die Forderungen der Moral selbst zu Kollektivvorstellungen werden, die sich mit den anderen Vorstellungen dieser Art mengen.

So eng ist die Verbindung beider geworden, dass Viele zu der Ueberzeugung gelangten, ohne Religion sei Moral unmöglich. In Wirklichkeit was es vielmehr das Bestehen der Moral, das zu manchen Auffassungen von Gott, Unsterblichkeit u. dgl. Veranlassung gab, die im höher entwickelten religiösen Denken eine grosse Rolle spielten, wie schon oben ausgeführt.[37]

The point of greatest significance in the citation above is the assertion that morality leads to God, immortality, etc. Only slightly less important, from the standpoint of intellectual history, is Kautsky's use of "Kollektiv-vorstellung" (collective representation). This is not a term he happened on by coincidence nor one so commonplace that he could pluck it unconsciously from the surrounding intellectual atmosphere. It was a term identified with and used extensively by Lucien Lévy-Bruhl in *Les Fonctions mentales dans les sociétés inférieures*, published in 1910 and translated into German as *Ueber das Denken der Naturvölker* in 1921.[38] In the *Geschichtsauffassung* Kautsky quoted this work, used the term "Kollektivvorstellung" frequently, even asserting that moral claims became

---

[34] *Ibid.*

[35] *Ibid.*, p. 355.

[36] Karl Kautsky, *Die Materialistische Geschichtsauffassung* (2 vols., Berlin: Verlag J. H. W. Dietz Nachf. G. m. b. H., 1927), I, 31-34, 300-305, 816-817; II, 80-81, 352-355, 808-809, 819-830 (hereinafter referred to as MG).

[37] Kautsky, MG, I, 301-302.

[38] *Ibid.*, p. 32.

collective and mingled with other collective representations, and criticized Lévy-Bruhl by arguing that the power of morality in a community does not depend on the existence of collective representations but rather on the existence of social forces which are based on definite social arrangements.[39] Despite Kautsky's attempts at maintaining a proper distance between Lévy-Bruhl and himself, his views on the relationships of morality and religion came increasingly to coincide not only with those of Lévy-Bruhl but with Durkheim's as well. These views are even more novel to and inconsistent with the original Marxist etiology of religion than the animistic position of Tylor.

This inconsistency can be illustrated both negatively and positively. From the negative perspective, one has but to recall that neither in "Religion I" and "II" nor in the *Geschichtsauffassung* did Kautsky speak of the importance to religion of modes of production, divisions of labor, and exploitation, nor did he suggest that religion functioned as a sanction for the ruling elite while serving as an opiate for the masses. From the positive perspective, it suffices to remember that Kautsky, in the works mentioned above, approached religion sociologically and functionally. Since he denied that it was a matter of private feelings, thoughts, solutions, and practices, he refused to investigate it from idiosyncratic positions, psychological as well as theological. To him religion was entirely a matter of communal concern, belief, and activity. In addition to functioning on behalf of common economic concerns, the ancestral gods also supplied their devotees with the social adhesive requisite to group survival. It is most noteworthy that, when speaking in this vein, Kautsky treated religion as a force providing for the moral and social unification of the entire group and not of some class or subdivision thereof. The positive and negative points itemized above, when taken together with their various implications, constitute a position like that taken by Durkheim, Lévy-Bruhl and others in the French structuralist tradition of anthropology.

Remembering that in *More* Kautsky had founded the existence of the gods upon fear and that in "Religion I" he had placed it squarely upon the dream, it is noteworthy to find him suggesting, in the *Geschichtsauffassung*, that it was the existence of morality which led to the gods.[40] A casual examination of this assertion makes it tempting to conclude that he had capitulated to the Durkheimians, that he had, at the very least, become "merely eclectic," or that he was simply an opportunist as Lenin would

---

[39] *Ibid.*, pp. 32, 300-304.
[40] *Ibid.*, p. 302.

have it. The assertion that it is more the existence of morality which leads to religion than religion to morality can be taken in two ways. It can be understood to mean that the moral requirements of human gregariousness lead to the gods in the sense that they would be emergent in the group mind or collective consciousness as Durkheim understood it, or it can be taken to mean that human moral requirements lead to the gods in the sense of resorting to them for aid in upholding a given way of life. In the second sense, the gods already exist, having been created by other and different forces. If Kautsky's views on religion in the *Geschichtsauffassung* are taken as a whole, it is clear that he intended the second of these two meanings. For example, refusing to reject Tylor's animism, even though both Durkheim and Lévy-Bruhl had criticized it soundly, he was still maintaining it as late as 1927: "Die Annahme solcher Wesen war nicht ganz aus der Luft gegriffen, sie fand ihren Ausgangspunkt in mancher Erfahrung, vor allem in einer Art 'innerer Erfahrung,' dem Traum."[41]

Five additional reasons can also be found for distuinguishing Kautsky's position of 1927 from that of the structuralists. First, noting that men seek to placate the gods even as they do their own human overlords, Kausky stressed the element of obsequiousness in religion to a degree not characteristic of the Durkheimians.[42] Second, he emphasized that primitive religion was an attempt at mastering the conditions which men encountered, particularly the economic conditions with which they had to contend.[43] This, too, received but relatively little stress among the structuralists. Third, like all Marxists with whose writings I am acquainted, but unlike the Durkheimians, Kautsky failed to take account of the nature and function of ritual and of its importance to religion. Fourth, in a similar manner, he never considered the importance to religion of group celebration. Fifth, and most important, he failed to analyze the sacred, a category of paramount importance to Durkheim and his followers.

I have already criticized Marx for having dropped the investigation of so-called natural religion too precipitately. Although Kautsky did not lodge this complaint against Marx explicitly, he conducted himself so as to avoid similar criticism. Minimizing the roles allegedly played by the fear of nature and of socio-economic forces, Kautsky, ever sensitive to ethnological developments, appropriated first the animism of Tylor and then certain Durkheimian views. In so doing he diverged sharply from the position

---

[41] *Ibid.*, pp. 32-33.
[42] *Ibid.*, p. 33.
[43] *Ibid.*

initially established by Marx and uncritically accepted by Lenin, but how successful were these departures?

Assuming that the spirit world, taken to be a dimension of reality, is created by dreaming; that the preliterate does not distinguish in kind between his own separable soul, wandering about in dreams, and the ubiquitous soul of the dead ancestor; and that the interests and needs of the ancestral spirits are on a par with the claims and requirements of living kin; wherein, then, does religion lie? Since these are presumably matters of fact, to the primitive, what enables them to produce religion? In other words, why should they not be taken as but one more dimension of the secular world?

Approaching the problem differently, one might consider the rise of monotheism as Kautsky conceived it. According to him, belief in one God required that a single spirit receive greater respect over a longer period of time than his rivals. But how did this happen? Did a given spirit appear more vividly in more people's dreams with greater regularity than did all other spirits? Did he make his dream appearances with such coherence and force that the dreamers awoke next morning with a clear-cut mandate to elevate that particular spirit above all others, develop a cult on his behalf, and follow his precepts? On the contrary, Kautsky argued that the rise of monotheism depended on the development of such social conditions as the growth of compactness of the tribe, the elevation of chieftans, the increased significance of the endogamous group, and the crucial importance of membership in family, clan, and tribe. The point here is not to suggest that Kautsky was entirely correct in his assessment of the social developments designated above but to show how little he said about the dream life in this context and to illustrate how tenuous its relationship must have been to the social developments in question. With the rise of the *Gentilverfassung*, the ancestor, according to Kautsky, was raised to preeminence. He became the object of a cult, his exploits were exaggerated, he was deified, and his ancestry was traced to a god.[44] The point here is not that the ancestor was encountered in dreams nor that he was a spirit, even an immortal one; the point is that the ancestor became sacred in association with a cherished way of life which he personified and defended as the tribe's archetypal figure, a way of life with which his descendants identified themselves.

Granted that it would be methodologically risky in dealing with the etiology of religion to minimize the importance of dreaming or, for that

---

[44] Kautsky, "Religion I," pp. 187-188.

matter, to overlook any psychic factor which might be essential to the projection of human qualities upon the external world, still and all, Kautsky placed undue emphasis on dreaming. Although it is impossible to know empirically how religion might be different without dreaming, it seems most unlikely that there would be no religion or that it would be radically different, if there were none. The Durkheimians were quite right in maintaining that it was not so much dream-encounters with the ancestors as it was the sacredness of the ancestors that mattered to religion.

In short, Kautsky's failure to undertake a thorough investigation of the sacred and the secular prevented his etiology of religion from becoming sufficiently comprehensive to account for all religious phenomena at the social level. Had he investigated the sacred in the detail made possible by the structuralists, he would probably have ended as they by emphasizing more than he had the power of religion to unify the social group and to serve ritualistically as the vehicle for celebrating its cherished ways of life, its values, and its aspirations.

Another weakness in his etiology of religion involves the degree of desirability which humans accord to posthumous experience. In a typically Marxist fashion, Kautsky degraded the significance of belief in life after death, contended that the idea of immorality "did not arise from a need of the soul," and sought to show that as long as the citizen of the classical commune believed his immortality to be guaranteed by the ongoing community he felt no need for personal resurrection. Kautsky wrote:

Actually, we find in the peoples of antiquity, who did not have a long cultural development in back of them, either no ideas at all as to life after death, or else the idea of a shadowy existence, arising out of the need for explaining the appearance of the dead in dreams: a miserable life that one had rather be without.[45]

This elicits three points. First, since elaborate mortuary cults appear to extend to the Upper Paleolithic and beyond (at least 15,000 years ago) it is absurd to speak of the so-called peoples of antiquity, such as the Greeks and Hebrews, as if they were not heirs of an extensive cultural development including funerary beliefs and practices.[46] Second, it can neither be shown empirically that ancient peoples had no idea of life after death nor that such ideas as they had could only have been based on the need to explain dream phenomena. Third, even if the Greeks and Hebrews felt aversion to Hades and Sheol respectively and lodged their claims to

---

[45] Kautsky, *Christianity*, p. 90.
[46] Noss, *Man's Religions*, p. 8; H. R. Hayes, *In the Beginnings: Early Man and His Gods* (New York: G. P. Putman's Sons, 1963), pp. 30-31, 37.

immortality in the survival of their groups, this neither implies that as individuals their needs, aspirations, and hopes were met nor that they were completely satisfied that death ends all. Furthermore, the Greeks and Hebrews in their aversion to the shadowy world of death may not be paradigmatic for all ancient peoples. Hence, in addition to factual weaknesses, Kautsky's methodology is questionable, rendering his conclusion unsound.

Nature Religions

The preceding section contains many of Kautsky's views on the earliest identifiable religions. Expository thoroughness requires the inclusion of four additional points on the nature religions, religions which he called polytheistic. First, Kautsky claimed that in normal times primitives pay little attention to religion, calling upon the gods only sporadically.[47] Second, he contended that whereas preagricultural nomads had few gods, agriculturalists possessed many since the latter had need of deities to preside over and to explain the various requirements and functions of agriculture and the divisions of labor involved therein.[48] Third, very early religions were localized inasmuch as group fantasy attached itself to special places, natural oddities, or objects (fetishes),[49] and inasmuch as religion was lodged in the group itself and in its deified ancestors; hence, such groups neither possessed a universalizable religion nor did they proselytize. Indeed, the more indifferent they were to the religion of other groups, the greater their own internal cohesion, according to Kautsky.[50] Fourth, such religions as these were serene, joyous, and tolerant.[51] This was particularly true of the early Teutonic peoples, for, if Kautsky was correct, their religion was an exuberant affair.[52] These rather unexceptional points occasion two comments. First, it may be inconsistent to say that the more indifferent a religiously idiosyncratic and isolated group is toward others the greater its internal cohesion and then to say that in normal times the members of such groups pay little attention to religion. It all depends on what religion is taken to be whether or not the individual pays little attention to it. Kautsky was confused on this point. Second, religions which are serene, joyous, and even exuberant, if such

---

[47] Kautsky, MG, II, 809.
[48] Kautsky, MG, I, 33.
[49] Kautsky, *Christianity*, p. 162; *More*, p. 74.
[50] Kautsky, "Religion II," p. 355.
[51] Kautsky, *More*, pp. 73-74.
[52] *Ibid.*, p. 74.

there be, are difficult to comprehend in the terms of exploitation, alienation, and palliation given by Marx, Engels, and Lenin. In entertaining such notions, Kautsky appears again to have dallied in the fields of heterodoxy.

Comparative Religions

Although Kautsky did not examine in detail the various historical religions outside the Judeo-Christian tradition, he did establish a position of great importance to comparative religion if true. He contended that it was scientifically inadmissible to distinguish one religion from another, for religion was simply that which was common to all so-called religions.[53] Since he took the doctrines of all religions to be cognitively vacuous, it sufficed to discover their common etiology, nature, and functions. Of etiology, enough has already been written, and since I shall examine Kautsky's views on the nature and functions of religion later, it will do here merely to note that he assumed all genuine religions to involve belief in spiritual beings and in a personal God or gods. Against the claim that original Buddhism was both atheistic and religious, he pointed out that atheism was true of Buddhism only insofar as it was a philosophy. As a religion, it was by no means godless, assimilating a host of older gods to itself.[54] Indeed, its broad and rapid expansion demanded no less. In any case it is not the mere idea of God that constitutes religion. When Kant for example, arrived at the postulation of God on the basis of practical reason, it was by no means a religious act but merely a metaphysical conception:

Der Glaube, das ist das Wesentliche jeder historischen, wirklichen Religion, dadurch unterscheidet sie sich von jeder Wissenschaft, jeder Philosophie, ganz abgesehen davon, ob ihre Resultate mit denen der Wissenschaft übereinstimmen oder nicht. Die Religion fordert volle *Gläubigkeit*, die Wissenschaft fordert *Prüfung*.[55]

RELIGION FROM BIBLICAL TIMES TO THE TWENTIETH CENTURY

Judaism: Biblical and Non-Biblical

Kautsky had little interest in Judaism as one religion among many. To him the Jews began religiously as did other peoples at a common level of

---

[53] Kautsky, "Religion II," p. 353.
[54] *Ibid.*
[55] *Ibid.*, p. 354.

development.[56] Initially they were polytheistic, and fetishistic, and viewed the after-life in Sheol much as the Greeks envisioned Hades.[57] Observing that all popular monotheistic religions emerged from peoples without developed art and industry who still clung to nomadic thought patterns,[58] Kautsky also noted that the Diaspora led to Jewish residence in metropolitan areas in which ethical monotheism developed out of specifically urban conditions.[59] Basically indifferent to the state yet tenaciously attached to their ethnic identity, the Jews of the Roman Empire lived, according to him, a contradictory existence involving tendencies toward universal ethical monotheism on the one hand and tribal ethical monotheism on the other.[60] Forced into the ghetto by Christians, the Jew became both the haggling merchant of tradition and the isolated intellectual who could not enter the modern world completely because of socio-economic restrictions and the conservative fetters of his religion.[61] Of all Jewish characteristics, however, the most notable one to Kautsky was urbanization:

We need only to note the influence of the urban environment on human beings at this day, the alterations in the country-dweller when exposed to the influence of city life, and then to recall that the Jews are the only race on earth that had constituted a purely urban population for approximately two thousand years: we now have an almost perfect explanation of Jewish traits. *They are an exaggerated form of urban traits in general.* I used the urban traits as early as 1890 in order to explain the Jewish character. The Jew has become the city dweller par excellence. The uniformity of the artificial environment imparted to the Jews everywhere a uniform mental type, in spite of all the variations in their natural environment, and all the differences in the inherited race elements. If this uniform type should be accepted as a race type, the descendent of the *homo alpinus* might be designated as the *homo urbanus.*[62]

To Kautsky, the greatest hope of the modern Jew lay in *"an energetic participation in the class struggle of the proletariat."*[63] Given proletarian victory, the Jew would be fully liberated and in this condition would

---

[56] Kautsky, *Christianity*, p. 162.

[57] *Ibid.*, p. 244.

[58] *Ibid.*, p. 163.

[59] *Ibid.*, p. 218.

[60] *Ibid.*, pp. 208, 220.

[61] Karl Kautsky, *Are the Jews a Race?* (New York: International Publishers, 1926), pp. 147, 245 (hereinafter referred to as *Jews*).

[62] *Ibid.*, p. 130.

[63] *Ibid.*, p. 239.

neither have cause to fear assimilation nor occasion to repine over the declining significance of religion, his own included.[64]

Primitive Christianity

With the writing of *Christianity* Kautsky returned by his own admission to an old love.[65] His purpose was neither to extole nor to stigmatize Christianity but to explain it from the standpoint of the materialist conception of history.[66] Initially Christianity arose among the proletariat, if by that one merely means the propertyless or those constituting the lowest classes of society.[67] More narrowly conceived, this society was, of course, Jewish and from it the early Christians inherited "monotheism, Messianism, belief in resurrection, and Essenian communism.[68] Broadly conceived, the society in question was Roman, many elements of which reinforced the Jewish fantasies itemized above. The Roman world witnessed the decomposition of traditional forms of government, production, and thought.[69] The civic *virtus* of the classic Roman and the *arete* of the Greek were destroyed leaving only public lassitude and servility.[70] The ruination of peasants and craftsmen and the misery of slaves denied inherent value to labor and left no hope for worthwhile work in a better society. The result was a futile yearning for resurrection and heavenly peace.[71] In these circumstances the gods, whom Greek science had nearly destroyed, were reborn, and the "sheep's nature" of men in the Roman Empire created heroes, saviors, and deified rulers to meet their needs.[72] Viewed in this way, it is little wonder that Kautsky denied the importance of ideas and heroes in the creation of Christianity, but affirmed instead that it was the product of objective conditions.

Unlike Bauer who denied historicity to Jesus, Kautsky was content to grant him existence but denied him an overpowering personality.[73] Furthermore, he denied uniqueness to Christian beliefs, contended that they were commonplace, requiring no sublime prophet for their revelation,

---

[64] *Ibid.*, pp. 214-242.
[65] Kautsky, *Christianity*, Author's Foreword, p. xi.
[66] *Ibid.*, pp. xi, xvii.
[67] Kautsky, *Christianity*, pp. 114, 272-274.
[68] *Ibid.*, p. 350.
[69] *Ibid.*, pp. 58-59, 86.
[70] *Ibid.*, p. 117.
[71] *Ibid.*, p. 45.
[72] *Ibid.*, pp. 99, 145.
[73] *Ibid.*, p. 382.

and claimed that we can know nothing of Jesus' views anyway.[74] But, according to Kautsky, Jesus was different from other Messiahs in that he bequeathed a communal organization with institutions adapted to holding his adherents together.[75] So outstanding was this organization that its very success led to belief in Jesus' resurrection and abiding presence. Since the idea of resurrection was important to those struggling to overthrow the decadent Roman social system, Christianity came not as a stranger but as a welcome friend.[76] Even so, it was not only the idea of everlasting life but also the communal organization designed by Jesus which permitted Christianity to vault from Judaism into the larger Roman world:

The notion of the Messiah could take root outside of Judaism only in the communistic form of the Christian community, of the crucified Messiah. It was only by faith in the Messiah and the resurrection that the communistic organization could establish itself and grow as a secret league in the Roman Empire. United, these two ideas—communism and belief in the Messiah—became irresistible.[77]

Reflecting (especially in Lk. 6:20-25, 16:19-31, 18:24-25, and Jas. 5:1) the fierce class hatred which characterized the Roman Empire, Christianity had enticed even the rich to enter its sacred precincts by the third century and had lost its class hatred.[78] Becoming anti-Jewish after the destruction of Jerusalem and transferring belief in the resurrected life in the Kingdom of God to faith in the immortality of the soul in Heaven or Hell,[79] Christianity evolved "from Judaism to Romanism, from proletarianism to world dominion, from the organization of communism to the exploitation of all classes."[80] Accompanying the recruitment of the rich and worldly to its ranks, an elitist bureaucracy developed in Christendom simultaneously with the establishment of doctrinal orthodoxy.[81] Despite social conditions similar to those in which Christianity was born, it took the developing Roman Church only four centuries to change primitive Christianity into its opposite.[82]

The most egregious deficiency in Kautsky's explanation of primitive

---

[74] *Ibid.*, p. 275.
[75] *Ibid.* p. 321.
[76] *Ibid.*, p. 325.
[77] *Ibid.*
[78] *Ibid.*, pp. 274, 276-77, 361.
[79] *Ibid.*, p. 351.
[80] *Ibid.*, pp. 309, 350.
[81] *Ibid.*, pp. 380-381.
[82] *Ibid.*, p. 388.

Christianity lay in his failure to take the eschatological framework of New Testament thought seriously. This does not mean that he ignored it. On the contrary, he attempted a cursory exegesis of several of the most important eschatological passages.[83] But very much like the theological liberals whose ideas Schweitzer sought to correct in *The Quest of the Historical Jesus*, Kautsky failed to understand the significance of eschatology. In writing *Christianity* he relied on a dozen or more important scholars, including Pfleiderer, Strauss, Wellhausen, Holzmann, and Harnack, but not once did he mention Schweitzer nor refer to his epochal work, even though it had been published two years before *Christianity*.

Noting that Jesus had said that his generation would not pass away before a galaxy of apocalyptic events, ending the age, had occurred (Mk. 13:30; Lk. 21:32), that he had informed his disciples that they would not have completed their trek throughout diminutive Israel before the Son of Man came (Matt. 10:23), and that there were some standing beside him who would not die before the Kingdom of God arrived in power and glory (Mk. 9:1), Kautsky, nevertheless, seemed unable to comprehend that anyone could accept these prophecies. This was his greatest mistake. Had he taken primitive Christian eschatology at face value, he could not have bemoaned, as he did, the failure of the New Testament to glorify productive labor,[84] could not have been righteously indignant over its failure to proscribe slavery,[85] and could not have made light of the contention that Jesus never intended to initiate an economic revolution.[86] The earliest Christians never entertained the notion that man could improve his earthly lot, nor was there any need to try, for the *eschaton* was at hand when the Son of Man, appearing on clouds of glory, would judge the quick and the dead, would establish the kingdom of righteousness, and would inaugurate the new age on behalf of the Heavenly Father.

Taken seriously, primitive Christian eschatology leaves in shambles Kautsky's novel conjecture that Jesus bequeathed his disciples an extraordinary organization replete with institutions well-designed to guarantee its survival. From the standpoint of belief in the sudden and cataclysmic end of the present world order, there would have been no more point in developing such an organization than there would have been in devising a scheme of socio-economic revolution or in recruiting the devil for

---

[83] *Ibid.*, pp. 301-302.
[84] *Ibid.*, p. 95.
[85] *Ibid.*, pp. 121-122.
[86] *Ibid.*, p. 284.

subterranean reform. As far as the New Testament is concerned, church organization developed spontaneously and in a variety of ways at least until the second century A.D.[87]

Failing to take a thoroughly functional approach to religion, Kautsky appears to have been both amazed and chagrined that Christianity could have been transmogrified in a mere three centuries from proletarian communism to world dominion and exploitation. Far more important and fundamental than these changes was the transformation forced on the Christian movement by the failure of its Lord to return as promised and by its unexpected entry into a world which was to have suffered cosmic tribulation, including a darkened sun, a bloodied moon, and fallen stars galore, but which witnessed no such prodigies. Of these matters involving the very survival of Christianity he had little to say beyond observing that the ongoing church, largely centered in urban areas, had to forsake its primitive communism suited to agrarian conditions and adjust to private property and commodity production.[88]

A second serious problem with Kautsky's materialistic explanation of Christian origins lies in his summary denial of charismatic greatness to Jesus. If, as he contended, the times were such that heroes were being made to meet human needs, then the times were also such that some were more likely candidates for myth-making and hero-worship than others. Since Kautsky wished to deny significance to ideas per se in the development of Christianity, it was important to him to note that Jesus' greatest moral teachings were already in the Old Testament and that Essenic communal organization was available for Christian appropriation. Kautsky was also aware that the apocalyptic and eschatological elements of the New Testament were commonplace to Intertestamental Judaism.[89] The parallelism Bultmann has shown between Jesus' parables and those of contemporary rabbis also reinforces Kautsky's position.[90] But, if one denies moral, religious, and intellectual uniqueness to Jesus, and if, contrary to Kautsky's opinion, one is also forced to deny him organizational genius, then what is left, if not charisma, to explain his apparent impact on early Christianity?

---

[87] Howard Clark Kee and Franklin W. Young, *Understanding the New Testament* (Englewood Cliffs, N. J.: Prentice-Hall, Inc., 1957), pp. 354-357.

[88] Kautsky, *Christianity*, pp. 352, 358.

[89] *Ibid.*, p. 236.

[90] Rudolf Bultmann, *Jesus and the Word*, trans. by L. P. Smith and E. H. Lantero (New York: Charles Scribner's Sons, 1958), pp. 57-61.

Finally, since by his own admission, the conditions which led to Christianity initially were the same as those which eventually led to the creation of its alleged opposite, one may question whether or not Kautsky possessed the variables necessary to explain early Christianity. If he did, then his interpretation of these variables, equally productive of contradictory results, is radically deficient or misconceived.

Roman Catholicism

In 1908, Kautsky wrote that we can have no certain knowledge of any "genuine doctrine of Jesus," but by 1913 he had learned somehow that priests had transformed Jesus' desires into their opposites.[91] He arrived at this conclusion first by taking the short-lived and localized communism of the Jerusalem Church as normative for Christianity and then by comparing it with the condition of the Roman Church under Constantine in the fourth century. Although there can be no doubt that Nicene Christianity was strikingly different from primitive Christianity, it cannot be shown, as Kautsky thought, that the Jerusalem Church faithfully reflected the moral, religious, and organizational intentions of Jesus; nor can it be assumed that the fourth century church was in fact different from what Jesus had intended it to be four centuries after his time, since there is no reason to believe that he intended a religious organization inspired by his person and teaching to endure indefinitely.

Although Kautsky deplored the loss of democracy and the simultaneous growth of bureaucracy and orthodoxy in the Catholic Church,[92] charged it with hypocrisy for preaching ethical universalism while practicing moral particularism,[93] took it to task for falsifying primitive Christianity,[94] and accused it of massive exploitation,[95] still and all, he did not employ the vehemence typical of the denunciations which Marx, Engels, and Lenin had hurled at Christendom. In fact, there were times when he seemed to regard the church as a useful, or even a necessary, social entity, if not a benign one. Illustrative of this point are his contentions that Christian law held the degenerating Roman State together while its priests "tamed the

---

[91] Kautsky, *Christianity*, pp. 21, 382; "Religion I," p. 182.

[92] Kautsky, *Christianity*, p. 380.

[93] Kautsky, *Ethics*, p. 98.

[94] Karl Kautsky, *Communism in Central Europe in the Time of the Reformation* (New York: Russell and Russell, 1959), p. 10 (hereinafter referred to as *Communism in Reformation*).

[95] Kautsky, *Christianity*, p. 388; *Communism in Reformation*, p. 29.

barbarious,"[96] that the church was the principal source and repository of knowledge for the peasantry,[97] and that it was indispensable to society at times, especially in the Middle Ages.[98]

To Kautsky, Catholicism was, of course, no single thing, and he never tired of distinguishing between the "old, feudal, popular Catholicism," represented at its best by Thomas More, and modern Jesuitical Catholicism, nor did he refrain from noting that the Church was sometimes less exploitive than at other times, and even progressive on occasion.[99] The greatest disappointment I find in his treatment of Catholicism lies in his failure to pursue the implications for religion of his own assertion that in dominating medieval life the church insinuated itself into all areas, including birth, death, and celebration.[100] Like Marx, Engels, and Lenin, he too failed to understand the importance of the rites of passage for religion.

Radical Christianity

The direct analysis of such major Protestant movements as Lutheranism, Calvinism, and Anglicanism played so small a part in Kautsky's thought that no special section dealing with them is warranted. Since his views on mainline Protestantism can best be expressed in the context of his opinions on types of radical Christianity, I will present them in due time in that way.

Class hatred, hostility to wealth, the adoption of communism, and interest in a better social order characterized primitive Christianity, according to Kautsky,[101] and made it revolutionary from the standpoint of existing society, but its passivity and lack of political rebelliousness rendered it incapable of changing that society.[102] Enduring indefinitely in a world order which was supposed to have been terminated, Christianity discovered itself capable of meeting the religious needs of the times and of appealing to all classes. Thus, the church developed as a permanent fixture in an ongoing world. Becoming institutionalized, bureaucratized,

---

[96] Kautsky, *Ethics*, pp. 8-9.

[97] Karl Kautsky, *Terrorism and Communism,* trans. by W. H. Kerridge (London: The National Labour Press, Ltd., 1920), pp. 10-11.

[98] Kautsky, *Communism in Reformation*, pp. 9, 29.

[99] Kautsky, *More*, pp. 74, 77-79.

[100] *Ibid.*, p. 36.

[101] Kautsky, *Christianity*, pp. 276-277, 324, 350; *Communism in Reformation*, p. 10; *Ethics*, p. 121.

[102] Kautsky, *Communism in Reformation*, p. 28.

and exploitive, the Roman Church either minimized or repudiated the social intentions of primitive Christianity. These intentions and characteristics were not entirely lost, however, but re-emerged in monasticism and broke out from time to time in what appeared to the church to be heretical movements.[103]

Kautsky referred to the social organization of primitive Christianity as "an equalizing communism" by which he meant "the division and distribution of the rich man's superfluity" among the destitute.[104] In other words, it was a communism of distribution but not of production. The doctrines of the New Testament reflecting this type of communism by no means led to its reappearance in medieval times. On the contrary, the exploitive conditions of the period resurrected it. Those who protested against these conditions, holding communal aspirations instead, merely found reinforcement for their views in the Scriptures. With reference to the Middle Ages, Kautsky wrote:

Thus the primitive Christian doctrine which had found its chief supporters among a tatterdemalian proletariat, now fell on fertile soil; the doctrine that poverty is no crime, but rather a providential, God-given condition, demanding earnest consideration. According to the teaching of the gospel the poor man was a representative of Christ. . . .[105]

Even though the church took these views to be heretical, at least when applied universally, it must be remembered that to Kautsky heresy was not really derived from ideological sources but was merely reflective of social conditions.[106]

Although monastic orders and sectarian societies in the Middle Ages traced the inspiration for their models of social organization to the primitive Christian communism of distribution, the two groups diverged greatly. To Kautsky, the monks, "having long ceased to be workers, had become exploiters, their communism consisting merely in the common consumption of booty."[107] Moreover, they supported the papacy and were given to asceticism and mysticism.[108] Unlike the monastic orders, such sectarians as the Waldenses, Apostolicans, Beghards, and Lollards, doting on New Testament apocalypticism, preserved the revolutionary fire of the first Christians. With the passing of the Middle Ages, such groups

---

[103] Kautsky, *Christianity*, pp. 389-390; *Communism in Reformation*, pp. 9, 14.
[104] Kautsky, *Communism in Reformation*, pp. 8-9.
[105] *Ibid.*, p. 7.
[106] *Ibid.*, p. 29.
[107] *Ibid.*, p. 14.
[108] *Ibid.*, p. 18.

became increasingly rebellious and political.[109] In this manner, they served as a transmission belt conveying the spirit of radical Christian equality and universalism to the plebeian movements of the sixteenth century. Thus, according to Kautsky, the heretical socialism of the Reformation came to play the same role then as that played by labor in 1848.[110] In making this point, Kautsky had in mind the Anabaptists (the industrious, if mystical, forerunners of modern socialism),[111] Thomas Münzer (the embodiment of heretical communism),[112] and the Peasant War.[113] Receiving their communism in an unbroken tradition from the Middle Ages, the Anabaptists could not, however, bequeath it to the modern workers' movement in the same manner, because portentious developments were about to occur:

As a real, effective force in public life, Christian communism came to an end in the sixtienth century. That century saw the birth of a new system of production, the modern State and the modern proletariat; and it saw also the birth of modern socialism.[8]

Meanwhile, Calvinism, its values already accepted by the rising bourgeoisie, was bestirring itself to sanction capitalistic society,[115] and Luther, convinced *"that communistic sectarians should in no case be permitted to thrive,"* was preparing to make his doctrines agreeable to monarchs and nationalists.[116] In addition to this, social conditions were so grievous for the masses by the sixteenth century that the Reformation acted as a catalyst in reintroducing the more sinister side of religion. Kautsky wrote:

This situation powerfully stimulated the religious-need, the longing for a better hereafter, the impulse to recognize an omnipotent God, who alone seemed able to make an end of the universal misery. At the same time religion lost its serene and benevolent character, and developed its darker and crueller sides. The devil reappeared, and men's imaginations were busy painting him in the blackest colours. The torments of hell were revived and partially realized on earth in the cruelties inflicted upon the living. Witch hunting and witch burning were concomitants of the bloody legislation against beggars and vagabonds.[117]

Unlike Marx who in comparison with Catholicism found Lutheranism in particular, if not Protestantism in general, to be progressive, Kautsky took

---

[109] *Ibid.,* pp. 24-25, 28.
[110] *Ibid.,* pp. 4-5.
[111] *Ibid.,* pp. 22-23, 256, 262, 291.
[112] *Ibid.,* p. 154.
[113] *Ibid.,* pp. 278-293.
[114] *Ibid.,* p. 293.
[115] *Ibid.,* p. 22.
[116] *Ibid.,* p. 118; *More,* p. 2.
[117] Kautsky, *More,* p. 77.

it as a whole to be regressive. It is clear that in comparison with Protestantism he preferred the old "Teutonic-Catholic" popular religion of pre-Reformation times and the religion of Thomas More both as More exemplified it personally and as he expressed it in his *Utopia*, this work being more progressive religiously than any church of the age.[118]

Religion in the Twentieth Century

According to Kautsky, "the various Protestant sects and Jesuitical, Tridentine Catholicism" constitute that which modern western man takes to be religion.[119] Since these groups were essentially developed from 1525 to 1648, Kautsky paid little attention to denominational movements after that time. He did, however, observe that it was the grim religion of the sixteenth century which collided with the philosophers of the Enlightenment.[120] Taking post-Reformation Protestantism and Catholicism to be paradigmatic and having no knowledge of other more benign forms of religion for purposes of comparison, these savants assaulted all religions as if they were equally superstitious and evil. It was largely in this vein that the early nineteenth century thinkers, including Marx and Engels, approached religion. Not until late in the century did such scholars as Tylor and Cunow make it possible to approach religion objectively. But with scientific methods available and with ethnographical data becoming ever more abundant, one could proceed in the twentieth century, as Kautsky thought he was doing, to the construction of an adequate materialist theory of religion.

The natural root of religion had already been smashed in the twentieth century by the advances of "industrial capitalism" and by "scientific thought."[121] Modern technological achievements were making men ever more competent to control their environment and to provide the necessities of life, and scientific explanation of natural phenomena was depriving the world of mystery and leaving ever smaller spheres of action to the gods. Many were abandoning religion for science, and theology was clearly losing power in society,[122] some theologians already having ceased to believe in God.[123]

---

[118] *Ibid.*, pp. 78-79, 242.

[119] *Ibid.*, p. 78.

[120] *Ibid.*, pp. 77-78.

[121] Kautsky, *Jews*, p. 12; "Religion II," p. 357.

[122] Karl Kautsky, *The Social Revolution*, trans. by A. M. and Mary Wood Simons (Chicago: Charles H. Kerr and Company, 1910), p. 11.

[123] Kautsky, "Religion II," p. 357.

Still and all, Kautsky discovered an increasing need for religion during the first third of the twentieth century. He explained this widespread urge to believe, at a time when belief was increasingly difficult, by reference to social conditions.[124] According to him, capitalistic society promoted an extreme degree of egotism which was detrimental to group feeling and unity.[125] The social dissolution which ensued was productive of religion. Conditions of exploitation, competition, restless striving for wealth, anarchy in production, and world conflict, typical of twentieth century capitalism, served as the nutrients which kept the religious growth alive through its one remaining (i.e., social) root.[126] In a society riven by class opposition, the exploitive group, seeing its way of life threatened by the dispossessed, resort to God as a policeman defending the traditional morality. Meanwhile, the dispossessed, having lost faith in the Established Church, seek, and miraculously find, a new and surprising disposition on the part of the old God to uphold new, proletarian, values.[127] When class struggles assume the form or religious struggles, religion, according to Kautsky, enters its last phase beyond which lies complete annihilation.[128] Given the ethical and political idealism of triumphant socialism, those who, in the future, might still turn to religion for comfort and enlightenment would be rare indeed.[129]

THE SUBSTANCE AND FUNCTIONS OF RELIGION

The Substance of Religion

Assessing Cunow's failure to define religion as unfortunate, Kautsky observed that there is scarcely another word more ambiguous and vague than it. In witness thereto, he noted that he had once used "religion" in three different ways on a single page.[130] There is perhaps no better way of approaching his final views on the essential character of religion than to examine each of the three meanings he crowed onto the page in question.

First, if one wishes to use the term religion in the best sense of the word, it means nothing, according to Kautsky, beyond self-sacrificial love

---

[124] *Ibid.*, p. 358.

[125] *Ibid.*, p. 356.

[126] *Ibid.*, p. 359.

[127] *Ibid.*, p. 356; *Communism in Reformation*, pp. 8, 20.

[128] Kautsky, "Religion II," p. 356.

[129] *Ibid.*, p. 358.

[130] *Ibid.*, p. 352.

for one's neighbor, or, in other words, practical idealism. "Im diesem Sinne predigt auch die Sozialdemokratie Religion, und zwar höhere Religion."[131] Granted that it could be christened in this way, Kautsky was not eager to do so, for to cast social democracy in the guise of a superior religion struggling to overcome its inferiors would be to enhance the importance of religion.[132] The point, however, was to recruit men for class struggles not religious struggles, since the latter had already become jejune.[133] Thus, while welcoming churchbelieving workers into the party, Kautsky preferred not to call it the true religion, even though it might be perceived in this way in the best sense of the word.

Second, Kautsky spoke of "religion-itself" by which he meant nothing more than attempts to solve those perennial conundrums of existence which, inaccessible to science, are mistakenly assumed by spiritualists to be amenable to metaphysics.[134] Herein lies a puzzle, for later in "Religion II" he observed that religion did not stem from the desire of the individual to explain insoluble riddles and that religion was not an attempt to gain ultimate enlightenment.[135] But in *More* he had said that the need for religion developed from the time man began to ponder until the emergence of science and that the nature religions were created by the need to understand natural forces.[136] He also made these points in both *Christianity* and *Ethics*.[137] If this constitutes neither a contradiction nor an oversight in Kautsky's thought, then, perhaps "Religion I" and the *Geschichtsauffassung* can throw some light on the problem, if not clarify it altogether.

In the former source, Kautsky had noted that at first there was no *philosophical need* to explain natural forces but only an economic need to control them.[138] He reinforced this point in the latter source by announcing that religion strove both to explain nature and to control it.[139] Kautsky seems to have assumed that if he could invariably link the explanatory aspect of religion with immediate, practical, needs, then he could deny that the explanatory elements of religion sprang from any innate mentalistic needs of mankind. Accordingly, all religious attempts at

---

[131] *Ibid.*
[132] *Ibid.*, p. 353.
[133] *Ibid.*
[134] *Ibid.*, p. 352.
[135] *Ibid.*, p. 358.
[136] Kautsky, *More*, p. 73.
[137] Kautsky, *Christianity*, pp. 144-145; *Ethics*, p. 5.
[138] Kautsky, "Religion I," p. 188.
[139] Kautsky, MG, I, 33; II, 809.

understanding the world were really attempts at controlling it. But, if so, what about the large number of modern people who, scientifically advanced and having no immediate needs to control natural forces as primitives did, nevertheless, continue to fall for what Kautsky called "spiritualistic swindles"?[140] His answer was that these needs were not inherent but were the result of the social disintegration produced by capitalism. Thus, the perennial questions of metaphysics, traditionally answered by religion, were not to him perennial but transient, occasioned alike by the need to control the natural environment and by the necessity of dealing with social distress.

But since science, no matter how advanced, does not in fact answer the metaphysical questions at issue, perennial or not, we shall have to wait until the complete triumph of socialism to get empirical data as to whether or not religious queries will continue to arise when the environment is under control, when production is made rational and society classless. It is impossible to determine at the moment whether or not religious specula-tion occurs only in response to the kinds of practical needs specified by Kautsky.

Third, in addition to speaking of religion in the best sense of the word and of "religion-itself," Kautsky wrote of actual religions, i.e., of the garden variety of historico-dogmatic faiths.[141] The actual religions of the world were, to him, the products of manifold social influences whereby men sought to control the spirit world for practical purposes.[142] Accordingly, he was quick to contend that the mere idea of God does not create religion,[143] that metaphysical constructions per se do not meet religious needs,[144] and that religion was not, originally at least, a striving for high ethical teachings.[145] Despite superficial similarities between metaphysical conceptions and abstract moral principles on the one hand and religion on the other, there could be no real religion to Kautsky unless there was active group faith in personalized spiritual beings whose disposition and power could be instrumental in meeting human economic and social needs. Ever at pains to emphasize the social nature of religion, Kautsky distinguished it from magic by noting that the former was a mode of collective activity whereas the latter was a form of private, egocentric,

---

[140] Kautsky, "Religion II," p. 358.

[141] *Ibid.*, p. 352.

[142] *Ibid.*, p. 358; *Christianity*, p. 308; MG, II, 808.

[143] Kautsky, "Religion II," p. 354.

[144] *Ibid.*

[145] *Ibid.*, p. 355.

practice.[146] Moreover, refusing to distinguish between the intellectual contents of religion and superstition, Kautsky viewed the former as the socially accepted pattern of dealing with the spirit world and the latter as the attempt of the individual to develop an idiosyncratic faith in opposition to prevailing opinion.[147]

The Functions of Religion

To Kautsky, as to Marx, Engels, and Lenin, religion was to be understood more in terms of function than of substance, and to him, as to them, religious functions could appropriately be subdivided into the spontaneous and the manipulative. Since the preceding pages contain much, explicitly or implicitly, about the functions of religion, it suffices here to give a critical summary. Kautsky's assertion that religion is a mode of practical striving efficacious in controlling the spirit world against nature, enemies, and social disintregration can serve as an outline for his views on both the spontaneous and manipulative functions of religion.[148]

By "nature" Kautsky meant to designate both the elemental forces which threaten man occasionally and the economic scarcity with which the world generally confronts him. Far from being an end in itself or a means toward meeting innate needs of the spirit, religion operates only in practical situations.[149] God, for example, loses religious significance when he is used as a factor in metaphysical explanation and not taken as an object of faith. By "enemies" Kautsky meant to identify not only external dangers to group life but also threats to psychological well-being. If social conditions, for instance, are such that the individual feels insecure, incompetent, and forsaken, religion will function in such a way as to provide security, assistance, and salvation.[150] In short, to all who have faith, but who cannot meet their own needs, it will supply consolation.[151] By "social disintegration" Kautsky had in mind those forces associated with class society and exploitation which weaken the social fabric by setting group against group. Since religion has functioned from the beginning as a means of social unity, it is not surprising to find it reasserting itself in conditions of social disintegration such as those typical of the twentieth century.

---

[146] Kautsky, MG, I, 301.
[147] Ibid.
[148] Kautsky, "Religion II," p. 358.
[149] Ibid.
[150] Kautsky, Christianity, pp. 101, 114.
[151] Kautsky, More, p. 72; "Religion II," pp. 358-359.

From the standpoint of manipulation, it was clear to Kautsky that the ruling class required religious sanctions in order to maintain its position. In the Middle Ages, for example, aristocrats used the Church for their own ulterior purposes even though they were contemptuous of it,[152] and in modern times the bourgeoisie have called upon religion repeatedly to help guarantee that the proletariat will respect the law and order which enable the propertied classes to flourish.[153]

As summarized, Kautsky's position is vulnerable to criticism at two important points. First, although it may be granted that religion functions only in the sphere of the practical, he did not conceive of the practical in terms broad enough to account for all relevant data. His analysis was deficient in accounting for the relationship of religion to ritual activities in general and to group celebration and participation in rites of passage in particular, and in accounting for the psychological significance of religion as an element in the *Weltanschauung* of the normal individual, whether or not the person in question has been made exceptionally needy by social conditions. Second, Kautsky permitted confusion to enter his thought by failing to distinguish between the kinds of morality which the Utilitarians have called "positive" and "critical" and between the kinds of society which Bergson referred to as "closed" and "open." In fact, Kautsky often spoke of the relationship of religion to morality and society as if these distinctions did not exist. For example, when he referred to religion as a means to the social unity of a primitive group and simultaneously affirmed that such religion was devoid of ethical striving, he was referring to religion in relationship to the "positive morality" of a "closed society," but when he spoke of the increasing necessity for and production of religion in times of diminishing social feeling and noted how classes in such circumstances could adopt old gods and put them to new moral uses, he was referring to the "critical morality" of a class or party in a relatively "open society." One is left to wonder whether or not the religion which unites groups but possesses no ethical striving is the same as the religion which can support the ethical striving of hostile groups in a society lacking unity.

To pursue a different tack for a time, Kautsky was perfectly aware that hostile groups, sharing a common tradition, could select divergent materials from their heritage which were useful to their respective class interests.[154]

---

[152] Kautsky, *Terrorism and Communism*, p. 11.
[153] Kautsky, "Religion II," p. 356.
[154] Kautsky, *Communism in Reformation*, pp. 8, 20.

When the ruling classes called upon God to support the "positive morality" which had been instrumental in their socio-economic success, he was quick to discern the class manipulation of religion for ulterior purposes, but when the dispossessed sought the blessings of God for their particular "critical morality" but the curses of God for what they took to be an evil "positive morality," Kautsky was not quick to discern the manipulation of religion for ulterior purposes. Thus, in addition to the categorial confusions, mentioned above, he occasionally selected data to suit partisan purposes.

The foregoing criticisms are not intended to suggest that Kautsky's position on the functions of religion is without merit. But, when to a lack of comprehensiveness one also adds a lack of analytic penetration, the result cannot be a thoroughly satisfying treatment of the subject at hand.

KAUTSKY: STALWART MARXIST OR RENEGADE?

This chapter began with Lenin's denunciation of Kautsky as a renegade, a vulgarian, and an opportunist. As the chapter unfolded it became clear that Kautsky had indeed revised some of Marx's and Engels' views on religion and had altered his own original position. He was, however, concerned to carry out these tasks in such a manner as to avoid being charged with what to him was the oprobrious label of "eclectic revisionism." The task now is to assess the degree to which he remained an orthodox and stalwart Marxist and the extent to which he was a revisionist, eclectic or not.

There are at least six points on which Kautsky remained in substantial unity with Marx and Engels. First, admitting as they had that there was interactionism between the substructure and superstructure of society,[155] he agreed with them that in the last analysis the mode of production was the determining factor in social formations,[156] that ideas were conditioned by their material base and that changes in ideas could be explained fully only in terms of socio-economic changes,[157] and that the understanding of religion required the study of actual conditions.[158] He reinforced these points by asserting that it was economic needs rather than mentalistic ones which led to God,[159] that it was social requirements rather than the

---

[155] Kautsky, MG, I, 817.
[156] Kautsky, *Christianity*, Author's Foreword, xiv; also p. 352.
[157] Kautsky, *More*, p. 62.
[158] Kautsky, *Christianity*, p. 23.
[159] Kautsky, "Religion I," p. 188.

needs of individual personalities which created religion,[160] and that heresy, for instance, was the product of conditions and not of religious fervor for unauthorized ideas.[161] Second, Kautsky, like Marx and Engels, denied that religious doctrines involving the supernatural could be true and, like them, refused in terms of intellectual form and content to distinguish between superstition and religion.[162] In witness thereto, Kautsky seldom, if ever, missed an opportunity to degrade religious conceptions to the realm of the fantastic, to ridicule such spiritualists as Maeterlinck, and to chide theologians for their errant ways.[163] Third, recognizing the profoundly conservative functions of religion in society, Marx, Engels, and Kautsky, nevertheless, agreed that religious ethics were relative and charged all who thought otherwise with hypocrisy.[164] Fourth, since the dream life which had initiated the fantasy of God could no longer support that idea,[165] since there was no inherent spiritual need for religion,[166] and since science and industry were progressively destroying it,[167] Kautsky, like his mentors, concluded that religion was withering away and that it would, one day, vanish.[168] Fifth, the failure to analyze the sacred, to examine ritual in sufficient depth, and to assess fully the significance to religion of belief in post-mortem existence constitute a common weakness in the thought of Marx, Engels, and Kautsky and reveal a common perspective on religion. Sixth, neither Marx and Engels nor Kautsky advised the forcible destruction of religion and its institutions.

Having noted six points in which Marx, Engels, and Kautsky were in complete or in nearly complete agreement, I should like now to turn to six points in which varying degrees of disunity can be discerned.

First, although he bore early witness to the twofold etiology of religion common to Marx and Engels, Kautsky modified it substantially by denying that natural religion was primary, by making it the second phase of an evolutionary development, and by denying that threatening social forces caused religious behavior prior to the mass production of commodities. Refusing to discount natural religion until the end of the Middle Ages,

---

[160] Kautsky, "Religion II," p. 354.
[161] Kautsky, *Communism in Reformation*, p. 29.
[162] Kautsky, MG, I, 301.
[163] Kautsky, "Religion II," pp. 358-359.
[164] *Ibid.*, p. 356.
[165] *Ibid.*, p. 358.
[166] *Ibid.*, p. 359.
[167] *Ibid.*, p. 357.
[168] *Ibid.*, p. 356.

Kautsky regarded threatening social forces as the primary cause of religious life from that time onward. Indeed, the religious revival he discerned just prior to World War I was an example of how a society involving class structure, capitalism, and exploitation could be productive of religion at a time when the forces leading to natural religion had become inconsequential among advanced peoples.

Second, by introducing animism to the original Marxist etiology of religion, Kautsky, like Engels, foisted a novel element upon Marxism. Unlike Engels, however, Kautsky was fully aware of the deed and unapologetic over keeping Marxism in step with what he took to be the newest in scientific anthropology. Although his adoption of animism altered Marx's conception of the origin of religion significantly, anticipations concerning the fate of religion, which Marx, Engels, and Kautsky relished together, were left untouched.

Third, since Kautsky had self-conciously combined animism with the materialistic explanation of religion, had modified Marx's etiology of religion, and was eventually to introject elements of French structuralism into the equation, he did not emphasize the role of fear in religion to the degree which characterized Marx and Engels. Consequently, he could not logically dwell upon the consolatory-palliative functions of religion so much as they had, nor did he. In short, man was not, to Kautsky, so craven a creature nor so oppressed by religion as Marx and Engels would have it. On the contrary, religion could to Kautsky be a joyous affair given the proper circumstances and was not invariably associated with the tribulations of class society. Moreover, as Engels had already noticed, religion could stimulate men to class action in opposition to exploitation; hence its effect could not entirely be that of an opiate.

Fourth, although Kautsky knew that the gods are made as men find themselves, that secular interests masquerade as sacred concerns, and that religion is often a celestial reflection of terrestrial forms, still he did not regard it as merely reflective, as an inessentiality having no history. On the contrary, given primitive man's dream experience and the social requirements of group life, religion was inevitable and had its own history, largely perhaps but not completely reflective of socio-economic factors as Marx and Engels had conceived them.[169]

Fifth, Kautsky took a more generous attitude toward medieval Catholicism than did Marx and Engels and appreciated the social utility of the church more than they. At the same time he was less enamored

---

[169] Kautsky, "Religion I," p. 182.

of Protestantism than either of his mentors. If the Reformation led to religious autonomy and was therefore preferable to Catholicism, it also introduced predestination and a more malevolent devil than had been suffered earlier. Clearly, Kautsky preferred More's religion to that of Luther or Calvin. Like Engels, but unlike Marx, Kautsky was quick to note resemblances between primitive Christianity and socialism and to feel partiality toward radical Christian sects whether lodged within Catholicism or Protestantism. In general, Kautsky was less hostile to religion than either Marx or Engels.

Sixth, although he may never have taken formal exception to certain concepts with which the young Marx characterized religion, they did not become trademarks of Kautsky's thought. I am thinking, for example, of Marx's assertion that religion is the self-consciousness of those who either have not yet found themselves or have already lost themselves. Such a view as this is inconsistent with Kautsky's animism and structuralism. To continue, he neither analyzed nor utilized the concept of alienation in his critique of religion. He spoke, rather, of specific economic and social fears and of their practical relationship to religion. Finally, the term "ideology" played only a perfunctory role in his critique.

Kautsky's most striking departure from the original Marxist position lay in the emphasis he placed on social feelings, morality, and group concern in the creation of religion within and on behalf of a given human group. This approach to religion stresses its utility and importance to group solidarity. Gone are such familiar Marxist themes as man's abject fear of nature, of his alienated condition in class society, and of his reduction to impotency by tyrannical forces of production.

Before arriving at a final assessment of Kautsky's credentials as a Marxist on the question of religion, it is appropriate to contrast him with his archenemy, Lenin. To begin with, in attitude toward religion, Lenin stood closer to Marx, whereas Kautsky was closer to Engels. While Lenin was giving essentially thoughtless, even atavistic, but always vehement expression to Marx's views on the subject, Kautsky was attempting to achieve scientific respectability for Marxism by trying, as Engels had haltingly begun to do, to keep it abreast of ethnographical advances. Developments which Kautsky took to be essential in constructing a revised materialist theory of religion would have been viewed by Lenin at best as instances of bourgeois anti-clericalism, at worst as counter-revolutionary claptrap.

To continue, Lenin could barely tolerate those who, for propaganda purposes, lapsed into theological jargon and would not suffer at all those who, whether god-seekers or god-builders, sought to reconcile Marxism with religion. Kautsky, on the other hand, was willing to cooperate with believers provided that their primary objective was to promote the proletarian cause and that religion remained strictly a private affair. Ever hostile toward religious exploitation and duplicity, continuously critical of god-seeking, and averse to god-building, Kautsky was convinced that the triumph of socialism would render all spiritualism irrelevant and obsolete. If, in the meantime, some misguided and overly imaginative workers mouthed the word "God," what possible difference could it make? It was far more important for Kautsky to keep Social Democracy free of compromising alliances and unsullied by association with various kinds of bourgeois liberalism, religious or political, than to worry over an occasional lapse from materialism.[170] But since Lenin was apprehensive that the slightest departure from materialism would permit agnostics to open the floodgates of faith, he sallied forth to do battle with philosophical skeptics. To Kautsky, it was unfitting for a Marxist to become as agitated, as Lenin clearly was, over mere ideas. Accordingly, he saw no need to write anything even remotely like *Materialism and Empirio-Criticism*.

Finally, it must be concluded that contemporary religion, whether in the party or out, did not pose a problem of intense concern to Kautsky as it did to Lenin on occasion, nor did he think that Social Democracy ought to be unduly exercised over it. Serene in the conviction that changing times and conditions would abolish religion, Kautsky was not given, as was Lenin, to devising tactics whereby its end might be hastened and its doom sealed.

With respect to the critique of religion, the way in which a single question is answered will determine whether Kautsky was a stalwart Marxist or a renegade. That question, is, "Does a naturalistic explanation of religion qualify as a materialistic explanation?" If so, Kautsky was perfectly orthodox, for at no time did he resort either to supernatural or to spiritualistic factors in comprehending religious phenomena. But since he utilized animistic and structuralist elements, in addition to economic factors in his explanation, he cannot be called a materialist in the narrow economic sense of the term. In any case, one point is clear: orthodox or not, Kautsky, unlike Lenin, was no vulgarian.

---

[170] Karl Kautsky, *Die Sozialdemokratie und die katholische Kirche* (Berlin: Hans Weber, 1906), Foreword, also pp. 30-31.

CONCLUSION

The foregoing pages are strewn with comments and analyses indicating what I take to be the theoretical, logical, and factual weaknesses in the treatments given to religion by Marx, Engels, Lenin, and Kautsky. The task now is neither to summarize nor to rehash these criticisms but rather to arrive at a general assessment of what might be thought of as the classical Marxist critiques of religion. Since every assessment contains at least some of the assessor's presuppositions and values, I make no pretense here of drawing conclusions based exclusively on objective data but confess to the insinuation of certain biases in the assessment which follows.

In his article entitled, "Naturalism Reconsidered," first delivered as a presidential address to a section of the American Philosophical Association, Ernest Nagel characterized naturalism in part as the position which takes for granted "the existential and causal primacy of organized matter in the executive order of nature."[1] Since I subscribe to this position, it is not surprising that I should take the greatest strength of Marxism to lie in its naturalism. Despite the fact that Marxism claims now and again to be more scientific than it really is and despite the possibility, if not the probability, that science is incapable of revealing everything about religious phenomena, still and all, the scientific methods of discovery and verification associated with a naturalistic orientation seem to me to offer the best hope of understanding religion.

The religious believer who disagrees with this has two options. First, he can fall back upon fideism or, second, he can rely upon some brand of natural theology. Should he choose to rest his case on faith alone, the Marxist can ask why he professes a given faith and not an alternative one.

---

[1] Ernest Nagel, "Naturalism Reconsidered," reprinted in Daniel J. Bronstein, Yervant H. Krikorian, and Philip Wiener, *Basic Problems of Philosophy* (3rd ed., Englewood Cliffs, N.J.: Prentice-Hall, Inc., 1964), p. 577.

In reply, the consistent fideist can only refer to his unique experiences and redouble his profession of faith à la Tertullian. He can not argue on its behalf. Thus, he is left with his own subjectivist interpretations of experience which to the outside observer explain nothing. Should the believer resort to natural theology and give reasons why he takes his faith to be true, he will be subjected not only to the merciless criticisms of Marxists but also to the non-Marxist criticism of Hume, Kant, and others in the modern analytic, positivistic, existentialist, and phenomenological traditions. In view of the decisive nature of these criticisms, it seems to me impossible to defend any variety of natural theology, unless there is a radical redefinition of traditional terms which is tantamount to their rejection. Thus, in comparison with the sinking sands on which all theologies are built, Marxism is founded upon the Gibraltar of naturalism.

Taking "the existential and causal primacy of organized matter" for granted, Marx and Engels extended its applicability beyond "the executive order to nature" so as to include especially the executive order of history. Accordingly, they developed a tripartite model of society which included an economic substructure composed of forces of production on which was erected a social structure composed of relations of production, all of which were topped off by an ideological superstructure composed of such symbolic effusions as ethics, philosophy, law, religion and the like. In developing this theoretical construct, Marx and Engels were the first, as Harris has noted, "to show how the problem of consciousness and the subjective experience of the importance of ideas for behavior could be reconciled with causation on a physicalist model."[2]

The materialist model of society which Marx and Engels constructed has not, however, received universal acceptance for at least six reasons. First, even though some, such as Lenin, have taken it to be thoroughly satisfactory,[3] others, such as Harris, have found ambiguity in it,[4] and still others, such as Plamenatz, have discovered it to be hopelessly confused.[5] Second, serious questions have arisen as to whether or not Marx's materialist model is also deterministic and, if so, in what way or ways.[6]

[2] Marvin Harris, *The Rise of Anthropological Theory: A History of Theories of Culture* (New York: Thomas Y. Crowell Company, 1968), pp. 230-231.

[3] Lenin, "The Three Sources and Three Component Parts of Marxism," LCW, XIX, 23.

[4] Haris, *The Rise of Anthropological Theory*, p. 232.

[5] Plamenatz, *German Marxism and Russian Communism*, pp. 23-35.

[6] Laird Addis, "The Individual and the Marxist Philosophy of History," in May Brodbeck, ed., *Readings in the Philosophy of the Social Sciences* (New York: The Macmillan Company, 1968), p. 318.

Third, problems have arisen concerning the kinds and degrees of social interactionism which Marx and Engels believed to occur between modes of production, taken to be ultimately decisive, and the relations of production and the items of ideology built thereon. Kamenka, for instance, has argued that "ideological factors do not merely act on the base" but that they "become part of it."[7] Fourth, it has been suggested that Marx and Engels' materialist model did not include enough material variables. To illustrate, Harris, who is sympathetic toward dialectical materialism, has, nevertheless, criticized Marx and Engels for minimizing "the modifying effect of environment upon the quantitative and qualitative characteristics of a 'definite stage of production'."[8] Fifth, in opposition to Marxism, many social scientists following Durkheim believe social facts to constitute a class which is *sui-generis*. While not denying interactionism, they reject any attempt at reducing social facts to allegedly more fundamental levels designed to give a causal explanation of social events in terms of psychology, economics, or biology.[9] Sixth, with respect to the religious element of ideology in particular, numerous investigators have maintained that many aspects of religion have only the most tenuous relationship, if any, to materialist variables functioning at the economic level. In relation to the emergence of religon, one thinks (a) of the noneconomic sources of fear mentioned by Malinowski and Radin;[10] (b) of the belief in immortality which Malinowski theorizes may have biological bases and which, without respect to biology, Montagu takes to be the "prototypic act of faith";[11] (c) of our biological and social heritage which Morris regards as demanding a center of authority and requiring the establisment of a "god-figure" as a surrogate for the dominant male of primate society;[12] (d) of the objective human need for a frame of reference which, according to Fromm, may also be an object of devotion;[13] and (e) of the need to

---

[7] Eugene Kamenka, *Marxism and Ethics* (London: Macmillan, 1969), p. 41.

[8] Harris, *The Rise of Anthropological Theory*, p. 233.

[9] Emile Durkheim, *The Roles of Sociological Method*, trans. by S. A. Solovay and J. H. Mueller and ed. by G. C. Catlin (Glencoe, Ill.: The Free Press, 1938), pp. 1-4.

[10] Malinowski, "Culture," *Encyclopaedia of the Social Sciences*, p. 630; Radin, *Primitive Religion*, pp. 5-7.

[11] Bronislaw Malinowski, *A Scientific Theory of Culture* (Chapel Hill: University of North Carolina Press, 1944), p. 174; Montagu, *Immortality, Religion and Morals*, p. 49.

[12] Morris, *The Naked Ape*, pp. 178-184.

[13] Fromm, *The Sane Society*, pp. 64-66.

adapt to the existential problems of hostility, frustration, defeat, despair, disease, and death which Yinger notes.[14]

The upshot of this is that Marx's historical materialism, unlike his naturalistic orientation, is not an unfailing source of strength. His materialist model of society, for example, is clearly incapable of accounting for religion on its own limited terms. Conceiving of religion as an inessentiality, Marx took it to be merely the reflection of the real world, but in so doing he confused the medium which does the reflecting with that which is reflected.[15] To maintain that religion has its own substantiality, so to speak, which commonly reflects socio-economic forms is not to deny that materialist variables of the sort Marx had in mind contribute to that substantiality; it is merely to deny that they account for it completely. Religion is, after all, not a single thing but more nearly a family or cluster of related phenomena.

Despite its limitations, however, the materialist theory of religion has much to offer heuristically. Kautsky's comments on Renan's *The Life of Jesus* illustrate this point strikingly:

Renan based his conception, not on the social conditions of the time, but on the picturesque impressions the modern tourist in Galilee receives. Hence Renan is able to assure us in his romance about Jesus that in Jesus' time this fair land 'abounded in plenty, joy and well-being,' so that 'every history of the origin of Christianity becomes a charming idyll.'

As charming as the lovely month of May 1871 in Paris.[16] As one who has read many a work of hermeneutics and apologetics, I can testify that it is a rare work of divinity which takes into account the real lives of real people, including their daily economic relationships. Accordingly, those who would understand religion in its total context must welcome Marx's materialist approach as the necessary antidote to the mentalistic strategies of theologians and apologists.

In addition to the decisive strength of its naturalism and the significant, if less than decisive, power of its materialism, Marxism possesses the virtue of always having approached religion functionally. In so doing, it has taken religion to be a unified set of phenomena amenable to objective study, has denied that scientific explanation must take the truth claims of dogmas into account, and has refused to categorize some faith positions

---

[14] Yinger, *The Science of Religion*, pp. 6-8.

[15] Paul Radin, "Economic Factors in Primitive Religion," *Science and Society*, I (Spring, 1937), 310-311.

[16] Kautsky, *Christianity*, p. 258.

pejoratively as superstitious while classifying others favorably as truly religious. Thus, despite its hostility toward religion and its failure to develop an adequate functionalist approach, Marxism has contributed to the climate in which the science of religion can flourish.

In conclusion, Marxism has little or nothing more to contribute of theoretical interest to the scientific study of religion. In the unlikely event that there are further contributions, they will come neither from Marx nor from Lenin but from the tradition inaugurated by Engels and developed by Kautsky. But that tradition has become so eclectic that any additional contribution it may make will bear only the slightest resemblance to Marx's original position.

BIBLIOGRAPHY

Primary Sources

Independent Works of Karl Marx Published Separately

Capital. Translated from the third German edition by Samuel Moore and Edward Aveling and edited by Friedrich Engels. 4 vols. Moscow: Foreign Languages Publishing House.

The Class Struggles in France: 1848 to 1850. Introduced by Friedrich Engels. Moscow: Foreign Languages Publishing House, n.d.

The Critique of the Gotha Program. Moscow: Foreign Languages Publishing House, n.d.

Economic and Philosophic Manuscripts of 1844. Moscow: Foreign Languages Publishing House, 1961.

The Eighteenth Brumaire of Louis Bonaparte. Moscow: Foreign Languages Publishing House, n.d.

The Poverty of Philosophy. Moscow: Foreign Languages Publishing House, n.d.

Pre-Capitalist Economic Formations. Edited and introduced by E. V. Hobsbawm. New World Paperbacks. New York: International Publishers, 1964.

Wages, Price and Profit. Moscow: Foreign Languages Publishing House, n.d.

Independent Works of Friendrich Engels Published Separately

Anti-Dühring. 3rd ed. Moscow: Foreign Languages Publishing House, 1962.

Dialectics of Nature. New World Paperbacks. New York: International Publishers, 1940.

The Origin of the Family, Private Property and the State. Moscow: Foreign Languages Publishing House, n.d.

The Peasant War in Germany. Moscow: Foreign Languages Publishing House, n.d.

Socialism: Utopian and Scientific. Moscow: Foreign Languages Publishing House, n.d.

Works of Marx and Engels in Collaboration Published Separately

The Communist Manifesto. Edited by Samuel H. Beer. New York: Appleton-Century-Crofts, 1955.

The German Ideology. Moscow: Progress Publishers, 1964.

The German Ideology. Parts I and III. Edited and introduced by R. Pascal. New York: International Publishers, 1947.

Germany: Revolution and Counter-Revolution. Edited by Eleanor Marx. New York: International Publishers, n.d.

The Holy Family or Critique of Critical Critique. Moscow: Foreign Languages Publishing House, 1956.

Collections of the Works of Marx and/or Engels

On Britain. Moscow: Foreign Languages Publishing House, 1962.

On Colonialism. Moscow: Foreign Languages Publishing House, n.d.

On Religion. Introduced by Reinhold Niebuhr. New York: Schocken Books, 1969.

Reader in Marxist Philosophy. Edited by Howard Selsam and Harry Martel. New World Paperbacks. New York: International Publishers, 1963.

Selected Correspondence. Moscow: Foreign Languages Publishing House, n.d.

Selected Works. New world Paperbacks. New York: International Publishers, 1968.

Werke: 39 vols. Berlin: Dietz Verlag, 1956-1970.

Writings of the Young Marx on Philosophy and Society. Edited and translated by Loyd Easton and Kurt Guddat. Anchor Books. Garden City, N. Y.: Doubleday & Company, Inc., 1967.

Works of V. I. Lenin

Collected Works. 45 vols. Moscow: Progress Publishers, 1960-1970.

The Works of Karl Kautsky

Are the Jews a Race? New York: International Publishers, 1926.

Communism in Central Europe in the Time of the Reformation. New York: Russell and Russell, 1959.

Ethics and the Materialist Conception of History. Translated by J. B. Askew. London: The Twentieth Century Press, Ltd., 1906.

Foundations of Christianity. Translated by Henry F. Mims. New York: Russell and Russell, 1953.

Die materialistische Geschichtsauffassung. 2 vols. Berlin: Verlag J. H. W. Dietz Nachf. G. m. b. H., 1927

"On Religion." Installment I. *Die neue Zeit,* I (November 7, 1913), 182-188.

"On Religion." Installment II. *Die neue Zeit,* I (December 5, 1913), 352-360.

The Social Revolution. Translated by A. M. and Mary Wood Simons. Chicago: Charles H. Kerr and Company, n.d.

Die Sozialdemokratie und die katholische Kirche. Berlin: Hans Weber, 1906.

Terrorism and Communism. Translated by W. H. Kerridge. London: The National Labour Press, Ltd., 1920.

Thomas More and His Utopia. New York: Russell and Russell, 1959.

Secondary Sources

Books

Addis, Laird. "The Individual and the Marxist Philosophy of History." *Readings in the Philosophy of the Social Sciences.* Edited by May Brodbeck. New York: The Macmillan Company, 1968.

Althusser, Louis. *Lénine et la philosophie.* Paris: François Maspero, 1969.

Bergson, Henri. *The Two Sources of Morality and Religion.* Anchor Books. Garden City, N. Y.: Doubleday & Company, Inc., 1954.

Bochenski, Joseph M. and Niemeyer, Gerhart, eds. *Handbook on Communism.* New York: Frederick A. Praeger, 1962.

Bociurkiw, Bohdan R. "Lenin and Religion." *Lenin: The Man, the Theorist, the Leader.* Edited by Leonard Schapiro and Peter Reddaway. New York: Frederick A. Praeger, 1967.

Calvez, Jean-Yves. *La pensée de Karl Marx.* Paris: Editions du seuil, 1956.

Casey, Robert Pierce. *Religion in Russia.* New York: Harper & Brothers Publishers, 1946.

Conquest, Robert, ed. *Religion in the U.S.S.R.* New York: Frederick A. Praeger, 1968.

Cunow, Heinrich. *Ursprung der Religion und des Gottesglaubens.* Berlin: Buchhandlung Vorwärts Paul Singer G. m. b. H., 1913.

Curtiss, John Shelton. *The Russian Church and the Soviet State: 1917-1950.* Boston: Little, Brown and Company, 1953.

Delekat, Friedrich. "Vom Wesen des Geldes, eine theologische Marxanalyse." *Marxismusstudien 3.* Edited by Erwin Metzke. Tübingen: J. C· B. Mohr (Paul Siebeck), 1954.

Desroche, Henri. *Marxisme et Religions.* Paris: Presses Universitaires de France, 1962.

Dewey, John. *A Common Faith.* New Haven: Yale University Press, 1934.

Dupré, Louis. *The Philosophical Foundations of Marxism.* New York: Harcourt, Brace and World, Inc., 1966.

Durkheim, Emile. *The Elementary Forms of the Religious Life.* Free Press Paperback. New York: The Free Press, 1965.

Eastman, Max. *Artists in Uniform.* New York: Alfred A. Knopf, 1934.

Feuerbach, Ludwig. *The Essence of Christianity.* Translated by George Eliot. Harper Torchbooks. New York: Harper & Brothers Publishers, 1957.

—. *Lectures on the Essence of Religion.* Translated by Ralph Manheim. New York: Harper & Row, Publishers, 1967.

Fischer, Louis. *The Life of Lenin.* New York: Harper & Row, Publishers, 1964.

Friedrich Engels der Denker. Basil: Mundus-Verlag AG., 1954.

Fromm, Erich. *The Sane Society.* A Fawcett Premier Book. Greenwich, Conn.: Fawcett Publications, Inc., 1965.

Gregor, A. James. *A Survey of Marxism.* New York: Random House, 1965.

Harris, Marvin. *The Rise of Anthropological Theory: A History of Theories of Culture.* New York: Thomas Y. Crowell Company, 1968.

Hook, Sidney. *From Hegel to Marx.* Ann Arbor Paperbacks. Ann Arbor, Mich.: The University of Michigan Press, 1962.

James, William. *The Varieties of Religious Experience.* The Modern Library. New York: Random House, n.d.

Kamenka, Eugene. *Marxism and Ethics.* A Papermac Book. London: Macmillan, 1969.

Katkov, George. "Lenin as Philosopher." *Lenin: The Man, the Theorist, the Leader.* Edited by Leonard Schapiro and Peter Reddaway. New York: Frederick A. Praeger, 1967.

Kline, George L. "Hegel and the Marxist-Leninist Critique of Religion." *Hegel and the Philosophy of Religion*. Edited by Darrel E. Christensen. The Hague: Martinus Nijhoff, 1970.

—. *Religious and Anti-Religious Thought in Russia*. Chicago: The University of Chicago Press, 1968.

Krupskaya, N. K. *Reminiscences of Lenin*. Moscow: Foreign Languages Publishing House, 1959.

Lefebvre, Henri. *The Sociology of Marx*. A Vintage Book. New York: Random House, 1969.

Leuba, James H. *A Psychological Study of Religion: Its Origin, Function, and Future*. New York: AMS Press, Inc., 1969.

Lévy-Bruhl, Lucien. *How Natives Think*. Translated by Lilian A. Clare. New York: Washington Square Press, 1966.

Lewis, John. *The Life and Teaching of Karl Marx*. New World Paperbacks. New York: International Publishers, 1965.

Ling, Trevor. *Buddha, Marx and God*. New York: St. Martin's Press, 1966.

Luijpen, William A. *Phenomenology and Atheism*. Duquesne Studies. Pittsburgh: Duquesne University Press, 1964.

Matthias, Eric. "Kautsky und der Kautskyanismus." *Marxismusstudien 5*. Edited by Iring Fetscher. Tübingen: J. C. B. (Paul Siebeeck), 1957.

Mayer, Gustav. *Friedrich Engels*. Translated by Gilbert Highet and Helen Highet. New York: Alfred A. Knopf, 1936.

McLellan, David. *The Young Hegelians and Karl Marx*. London: Macmillan, 1969.

Monnerot, Jules. *Sociology of Communism*. Translated by Jane Degas and Richard Rees. London: George Allen & Unwin Ltd., 1953.

Montagu, Ashley. *Immortality, Religion, and Morals*. New York: Hawthorn Books, 1971.

Payne, Robert. *The Life and Death of Lenin*. An Avon Book. New York: The Hearst Corporation, 1967.

—. *Marx*. New York: Simon and Schuster, 1968.

Plamenatz, John. *German Marxism and Russian Communism*. Harper Torchbooks. New York: Harper & Row, Publishers, 1965.

Radin, Paul. *Primitive Religion*. Dover Paperback. New York: Dover Publications, Inc., 1957.

Rotenstreich, Nathan. *Basic Problems of Marx's Philosophy*. New York: The Bobbs-Merrill Company, Inc., 1965.

Sumner, William Graham and Keller, Albert G. *The Science of Society*. 4 vols. New Haven: Yale University Press, 1944.

Stepanova, Yelena. *Friedrich Engels*. Moscow: Foreign Languages Publishing House, 1958.

Terray, Emmanuel. *Le Marxisme devant les sociétés "Primitives": deux études*. Paris: François Maspero, 1969.

Tucker, Robert C. *Philosophy and Myth in Karl Marx*. Cambridge: Cambridge University Press, 1961.

Valentinov (Volsky, N. V.). *Encounters With Lenin*. Translated by Paul Rosta and Brian Pearce. London: Oxford University Press, 1968.

Wach, Joachim. *Sociology of Religion*. Chicago: The University of Chicago Press, 1944.

Wetter, Gustav. *Dialectical Materialism: A Historical and Systematic Survey of Philosophy in the Soviet Union.* Translated by Peter Heath. New York: Frederick A. Praeger, 1963.

Wilson, Edmund. *To the Finland Station.* An Anchor Book. Garden City, N. Y.: Doubleday & Company, Inc., 1953.

Yaroslavsky, E. *Religion in the U.S.S.R.* 2nd ed. Modern Books Ltd., 1932.

Yinger, J. Milton. *The Scientific Study of Religion* London: The Macmillan Company, 1970.

Articles

Barnhart, J. E. " 'Anthropological Nature' in Feuerbach and Marx." *Philosophy Today,* XI (Winter, 1967), 265-275.

Blanchard, Yvon. "Marx et la Religion." *Dialogue,* V (March, 1967), 592-602.

Diamond, S. "Marx's 'First Thesis' on Feuerbach." *Science and Society,* I (Summer, 1937), 539-544.

Feuer, Lewis. "Lenin's Fantasy." *Encounter,* XXXV (December, 1970), 23-35.

Gladden, James W. "The Condition of Religion in Communist Europe—Twenty Years After Tobias." *Lexington Theological Quarterly,* VI (October, 1971), 102-114.

Hammen, Oscar J. "The Young Marx, Reconsidered." *Journal of the History of Ideas,* XXXI (January-March, 1970), 109-120.

Hodges, Donald C. "Marx's Contribution to Humanism." *Science and Society,* XXIX (Spring, 1965), 173-191.

—. "The Unity of Marx's Thought." *Science and Society,* XXVIII (Summer, 1964), 316-323.

—. "The Young Marx—A Reappraisal." *Philosophy and Phenomenological Research,* XXVII (September, 1966-June, 1967), 216-229.

Kojève, Alexandre. "Hegel, Marx and Christianity." *Interpretation,* I (Summer, 1970), 21-42.

Kon, Igor S. "The Concept of Alienation in Modern Sociology." *Social Research,* XXXIV (Autumn, 1967), 507-528.

Lamont, Corliss. "A Reply to Joseph Needham." *Science and Society,* I (Summer, 1937), 495-498.

Lobkowicz, Nicholas. "Karl Marx's Attitude Toward Religion." *The Review of Politics,* XXVI (July, 1964), 319-352.

Löwith, Karl. "Man's Self-Alienation in the Early Writings of Marx." *Social Research,* XXI (Summer, 1954), 204-230.

Mayo, H. B. "Marxism and Religion." *The Hibbert Journal,* LI (April, 1953), 226-233.

Radin, Paul. "Economic Factors in Primitive Religion." *Science and Society,* I (Spring, 1937), 310-325.

Rosen, Zvi. "The Influence of Bruno Bauer on Marx's Concept of Alienation." *Social Theory and Practice,* I (Fall, 1970), 50-68.

INDEX